IØ1Ø5181

About the Authors

Meghana Nayak is Associate Professor of Political Science and teaches in the Women's and Gender Studies Department at Pace University-New York. She has published in *International Feminist Journal of Politics*, *International Studies Review*, *Women and Politics*, and has a chapter in *Theorizing Sexual Violence* (edited by Renee Heberle and Victoria Grace). Her work focuses on social movements, the politics of gender violence, and feminist and critical approaches to hegemony, security, and identity.

Eric Selbin is Professor of Political Science at Southwestern University and a University Scholar. His books include *Revolution, Rebellion, Resistance*, *Modern Latin American Revolutions*, and *Understanding Revolutions* (with John Foran and Jack Goldstone). In 2007 he was selected as one of Southwestern's all-time 'Fav Five' faculty and received an exemplary teaching award in 2001–2.

Decentering International Relations

Meghana Nayak and Eric Selbin

Zed Books

LONDON & NEW YORK

Decentering International Relations was first published in 2010 by Zed Books Ltd, 7 Cynthia Street, London N1 9JF, UK and Room 400, 175 Fifth Avenue, New York, NY 10010, USA

www.zedbooks.co.uk

Copyright © Meghana Nayak and Eric Selbin 2010

The rights of Meghana Nayak and Eric Selbin to be identified as the authors of this work have been asserted by them in accordance with the Copyright, Designs and Patents Act, 1988

Designed and typeset in Adobe Garamond by Kate Kirkwood
Index by John Barker
Cover designed by Rogue Four Design

All rights reserved. No part of this publication may be reproduced, stored in a retrieval system or transmitted in any form or by any means, electronic, mechanical, photocopying or otherwise, without the prior permission of Zed Books Ltd.

A catalogue record for this book is available from the British Library
Library of Congress Cataloging in Publication Data available

ISBN 978 1 84813 239 9 pb

Contents

Acknowledgments

Acknowledgments are a joy and a challenge, a bitter-sweet moment of immense gratitude married to a sense of inadequacy – certain you are forgetting someone who made an important contribution or tried to prevent the errors you will no doubt find. The mistakes are all our own and not due to those who did so much to make this experience such a joy.

We are both grateful to our home institutions, Pace University and Southwestern University, for their support and the opportunity they provide to interact and work with some amazing colleagues and exceptional – in any number of ways – students, who inspire and challenge us. Zed Books has been a warm home, from Ellen Hallsworth's initial enthusiasm to Ken Barlow's gentle (and brave) guidance. The deft touch of both Mike Kirkwood and Kate Kirkwood was invaluable. Cindy Weber's incredible feedback and encouragement was the essence of collegiality. It is a delight to recognize our debt to the University of Minnesota's Political Science Department and our mentor, Kathryn Sikkink. We have many others to thank.

Meghana: I wanted to participate in this project because of my students and I hope that there is at least one moment in this book that inspires them to really think about what they're doing when they study IR. I believe academia can be a site for political struggle, inspiration, and social change because of two classes I took while I was an undergraduate at Southwestern University. First, on a whim, I took Introduction to Women's Studies with Helene Meyers; to this day, I try to summon her spirit, passion, and intensity when I teach. Second, I decided to take Comparative Politics with Eric Selbin in my junior year, simply because my friends raved about him. He pushed and challenged me to think about politics in ways I never thought possible. Helene and Eric continue to mentor me in various ways, and I'm delighted to call them colleagues and dear friends.

2

It was immense fun to write a book with my first political science professor. Somehow, Eric put up with my endless questions and concerns. He's one of the funniest and kindest people I've ever met, and, in between laughs, he managed to teach me a thing or two about revolution and resistance. Both of us, of course, have many people to thank at the University of Minnesota, where we both received our PhDs. Frankly, throughout my time there, from 1997 to 2003, I felt, in more ways than I can count, completely out of my element. But the folks I met there, particularly the ever-patient and brilliant Kathryn Sikkink, Raymond Duvall, and Richa Nagar, and countless other professors and peers in Political Science, Feminist Studies, and the MacArthur Program, took me seriously and shaped my research, teaching, and activism. In 2003, I moved to New York for a job at Pace University and found a community that supports my work and is committed to students. I don't think I could do without the friendship, support, and generosity of my colleagues, particularly Christopher Malone in Political Science, or the enthusiasm of my students here, past and present.

I'm also incredibly grateful to the people I interviewed, all of whom are engaging in immensely important decentering work. Many people have read various versions of this book, fully and unconditionally supported why I was working on this project, suggested people to talk to, wrote amazing work I could cite, and/or sent me their manuscripts: Cynthia Weber, Himadeep Muppidi, Susan Kang, Wanjiru Kamau-Rutenberg, Mohan Nadig, Jennifer Suchland, Jonneke Koomen, Alina Sajed, Thomas Kim, Walleska Lantigua, Roohi Choudhry, Andy Marra, Lorenda Pinder, and Alejandra Lopez. Conversations with Emily Hardt, Catherine Beebe, and Sachita Shenoy made me think carefully about what I was writing and why, and helped me remember to be hopeful about *everything*. Goldspot's vibrant and beautiful music got me through many writing blocks and served as a source of inspiration. My beloved borough of Brooklyn deserves a shout-out; there's an amazing community of writers, artists, activists, and thinkers here. Finally, endless gratitude and love to the following: Mom, Dad, Niraj, Chanda, Jayant, Neha, Arunapachi, and Nayantara akka.

Eric: First and foremost I want to thank Meghana Nayak. For the past fifteen years she has pushed and prodded, taught, and inspired me. As befits a book inspired by students, thanks are also due to three sets of them that have influenced what you see here.

At the University of Minnesota it was my good fortune to be on the periphery of an exceptional cohort of IR graduate students who kindly let a mere comparativist hang around and listen. I learned a great deal from Michael Barnett, Roxanne Doty, Kathryn Hochstetler, Cynthia Kite, Rhona Leibel, Eric Mlyn, Himadeep Muppidi, Sheila Nair, Jutta Weldes, and Alex Wendt that informs my thinking still, though without Cindy Kite's tutelage it is not at all clear to me I would have known what to do with any of it; if I have, I am in her debt, not least for conversations years later during sun-drenched Umeå summers. It is a testament to Bud Duvall and Brian Job as scholars and teachers that they created an atmosphere in which we could think and play and take risks, and what I owe Kathryn Sikkink for the model of scholar and teacher she offered is incalculable. Few if any of these folks are likely be enamored with what is here, but my appreciation is great.

Somewhat more directly, this book is the result of an exceptional set of students I have been lucky to work with at Southwestern University, not least my co-author. On this particular subject, why we construct IR in the ways we do, why it matters, and how things might look differently if we began from elsewhere (or even elsewhen), Jennifer Suchland, Sara Alvis Daly, Farhana Qazi, Annaliese Richard, Chakira Hunter, Henrietta Muñoz, Ana 'Dr Pink Shoes' Villalobos, Olivia Travioso, Meagan Elliot, Alex Rutledge, Jacob Beswick, Rakhee Kewada, and Diana Parra all made me think and taught me a great deal. The support of Southwestern University's Provost James Hunt and the University Scholar program has been invaluable, and the Political Science Department a congenial and encouraging home.

Finally, I would be remiss not to note another set of 'students,' IR scholars, who have been instrumental in the development of my thinking about IR. For some twenty years Cynthia Weber has inspired, intimidated, and amazed me; during that same time Kevin Dunn, Kathy Hochstetler, Cindy Kite, Meghana Nayak, Anne Sisson Runyan, Jennifer Suchland, and others have answered my questions and questioned my answers.

As always, my work is dedicated to three incredible women who so warmly and graciously share their lives with me on a daily basis. Helen Cordes, Jesse Cordes Selbin, and Zoe Cordes Selbin are the epitome of love, joy, generosity, warmth, and kindness – and more fun than anyone has any right to have; y'all pass a good time, ya hear?

Chapter One / Introduction

Us, Them, Over There

'What they really need is education.'

'So, what can we do to help?'

'We shouldn't impose our way of life on them, especially when they're not ready and don't want it. Some people just aren't used to democracy and freedom.'

'They should take care of their own problems; we have enough of our own.'

'The US is not the world's policeman.'

'They hate our way of life and everything about us.'

No doubt, comments like these are quite familiar to the reader. You may have heard them in a classroom, at work, during a dinner conversation, or while watching a news program. Have you noticed how quickly a conversation about some issue in the world shifts to what 'we' should do (or not do) about 'them,' living 'over there'? We lose the nuances of the situation in question and start debating whether the US should 'stay out of it' or 'go in' because only it is capable of doing so. We are confident that our information is solid, intentions good, motives pure, and capability to engender change evident. In this book, we claim that we impoverish our understanding of the world by always beginning from – or inserting, referencing, gesturing towards – the US. In this way we treat the US/the North/the West as actors and all beyond this reference point as mere issues to be figured out or theorized by 'us.' We rely upon concepts and theories that lead us back to an 'us–them–over there' frame that seems to recycle endlessly.

When we teach or learn International Relations (IR), we are purportedly attempting to understand for whom power works and how,

1

with the added dimension of where power resides. Thus, the outsized role the US has come to play in world affairs cannot (and should not) be ignored. At the same time, it is a common mistake to read the US as some omnipotent potentate endowed with particular gravitas and uniquely equipped to understand and solve the problems of the world and its population at every level from the local to the global. The world's people do not greet their day wondering what it is 'we' think or what it is 'we' want them to do. And, surely, there must be a way to speak about those directly affected by US hegemonic power without lapsing into multiple, barely substantiated presumptions. While the US has had a disproportionate role in shaping certain processes and situations for some hundred years now, the myriad possibilities of global politics are not delimited by US actions or power.

This book claims that IR – as a body of knowledge and set of discourses, as a discipline/field of study in which we participate as scholars, theorists, and students, and as a field of 'practical' political decisions and structures[1] – is 'centered.' This centering has four main attributes. First, IR focuses primarily on and legitimizes the actions and decisions of the US and the global North/West. Second, IR privileges certain political projects, such as neoliberal economic policies, state-centrism, and Northern/Western liberal democracy.[2] Third, IR legitimizes the most privileged socio-political players and institutions, in both the Global North/West and the Global South,[3] to produce knowledge and make decisions about the rest of the world, thus replicating or maintaining certain unequal power relationships. Finally, IR examines certain understandings of political concepts (such as sovereignty) and particular narratives that can elide, distort, or completely miss multiple ways of understanding and living in the world. Why do our studies, questions, policies, and research always start and end this way – in the center, in the North/West?

When we say 'North/West,' we mean primarily the US, but also Great Britain, 'Western' European countries, and, depending on context, limited others.[4] It is not always entirely clear, beyond geography, what makes these places 'Western,' but countries, people, scholars, and institutions ensconced in the Global North/West represent themselves as 'universal,' developed, and civilized – erasing how they got into privileged military, economic, socio-cultural, diplomatic, and political relationships with the so-called Third World/Global South.[5] Think of the 'center' as the nucleus: this is where decisions are made, discourses are legitimized, and people and entities are put in positions to further entrench the most privileged ways of thinking about the world.

How do you see the 'centers' of power operating? Who is in your 'we,' and who is (most) decidedly not? Even when you say 'we' should hold 'our' government accountable for 'our' foreign policy because 'our' taxes are paying for unpopular wars, have you asked yourself what benefits you derive from being a part of this 'we'? Do you ever wonder if the peasants, farmers, oppressed women, child soldiers, sick and dying, poor – or others you study, categorize, and write about – are sitting around somewhere wondering about you, ready to compile a list of recommendations about what to do about you and your problems? If you are a student or scholar of IR, or any discipline that explores global politics, if you are part of a governmental or nongovernmental organization with an international focus, if you practice international law or engage in international commerce, or if you are an activist involved in various global issues, we would like you, with us, to question what we have been taught, by whom, and how, and the effects of what we study and do. Even if you believe you have nothing to do with IR theories, scholarship, professors, or organizations, they have something to do with you; and the way you think, live, and act in the world matters fundamentally.

We are articulating the thorny recognition that IR, as we practice, teach, learn, and fund it, is more likely to reinforce domination than to encourage discussion and dissent; despite our very real desires, this is the case no matter how good anyone's intentions are (a point to which we will return).What kind of way is this to think about, to 'do,' IR? And, what can and should we do about it? As two professors of political science located in the US, we have found that it is often difficult to teach, learn, and speak about IR in any other way. We return to our offices after class, wondering whether we offered adequate challenges to, and rethinking of, the usual ways of doing IR. So this book emerged out of a seemingly simple question: given how Northern/Western scholars, practitioners, analysts, discourses, concepts, and political projects dominate IR (the discipline, the body of knowledge, the practical politics), is it possible to decenter IR, to decenter the US and the Global North?

Fundamentally, we want to make three points which frame our response. First, we wish to recognize the narrative(s) that have dominated and hence disciplined the field of IR. In other words, we examine the 'story of IR.'

Second, the notion of decentering is more than simply a matter of semantics or an abstract game, more than an opposition to or the flip side of centering. We aim to call out the 'centeredness' of IR, whether that means the focus on the North/West, and the US in particular, as the center of the world, the role of certain institutions, universities, scholars, and practitioners in creating 'knowledge' about 'Others,' or the material effects of power relationships on people's daily lives. A centered IR erases how we got here, and privileges sovereignty, hierarchy, and certain kinds of power over intersubjectivity, agency, identity, engagement, responsibility, and accountability (Agathangelou and Ling, 2004: 44). To decenter IR from its Northern/Western anchors requires us to challenge the politics, concepts, and practices that enable certain narratives of IR to be central; decentering is also a way to put forth and participate in other kinds of narratives and politics that have different 'starting' points. In particular, this book focuses on how the specific, pressing issues of *indigeneity, human rights, globalization,* and *peace and security* are simultaneously normative inventions/categories meant to sustain (and even extend) particular power structures *and* sites for insurgent and subversive attempts to live IR at the margins.

Third, we articulate a set of questions we believe are or should be critical for decentering IR's narratives. We explore what it means for us, as the authors, to join conversations 'at the margins' of IR. In effect, to decenter IR is to start with the possibility of a world that operates and is shaped in ways that are fundamentally different from what we 'know.' We aim to recognize our privileges as loss and our marginality as power, and to connect with people who are remaking their worlds.

The Story of IR

Critical IR theories, varied as they may be, generally challenge the world as 'given,' thus tracing and revealing power structures that are accepted as natural and inevitable. A significant number of critical IR scholars have argued that IR perpetuates and legitimizes particular 'stories' or narratives, so what follows might be familiar to you. In story of IR as it is told, the fifteenth century heralded the advent of the 'Age of Discovery' (or 'Exploration'), when 'the Europeans' (hardly, it merits note, a monolithic crowd) began to set out principally by water for more distant lands. 'Western Europe' (primarily Portugal, Spain, France, Great Britain, and the Netherlands, and eventually by extension some of the 'white' settler regimes) stood as the repository of knowledge, wisdom, and vision, and it set out to 'discover' a wider world. Generously, as the story unfolds, in return for little more than raw materials and some traded goods, these Christian Europeans brought civilization to the benighted in the disordered, and hence discordant, morass.

The world beyond (sometimes *just* outside, such as Russia, or even *within*, as with Ireland) Europe's still ill-defined borders cried out, the Europeans believed, for the order and rigor they, with the best interests of all human beings at heart, could provide. In this era, states were still in formation, and territorial sovereignty as an organizing principle partly aimed to deal with religious differences and to prevent the intervention of the Pope, Holy Roman Emperor, and various others into the emerging state's internal affairs. But from early on sovereignty and the modern state system were also deployed to mark a difference from and to discipline and control the colonized world (Anghie, 2005). Whatever violence, atrocities, or oppression occurred during colonialism receive no mention in the story, or pale in comparison to the achievements of industrialization and civilization. As Krishna (2001) reveals in his examination of encounters between Europe and Africa, Spain and Mexico, and Great Britain and India, IR discourse misrepresents, simplifies, and deeply distorts the importance of these dramatically lopsided interactions.

Certainly, colonization presaged the Age of the Enlightenment and the concomitant self-styled and self-anointed onus for the North/West, the 'white man's burden,'[6] which would increasingly be the framework for the liberalism and rationalism that defined the nineteenth century. As the story continues, it marks the twentieth century, however specified,[7] by a number of great calamities and innumerable tragedies produced by human actions. Eventually a US protagonist emerged, having 'matured' during its experiences in World War Two, ready to take on Great Britain's abandoned role of hegemon – abandoned, it is worth noting, after defeat and rejection. This 'great' war apparently deeply shaped the world we live in and profoundly framed and ineluctably structured the rise of a field of study known as International Relations. As decolonization increased the number of sovereign states, the US and its mainly European allies increasingly created and institutionalized regimes of 'global governance,' so as to manage the conflict with and within the so-called developing world. Of course, not all countries and regions decolonized in the same way or at the same pace – we may compare, for example, South America and South Asia, or question whether indigenous peoples experienced decolonization. The post-Soviet and southeastern European states that gained independence in the 1990s present a further challenge, having had different experiences from each other, from decolonized countries, and in relationship to Russia.

But the story continues nonetheless: the locus of knowledge (and, indeed, 'truth') is firmly entrenched in the North/West; the scholars, policy makers, and practitioners who are charged with the creation, protection, and 'dissemination' of that knowledge are lodged in, represent, or are somehow tied to the North/West. The story lets some of us – and only some of us – be storytellers (of this story or close iterations) and come up with ways to help the rest of the world 'catch up,' even though 'we' know that it really cannot and will not. The story, it should be noted, deftly interweaves pragmatic politics and the discipline/field/ discourses of IR. For too long, this story has bluntly or subtly driven our understanding of 'international,' of 'relations,' and of what constitutes legitimate knowledge worthy of our attention. It is a story with a Euro- and Anglo-centric chronology of discovery and enlightenment (colonialism), the 'world' wars, pre- and post-Cold War (which was often quite hot in parts of the world far removed from the primary antagonists), and pre- and post-9/11, as if all of the world is similarly shaped by these events and singularly obsessed with joining the 'march of progress' and being on the 'right' side of history.

Agathangelou and Ling discuss how IR

> comes to resemble a colonial household . . . seek[ing] to stave off . . . 'disorder' ['anarchy'; 'local traditions of thinking, doing, and being'] by imposing 'order.' But the House does so by appropriating the knowledge, resources, and labor of racialized, sexualized Others for its own benefit and pleasure while announcing itself as the sole producer-father of our world. Others qualify as 'innocent' children, wards, or servants at best, or 'unteachable' barbarians at worst. (2004: 21)

This 'House' of IR,[8] as Agathangelou and Ling call it, is not open to just anyone; whether a state, policy maker, organization, or academic,[9] one has to behave and follow the norms and mores (or at least seem redeemable) to gain entry into the House of IR. Agathangelou and Ling (2004: 23–35) discuss how the theories and schools of thought in IR 'fit' together in this hierarchical House. We explain these theories in more detail in our notes because their relevance is not just for political science majors and IR scholars; they are not just academic jargon. Rather, they are fundamental narratives about how the world works, recommending certain kinds of decisions (made by only certain actors) about the problems and issues around the world. Indeed, the theoretical positions (and accompanying ontological and epistemological presumptions)[10] described determine the very definition of what constitutes a 'problem.'

In the House, Agathangelou and Ling (*ibid.*) posit a father realism[11] and mother liberalism,[12] their 'caretaking daughters,'[13] neoliberalism, liberal feminism, and standpoint feminism, and a 'bastard heir,' neo-realism.[14] These schools of thoughts constitute, in a sense, the 'center' – indeed, a central *structure* – that maintains order and control over other ways of thinking and being. These theories take the world order as 'given,' employing positivist epistemology and empiricism to provide 'solutions' such as militarized intervention, structural adjustment programs, and other policies enabling the North/West or privileged portions of society to 'deal' with the 'rest' and to keep ongoing power relationships and structures in place. Upstairs are the semi-estranged 'rebel sons' (Marxism, Gramscian international political economy, post-modern IR, pragmatic/liberal constructivism)[15] and 'fallen daughters' (postmodern feminism, queer studies).[16] They are on the 'borders' of discourses and policies in IR because of their varying focus on issues of class, ideology, language, identity, gender, race, and sexuality; at the same time, they are indebted in many ways to Eurocentric and Anglocentric thinkers and concepts. Downstairs one finds the 'laborers,' who provide their services to or are tolerated on the periphery of the center: the native informant servants (area studies and comparative politics experts),[17] Asian capitalist countries,[18] and peripheral and transitional economies.[19] Outside (meaning, not interested in 'acceptance' into the House (*ibid.*: 32)) are Orientalism,[20] the terrorist network, Al Qaeda,[21] postcolonial IR,[22] and worldism.[23]

How can we speak about the world in meaningful ways or offer critical analysis if we are doing so within a discipline that favors a (neo)colonial order and the attendant gender, race, class, sexual, and labor divisions in academia and the world? When we focus on one theory versus another, rather than the whole body of theories and the field of IR, we can fail to recognize that it's not simply a discipline with a happy variety of perspectives, some more unconsciously or unintentionally privileged and thus central than others, with North Americans somehow simply more participatory than others for no particular reason. The discipline *ensures* (may, indeed, demand) *as* a discipline that some perspectives will be privileged and some subject positions will be preferred (even within the context of doing critical IR theory).

In the light of these comments, we should mention a bit more about ourselves. The writing of this book brings to mind Deleuze and Guattari's delightful and provocative declaration that opens *A Thousand Plateaus*: 'The two of us wrote *Anti-Oedipus* together. Since each of us was several, there was already quite a crowd' (1987: 3). We hope you will join this welter of voices. Meghana is the daughter of immigrants from India and was raised in Texas; Eric is a first-generation son of political activists, raised Jewish in Louisiana. Meghana was a psychology/women's studies undergraduate student intent on medical school until she took Eric's class on comparative politics, which nurtured her commitment to understanding the politics of gender violence. She eventually headed off to Eric's alma mater, the University of Minnesota, for a PhD in Political Science. We had the same dissertation advisor and constructed our academic identities, at least in part, via that program's contributions to the constructivist (liberal and critical) school of thought. We ply our trade on what might reasonably be considered the semi-periphery of the academy, because of the kinds of questions we ask, because critical feminist, postcolonial, and Marxist-Gramscian theories inform our work and activism, and because we tend to hang out with the 'Rebel Sons' and 'Fallen Daughters' of IR. At the same time, we are committed to fully shaking IR (inclusive of our own influences and presumptions) to its core. Thus it seems appropriate to turn next to precisely what we mean by decentering.

Centering and Decentering: More than a Matter of Semantics

Whenever we say 'decenter' in this book, we are signaling to the reader that we are talking about interrogating, disturbing, engaging, reframing, challenging, mocking, or even undoing mainstream, privileged ways of viewing the world.[24] That means we first find the concept, theory, or discourse that seems to be the 'natural' starting point of how we think about ourselves and the world, but that we can also politicize and use to think about and do IR in different ways. As such, the rest of the book is devoted to the concepts – *indigeneity, human rights, globalization,* and *peace and security* – that we think do just that.

Many might think we should start with concepts such as power, the state, sovereignty, hierarchy, anarchy, or others typically 'understood' to be the defining foci of IR. However, we argue that the stranglehold that these concepts have on IR and the trappings of these categories have been made possible by the image of the 'native,' the idea of 'human rights' as the quintessentially modern marker of civilized societies, the inevitable march of 'globalization,' and the imperatives of 'peace and security.' We contend that it is these concepts – innocent and merely descriptive as they may sound – that have *enabled* IR to *center itself,* by reproducing, enabling, and privileging particular power relations in the world, in the media, and in the classroom. These are the very power relations that mainstream scholars defend (and, in some cases, consciously or not, seek to maintain and extend) and critical scholars critique (though they too can perpetuate this dominant paradigm). In other words, it is through these concepts that IR anchors itself to particular players (the US state, the North/West, an international financial institution, a university) that are supposedly the most important, relevant, or significant actor (the 'center'), to particular productions of knowledge by those actors about others in the world, to specific policies and decisions, and to restrictions on what is appropriate to study in the discipline.

In the chapters that follow, we figure out what exactly each of these concepts 'accomplishes' for IR, ask how it came to be that way, and examine the implications. We also explore how those same concepts can *decenter* IR. This means that we explore other places to start, and ask how scholars, activists, practitioners, and theorists in multiple locations both critique and use those concepts to 'do' IR in a different way. Thus, decentering is not simply a critique; it also involves an imagining of how else we might speak about, experience, and change the world in ways that are not merely circumscribed by, or a response to, or otherwise signified by the center. How, in other words, can we use the categories of indigeneity, human rights, globalization, and peace and security to unravel, challenge, and rethink IR as a discipline, a field of study, discourse, policy-making, and the sum of political interactions?

At the same time, we must understand the relationship between the center and the margins, because local, marginalized, multiple subjects do not exist in a world without forces of exploitation and oppression. And we decidedly say 'between,' because if doing IR from the center is problematic, so is claiming to do so 'only' from the margins. Rather, we are seeking to do IR from places, positions, and perspectives that are trying not to be beneficiaries of the story of IR (even though in many ways, we might be constructed by or complicit with that story). While we want to intervene in the endless gesturing towards the North/ West, this does not mean we will stop talking about the US or refuse to address the North/West in this book. Instead, we examine how the way we talk about, share, and experience these narratives may center and decenter the North/West and the disciplinary methods, pedagogies, and understandings of IR.

A variety of other disciplines and intellectual traditions have employed 'decentering' to indicate, in effect, attempts to radically shift, denaturalize, and make 'less central' the very components and tenets that make hegemonic politics possible. Within IR, critical theories certainly confront and disrupt hierarchical power relationships and underscore 'practical political resistance to the production and reproduction of empire, in that any inordinate concentration of power is seen as not desirable' (Duvall and Varadarajan, 2003: 78). Explicit examples of decentering IR in the way we describe are not numerous, but we find particularly useful Agathangelou and Ling's call to replace the 'obsessive fear of disorder' that rules IR with an appreciation and understanding of difference, dialogue, open-ended questions, and the messiness, complexity, and even beauty of our lives (2004: 22). The authors describe a shift towards 'worldism,' guided by Mahatma Gandhi's 'oceanic circle,' a model of connectedness based less on destroying the center and more on deriving strength and clarity as to how we are living and relating together. This shift from the House of IR to worldism is necessary in order to decenter, unsettle, relativize, and provincialize IR.[25] Let's politicize what the world is about, what is done to make that world endure, and the effects of what we do about it.

How and Why We Question IR

We have questions – quite a lot, actually, not least about the ontological and epistemological foundations of IR – and frighteningly few answers. But we hope that by engaging with you in this exercise, through the concepts of indigeneity, human rights, globalization, and peace and security, we will come up with some more answers, at least for now. In our estimation, while answers may come and go, it is the questions that remain. If at the end of this book you have more questions than answers, we will be delighted – though this may present a problem if someone asks you what it is about or if anyone is hoping to quiz you on the contents of this book. Perhaps, in fine Talmudic fashion, you can simply respond to their queries with questions of your own.

In 'doing' IR, we pose the questions which critical/alternative IR theorists, to their great credit, raise, but we wish to turn those questions back onto them/us. Is it possible to break the chain of signifiers, that is, the discourse, which always leads back to the US and its (largely) European allies? In what ways do we rely on intellectual histories that were written by and for only certain subjects in certain locations? In what ways do we gaze upon those who are always already the questioned subject, those whom we presume could never theorize or ponder, or even articulate, how the world works but rather only serve as fodder for our theories? How do those geographically 'outside' of the North/West participate in 'centering' IR? How do those one might consider 'part' of the North/West – by citizenship, job, location, residency – participate in decentering IR? How do we participate in the production and circulation of certain meanings? What is our complicity with relations of power? How do we stop denying and seek to understand the losses and silences in how IR has been practiced, written, and narrated? The implications of these questions are significant – how do we respond?

So as to craft a response, we critique, take on, and grapple with a multiplicity of theories, actors, institutions, practices, and narratives. No one and nothing is 'innocent,' in a sense. This is not to neglect the dedication, commitment, and hard work of so many academics, practitioners, and activists, many located in the very institutions or promoting the very processes we may critique. Rather, our hope is to open the door to the difficult, uncomfortable, and tense conversations that will help us see better how power works. We have tried with each other, and the many people who gave generously of their time, to decipher/explicate our privileges and (mis)education as North American IR scholars and activists. Accordingly, we have sought out and engaged in conversations with scholars and activists living and doing IR in a 'decentered' way. We did this to indicate the ongoing, organic *practice* that is IR. Some of these scholars and activists are based in the North/ West; others are not. Just as we are allies of various social movements, we are and seek allies of attempts to decenter the US in terms of its politics and academic and institutionalized power, and to decenter the usual ways of doing IR.

We are extremely well aware of our positions of power, of the authority that adheres to and is inherent in such positions, and of the risk of inadvertently implying that we 'speak for others.' So, we are not simply inserting case studies from around the world, or even (solely) voices from the Global South. We are not seeking some type of martyr-like self-marginalization or an IR from a prototypical 'oppressed' subject position. We are not seeking to speak 'for' the entire rest of the world in order to 'center' *them*. Rather, we are seeking to hold ourselves and our peers accountable as we figure out our place in the world. At the same time we recognize the borderlands and margins within the North/West where the 'periphery' is not the literal peripheral but rather the place where we learn how the world works and for whom, and how people come together to make things better for themselves and others. We also recognize that elites, countries, and institutions in the Global South and the putative 'periphery' can (and perhaps must) mimic the center, legitimize Western-centric IR metanarratives, and discipline the boundaries of IR as a field of study, as a practice. Indeed, we often found that various universities outside of the US use an IR curriculum that is disconcertingly similar to the ones we critique. We also discovered that peers in the US gave us much to think about with their provocative theories, carefully researched case studies, and thoughtful efforts to reconcile what they both enjoy and fear about living in the North/West. So, we really can't assume anything just based on someone's location; the so-called distinctions between the North/West and the Global South are not always clear, evident, or even distinct.

'Doing' IR, as a scholar, student, practitioner, or activist, requires and demands reflexivity, accountability, responsibility, and, sometimes, an acceptance of not knowing/mastering it all or even much, if any. This is not an easy position for an activist, intellectual, or policy maker to adopt. There is no vanguard party, there is no dogma, there is no we–them; this is not, in any traditional sense, a revolution – but then 'traditional' conceptions of revolution seem less and less useful (and may never have been as useful as we imagined; see, for example, Foran, 2005;

Gilly, 2005; Khasnabish, 2007; Selbin, 2010). Still, this does represent a type of resistance, and it is a rebellion (of sorts). We do not say this glibly, since any academic claim to resistance (not to mention rebellion or revolution) should be viewed with suspicion. Nonetheless, guided by Mexico's modern-day Zapatistas' claim that 'it is not necessary to conquer the world. It is sufficient to make it new. Us. Today' (Marcos, *et al.*, 1998: 19), we call on us all to actively confront the 'usual' ways we proceed.

An Insurgent IR

A recent International Studies Association (ISA) conference panel captured many of the concerns we are describing here.[26] One of the panelists revealed the dismal statistics about the very small number of African IR scholars participating in ISA conferences. Two-thirds of ISA's membership, he noted, comes from North America, mainly the US, while Latin America and Africa have the weakest representation. This prompted others to comment that the entire conference and the most 'reputable' IR journals are in English. If the ISA is no longer 'white guys with ties talking about missile size' (a snarky if disturbingly accurate appraisal *circa* the late 1980s – see also Cohn, 1987), it remains the case that IR is in thrall to the North/West's vision of itself as the repository of truth and enlightenment, the arbiter of what things are and how they should be, and the center of world affairs – to understand the world (never mind consider changing it), you must begin from 'here.'

This is not just a problem with IR not having 'enough' people from around the world involved in a discipline and field ostensibly *about* the world – though this would seem to be worth noting. This is not just about visibility – especially simply for the sake of visibility; many of us in the North/West have learned of late how to finesse that. As another panelist noted, it is about the realization that when many African students and scholars read about 'Africa' in International Relations texts and journals, they don't recognize themselves. IR scholars, policy makers, and activists rarely talk about the world without using the North/West – and the US in particular – as the reference point.

What is needed is to challenge *who* knows, what is constructed as *knowable*, and what is *done* with knowledge. Many other disciplines came to this view long ago – Said's *Orientalism* (1979) changed comparative literature and soon thereafter some of the social sciences and humanities disciplines. Political science, IR in particular, stands out, for all its sophistication and sensitivity, as surprisingly facile and resistant to the fundamental challenge and opportunity such a perspective presents.

Steve Smith (2002) claims that what sets US IR apart from variants elsewhere is the former's epistemological commitments to positivism/ rationalism and consequential inability to think through difference and account for inequalities. Like Smith, Waever (1998) examines how US IR, in particular, developed and asserts itself through the primacy of rational choice scholarship, expecting the rest of IR scholarship to follow suit. In the context of the close relationship between academia and the policy world, US IR aims to 'export' its knowledge to the rest of the world, feigning to be a 'transcultural, transhistorical standard of scholarship' (Smith, 2002: 82). In so doing, US scholarship and policy-making simultaneously draw upon Eurocentric thought while setting themselves aside as different and 'exceptional' in their analyses and policies; at the same time, crucial differences among Western powers notwithstanding, there is (apparently) no question that it is the North/West, the center, that will produce knowledge, make decisions, and govern the rest of the world (Nayak and Malone, 2009). In other words, Northern/Western IR more generally fails to recognize non-Western subjects as *thinkers* rather than 'objects' (Shilliam, 2008).

Thus, there are multiple salutary efforts afoot to explore what it would take (and mean) to make IR truly inclusive with regard to concepts, areas of study, policy suggestions, and the universities at which scholars are located.[27] In a sense, in order to 'democratize' IR, we are guided in part by notions of everyday or 'ordinary' democracy such as Pogrebinschi's (2007). Deploying 'democratization' opens us to charges of emulating the very sort of dynamic (Northern/Westernization and liberal, bourgeois democratic, where the parameters are pre-established) we want to confront; thus, we claim that the mere fact of being 'inclusive,' by using different types of theories to address IR, or considering perspectives from the Global South, is not enough.

Thus many seek inventive ways, through critical pedagogy, to learn and tell stories about the world, tracing where and how power exists and circulates. Pedagogy refers to how knowledge is produced, deployed, and disseminated. A *critical* approach entails

reading, writing, and speaking which go beneath surface meaning, first impressions, dominant myths, official pronouncements, traditional clichés, received wisdom, and mere opinions, to understand the deep meaning, root causes, social context, ideology, and personal consequences of any action, event, object, process, organization, experience, text, subject matter, policy, mass media, or discourse. (Shor, 1992: 129)

If we are to read 'decentering' international relations as a call to dismantle and disrupt the epistemological practices that made and make possible colonial encounters (Denzin, Lincoln, and Tuhiwai Smith, 2008), then critical pedagogy is crucial to this project. In our classrooms, we know that pedagogy plays a socializing role, particularly by legitimizing nationalist myths and mythologies about others, reproducing certain historical narratives, focusing primarily on certain schools of thought, and thinking about only certain people in the world (Chong and Hamilton-Hart, 2009). Further, we do not believe there is 'objective social science' (or humanities or natural sciences) and are not clear it would be a good thing if there were.[28] The hunt for 'objective' data that are distinct from the subjective states of people, couched in seemingly 'scientific' language and methods, in search of reliability and replicability, may not be helpful; such data may well obscure more than they illuminate. Everybody starts from somewhere, everyone stands in some place, and all of us are ineluctably shaped by our circumstances. How could it possibly be otherwise? That's why we ask ourselves, each other, and our students: How do you know what you know? How do you challenge received wisdoms from a variety of sources of information? How do you inform your political sensibilities and analyses? And, what kinds of connections are there (or not) with communities you read about?

For example, feminist scholar Simona Sharoni uses a matrix of privilege, originally developed by the former non-profit organization Children's Creative Response, to provoke conversation about identity, difference, and power.[29] Feminist IR scholar Cynthia Enloe assigns anthropology texts and asks students to assume the subject position of someone who is directly affected by the policies and processes discussed in class. But, she is careful to point out that examining how various people live international relations is not about tokening or exoticizing them – easy to say, much harder to do. She offers the following example, in which a professor might take

a Mexican male corn farmer, a Canadian supermarket woman worker, the son of an elite Mexican politician, a woman urban neighborhood activist in a working class section of Mexico City, a Canadian male foreign affairs officer responsible for NAFTA negotiations – and ask the students to imagine two of these people meeting.[30]

Enloe's many books (2000, 2001, 2007) are replete with examples of examining everyday experiences of IR: the food we buy, the labels on our clothes and shoes, the 'curiosity' with which we should question what we learn from classroom lectures, advertisements, tourism, labor practices.

If such 'thought exercises' seem an unlikely source of rebellion, they are nonetheless sparks of hope in people (re)imagining their world. Some of our conversations are with or inspired by, for example, spoken word artists and musicians. If these people do not seem like producers of IR, that reflects our impoverished views far more than the reality of their lives and worlds.

Another approach to rethinking IR and connecting it to our lives is through interdisciplinary scholarship. Some explore topics such as science fiction (Weldes, 2003), music (Franklin, 2005), and punk politics (Dunn, 2008), while others draw upon innovative work in other disciplines and fields, such as postcolonial theory, feminist studies, geography, anthropology, economics, comparative literature, and performance. Such studies reveal the myopias of IR theory and practice. Chowdhry and Nair's edited volume (2002), for example, reveals how we can use critical theories of IR, particularly in the context of postcolonial studies, to rethink representational practices, international hierarchy, and the intersection of race, gender, and class in questions of justice. Other scholars draw upon various feminist and queer theorists to rethink how we study states and institutions. We can, for example, decenter IR's role in deploying essentialized norms about gender, sex, and sexuality through studies of the World Bank's promotion of heteronormative families (particularly through gender mainstreaming policies) and certain gendered subjectivities that 'fit' the neoliberal world order (Bedford, 2009). Or we can explore the 'hysteria' over the imagined emasculation (through invasions or failed military attacks) of states and communities (Weber, 1999; Parpart and Zalewski, 2008).

Many others consider the deficiencies of IR theory when applied around the world, urging an examination of multiple empirical examples so as to rethink concepts such as sovereignty. Tétreault and Lipschultz's *Global Politics as if People Mattered* (2005) investigates people's 'actual' experiences with nation-states, economics, and migration. Two new volumes focus on how Northern/Western IR theory misrepresents experiences in the rest of the world, and how to use interpretations emanating from countries and perspectives around the world to transform the way we study and think about various IR issues (Acharya and Buzan, 2009; Waever and Tickner, 2009). Consider also the edited volumes *International Relations Theory and the Third World* (Neuman, 1998) and *Africa's Challenge to International Relations Theory* (Dunn and Shaw, 2001). On the other hand, Tsygankov and Tsygankov (2007) consider how non-Western IR might rely (too) heavily on Western IR perspectives, forcing us to ask why and when Western IR is legitimized around the world. Darby's claim that the 'international has been appropriated to stand for the experiences and interests of the powerful' (2006: 6) underscores the relevance of the production of knowledge to North–South relationships (Darby, 2000, 2006).

To complicate matters further, Brown (2006) emphasizes that IR theory is not only problematic when applied to Africa but is problematic in and of itself. Perhaps Northern/Western IR willfully misrepresents not just the rest of the world but the North/West itself – particularly its self-representation as a hermeneutically sealed entity that can be known. This is, obviously, no small claim and provocative; it is crucial to our project here.

In addition, Shani (2008: 723) asks whether critical IR scholars can really open up space for challenges to Northern/Western normative epistemology when they fundamentally rely upon secular Eurocentric historicism; for almost all scholars, the starting points are Hegel, Marx, Foucault, Gramsci, the Frankfurt School, or Habermas. Shani, in an attempt to delineate what a less Eurocentric IR might look like, claims that critical IR is still firmly located in – in terms of speaking to and for – the North/West. He demands that, as we examine the scholarship that aims to 'include' the rest of the world, we ask: Who gets to include whom? Is there an uncritical acceptance of the territorialized nation-state? Are Northern/Western theories, critical or not, granted a status superior to non-Northern/Western theories? Shani examines critical Islamist discourses on modern Islamic nationalisms (such as Turkish Kemalism) and *salafism* (a militant, ideological stance advocating a return to a 'golden' age of Islamism and drawing upon, in some ways, late-nineteenth century Islamic responses to European colonialism) and critical Sikh discourses on the Khalsa Panth (which governs baptized Sikhs) in order to challenge the assumption that non-Western discourses are necessarily 'derivative' of Western discourses. He thus compels us to rethink solidarity, community, and sovereignty in the context of non-Northern/Western transnational communities that are at the forefront of what post-Westphalian life looks like (*ibid.*: 727).

In effect, we have to consider who we are when we are doing IR. What are we missing or ignoring? At whose cost? What is our stake in the theories, policies, and decisions we write about or support? As such, we appreciate Sankaran Krishna's interrogation of the aesthetics of the discipline (1993, 1999). He recently pointed out at a conference that 'Third World students' stay away from critical IR because the idioms are too hard or they are uncomfortable with the theory's use of overly stylized English.[31] He asked, can a refugee feel at home in critical IR, or would they seek out poetry instead? While we believe that theory is not separate from praxis, we recognize the perception that many theories are 'inaccessible,' requiring years, time, intellectual community, patience, and many iterations before one might feel comfortable saying 'I'm politically committed' to this or that theoretical framework. Accordingly, when we do IR are we implicitly saying that only some of us can understand it, while the rest of us 'live' it? Do students leave or switch out of political science and IR because what they read seems to have nothing to do with the lives they live? How *are* we living IR day to day: when we travel, read the news, purchase a product, or visit a museum?

Muppidi (2010) seeks to expose such profoundly colonial indicators and holds us all accountable for who we are as scholars and students; he demands that we consider how our scholarship maintains and even extends the global colonial order. If some forms of knowledge, discourse, and representation of 'the colonized' are no longer 'acceptable,' others are invisible but equally important in upholding the very power relationships that enable colonialism and imperialism. Thus, Muppidi (*ibid.*) offers a sophisticated and nuanced demonstration of the subtlety of IR's role in racialization and the imposing endurance of the colonial order. It would be far easier for all of us to consider and confront it if it were simple, linear, and readily visible. Instead, it is insidious, sometimes unintentional, messy, and painfully provocative when raised in IR circles; we know, we have been in the room.

Indeed, Krishna argues that IR is 'predicated on a systematic politics of forgetting, a willful amnesia, on the question of race' (2001: 401). The discipline does so through abstraction, or 'theory building,' rather than historicized, descriptive analysis; this is rooted in the need to erase the violence that has made possible the type of international relations and global politics most upheld (and, indeed, extended) by mainstream scholars (Krishna, 2001). In other words, what we see around us and how we see it is so partly because of the theft of land, violence, and slavery. This is not meant to suggest a frame of victimization or to set up a 'noble' Global South; it is meant to recognize the 'reality' of the world's immense majority and the relative paucity of knowledge about what undergirds 'our' 'knowledge.'

For our purposes here, we point to Krishna's questions for scholars and students of IR that are, in part, motivating us: How and why do we 'find ourselves inhabiting a discipline that has excised questions of inequality, genocide, the theft of lands and cultures, and has, in their stead, centered on issues such as combating terrorism, securing sovereignty, and winning the games that nations play' (*ibid.*: 421)? Similarly, Chen, Hwang, and Ling (2009) speak about what IR 'brackets,' that is, what is marked as insignificant or irrelevant, and hence shunted aside: unlearned, forgotten, contained. Their project proffers a 'dialectics of subjectivity,' 'transnational solidarities,' and taking seriously multiple world views, hybridities, in-between places, and daily encounters that are a part of the world left out of the study of IR. They also question when and how the study of relations in the world gets reduced to an industry of legitimizing (and thereby validating and authorizing) foreign policy and technocratic elites of nation-states. Inayatullah and Blaney explore how doing IR from below reveals 'that contemporary international relations is an expression of the Western theory of progress' (2007: 672). Here is the IR story again in all its glory. We would add, how and why do we find ourselves always challenging, rebuking, and returning to not just 'the state,' but certain states: the US, Great Britain, and occasional others?

In sum, the works we draw upon and engage with here 'get' the pathology of power, the colonial desires, that permeate IR. The stories of IR can be terribly and historically dishonest and anachronistic but are still taught in classrooms, appear in journalistic analyses, and dominate the scholarship and policy reports. The way we produce, deploy, and employ knowledge not only affects people's lives but sometimes costs them – simply (not that there is anything simple about it) because of how we theorize the world. It is urgent that we not only recognize this, but do something different, act. This should not, indeed, must not, produce paralysis but rather demands that we recognize and collaborate with people who are doing and living IR in ways that never make it into most classrooms or journals.

In the following chapters, we will work our way through how we might decenter the concepts of indigeneity, human rights, globalization, and peace and security – and, thus, IR – and consider the implications and ramifications of doing this. Accordingly, in each chapter, we will investigate those presumptions and the production of knowledge, take a close look at how activists and scholars participate in decentering IR, and put forth possible pedagogical and scholarly interventions readers can consider. We will recast familiar topics and issues. In other words, we will endeavor to map what a decentered IR might look like and how it might operate. This will be a fraught process and mistakes will be made; perhaps they must be made if we are to make any headway.

Chapter Two / Indigeneity

Rethinking IR's Tourism – Northern/Western Fantasies of Indigeneity

Baz Luhrmann, of *Moulin Rouge* fame, recently directed a Tourism Australia television commercial that can now be seen on YouTube and blogs. The advertisement's opening scene quickly indicates via a phone conversation that a woman in New York City is having romantic problems with a man. They both appear to be white. That night, while she sleeps, a young, naked brown boy creeps barefoot, leaving muddy footprints behind him in the streets, into her bedroom and whispers into her ear, 'Sometimes, we have to get lost to find ourselves. Sometimes – we got to go walkabout.' He then sprinkles 'magical' dust into her hands. The woman and the man suddenly find themselves swimming in a breathtaking scene in Australia, one that is removed from time and place, depicting travel as fantasy. As they reconnect, the man says, with immeasurable relief in his voice, 'Glad you're back,' to the now relaxed woman, no longer a busy career woman, and ready to devote herself to her man, seduced back into both nature and what is 'natural' by a young (presumably aboriginal) boy.

Tim Jones, a marketing manager at Tourism Australia, explains in an interview:

> When you go 'Walkabout' you leave the pressures of everyday life behind to rediscover what is important to you. This concept is intrinsically linked to the cultural and traditional beliefs of the Australian Aboriginal people, making it uniquely Australian.[1]

Many things about this advertisement should ring familiar; three are likely to jump out: first, there is the wrenching of an aboriginal adolescent rite of passage into some sort of Northern/Western fantasy of a few days' vacation; second, there is the appropriation of supposedly timeless, static 'traditions' imputed to people historically discriminated against and displaced by the very governments using marketing tools and branding consultants to draw in tourists for some type of 'real' experience; third, there is the romanticization of those usually reviled or seen as disposable, for politically or economically expedient purposes. And, just to complicate matters a bit (see Enloe, 2001), it is hardly the case that those being woven into Northern/Western fantasies are not availing themselves of the situation as well. It might, in other words, be a little too tempting to posit the wicked, Western ways against poor, dumb, ignorant natives who don't know any better and have no idea when they're experiencing exploitation. Instead, it is possible and common for people to understand quite well when they're being 'screwed over' and to look for places around the edges to see what they can leverage out of the situation.

As we do IR, we must ask in what ways we are tourists, explorers, and adventurers in other people's worlds. How do we exploit and neglect others? Who do we categorize and 'brand'? Whose existence is simultaneously denied yet deployed conveniently to prove our theories or accomplish our political and economic agendas? Where do we travel, as voyeurs, in hopes of connecting with, exploring, or discovering some 'real' knowledge (with or without a magical dose of fantasy) about what some place, some peoples, must be like? Who cannot travel, and who do we presume never would travel to look at 'us'?

These questions beg us to begin by understanding what is meant by indigeneity – by indigenous, first, or aboriginal peoples. This concern will run through the chapters to come, since indigeneity cuts to the core of so many other concepts. Human rights departs from here, globalization is implicated here, and ever more of today's issues of peace and security are (d)riven by tensions related to indigeneity. If we can problematize this concept and show how intensely knotty it has become, we believe we can see how these other more familiar matters of human rights, globalization (and associated topics such as development, economics, and the environment), and peace and security are equally susceptible. These three topics make up the core of almost any introduction to an IR course and are, by and large, the stock in trade of various graduate-level courses. Yet, undergirding them all to some degree is indigeneity.

The Category of Indigeneity

IR is profoundly peopled and stated (in several senses). In the previous chapter, we very briefly discussed some of these peoples and states, using the particularly apt 'house' metaphor from Agathangelou and Ling (2004). But who or what constitutes a 'native'? As we answer this question, we point out how the category of indigeneity – the image and idea of the native – serves to center IR in three essential ways: (1) by justifying the existence of the state and its importance as a central concern of IR; (2) by empowering institutions and states to decide, classify, and interrogate indigenous peoples' identities and rights; and (3) by entrenching Northern/Western understandings of land and private property.

First, even though indigenous peoples are seemingly 'absent' (or, alternatively, some type of undifferentiated mass) in IR theory, discourse, and policy, they are crucial for maintaining the critical nation-state 'origin myth.' This brings us to our claim: in a profound and underappreciated sense, indigeneity was the 'first' IR topic. This may seem like an odd thing to say. After all, there is a propensity in IR to proffer Thucydides as the first IR theorist and his *History of the Peloponnesian War* as the *ur* ('original') text, which serves several purposes: it roots IR deeply in the Northern/Western canon reliant on Greco-Roman custom,[2] suggests that IR is as old or older than other fields of political study,[3] and positions realism as the sort of *echt* ('true') IR theory. We start IR classes with realism, not indigenous peoples.

It is also difficult to think of indigeneity as important because another origin or source point for IR is typically the European 'state-making' (defined largely by war-making)[4] of the sixteenth and seventeenth century, culminating in the Peace of Westphalia (1648).[5] Thus, we realize it may seem counter-intuitive to speak about aboriginal and indigenous peoples, rather than the state, as a centering concept, particularly when we go on and on about the US and Western European *states*' dominance in the world. After all, practically every IR textbook begins and ends with the state in some manner; international relations is defined as relations between states. The purportedly crucial Westphalian moment – the creation of functionally similar, territorially bound nation-states and state sovereignty based on a seventeenth-century model of Europe – gives us the modern state system and hence the modern world.

In this system, each state's sovereignty is defined by the right to control its own affairs without outside interference and by its control over territorially bounded populations defined as *citizens*. Citizens receive a 'legal-juridical status,' entitling them, allegedly, to the state's protection (more on this in Chapter 5) in exchange for performing duties and fulfilling obligations such as abiding by the laws and paying taxes (Ling, 2010: 101).The implication of citizenship, of course, is that there are different people in different places fruitfully grouped into 'us' and 'them.' The state and citizen align in the 'nation-state,' whereby the state represents the nation, or political community of citizens loyal to the sovereign.

But while the nation-state concept is powerful, its reality (as it were) is suspect. Quick! How many true 'nation-states,' with a single people united by a deep sense of shared culture and identity (a nation) located in a geographically bounded territory under the control of a sovereign government with a monopoly over the use of force (a state), can you name? Japan? Well, except for the relatively few Ryūkyū and the Ainu and assorted Chinese and Koreans. Finland, perhaps? Ah, but there are the Sami as well as Romani, a smattering of Russians and Estonians, and, if you ask the Swedes, *all* those Swedish-Finns. How about Iceland? Hard to argue with that one, but a single case is hardly helpful and certainly belies the notion that we live in a Westphalian world of nation-states.

More to the point, what about those who lived in different types of communities when others arrived to arbitrarily designate and map the territory and to impose a belonging accessed only through citizenship – available to certain private-property holders who pledged allegiance to the eventually created nation-state but *not* available to those who were 'different'? The lines drawn on maps cut through families and communities. Indeed, Inayatullah and Blaney illustrate how the Westphalian myth could only allow the 'birth' of the nation-state system (for colonizers) by dealing with difference through the 'deferral of a genuine recognition, exploration, and engagement' (2004: 44). Instead, the frame is one of danger and disorder, whereupon difference is read as degenerate, backward, and pre-modern.

Accordingly, the 'intellectual origins of IR closely align the field with a legacy of colonialism and religious cleansing' (*ibid.*: viii). Naming this difference, pointing out these 'Others,' was important to the development of IR, necessary to create an order, indispensable to justify behavior, essential to rationalize exploitation, and crucial to the construction of domination.[6] If it were not for the native, in other words, we would not have realized how we needed to organize ourselves politically and, it goes without saying, in a civilized way into these entities we call nation-states. *They* live primitively in their tribes; *we* are civilized with our states. Thus, lurking behind our passports and citizenship status is the native – the denial, murder, and enslavement of whom made possible the modern nation-state.

So, indigeneity centers IR in the sense that it legitimizes the territorial organization of the world into nation-states. In order for the state to remain the basic unit of analysis in IR and, accordingly, for Northern/Western understandings of sovereignty to prevail in IR theory and Western policy-making, there has to be a concept of something primitive, regressive, vaguely dangerous, and vestigial (left behind) in the (putative) state of nature. Terms such as '*Indian* and *American Indian*, like *Native American*, *aboriginal*, and *indigenous* emerged as a product of a co-constitutive relationship with terms such as *colonizers*, *settler*, and *American*' (Bruyneel, 2007: ix, italics in original). Consequently, indigenous peoples did not *always* see that they had something in 'common' in opposition to 'Europeans' (*ibid.*). They *became* native peoples in contradistinction to colonizers and state-making. Yet we easily forget this point. As Smith argues, the critiques of US President Bush's 'unconstitutional' behavior after 9/11 or of US 'empire,' 'still unwittingly or implicitly take the US Constitution as their original story, presuming the US nation-state even as they critique it,' thereby masking the 'genocide of indigenous peoples that is its foundation' (Smith 2008: 310, 311).

The second manner in which indigeneity centers IR has to do with the accordance of rights and justice to indigenous peoples. The context is one of Northern/Western juridical categories which 'give' *them* rights while leaving undisturbed 'civilization,' state sovereignty, and Northern/Western institutional arrangements which are constructed and construed as both universal and enduring.[7] In this process, the North/West has also granted itself naming rights, the right to distinguish territory/ies (and adjudicate amongst claimants), and to support/fund lifestyles that are in harmony with contemporary understandings of civilization and late modernity. This is not to avoid or neglect how people claim and name themselves as native, *indios*, indigenous, and so forth. Rather, this is about constructing categories and extending and granting rights to those who supposedly comprise that category. Citizenship strictly determines inside and outside, with indigenous people as the permanent outsiders living 'inside.'

The achievement of 'indigenous rights' has thus become increasingly dependent on a patchwork quilt of post-World War Two international organizations designed to redress what were conceded by many to be inequities and serious, even tragic, mistakes.[8] But the United Nations (an intergovernmental organization with member states), human rights organizations, and international law (a regime that protects state sovereignty) have not responded with any sort of consistency. There seems to be little support, for example, for reparations in those places with the greatest number of indigenous people. Australia, Canada, New Zealand, and the United States, for example, were the four dissenting votes on the United Nations' 2007 passage of the Declaration on the Rights of Indigenous Peoples (there were also eleven abstentions); there is little more support in places such as Russia, Mexico, or Guatemala. Yet others elsewhere and sometimes even in these places are designated or acknowledged as deserving some type of reparations or support. The reasons are not always clear. What *is* clear is that the entities (nation-states, the UN, international law) that grant or name those rights are rarely, if ever, interrogated as much as the people striving for justice.

So, what must indigenous peoples do, and how must they represent themselves, in order to 'get' rights and accompanying privileges? Nair notes that 'indigenous delegates are involved in the discursive production of "indigenous place" in the UN' and 'most often, indigenous identities are understood as a political strategy used by the respective communities' (2006: 6). She cites: (1) 'the Maasai attempts in Tanzania to link their fragmented identities together in terms of "indigeneity" ... in turn gave them better visibility, increased legitimacy, and improved donor support,' (2) 'in Indonesia, tribal people articulate transnationally recognized indigenous identity as a strategy,' and (3) 'tribes in [the] central region of India (Jharkhand region)' do the same (*ibid.*). In Nair's estimation it is thus that indigenous peoples have rights, 'but collective rights determined by their nativity' (*ibid.*: 7). Natives, in other words, must constantly define themselves, be defined, and wait for established organizations and authorities to 'allow' them, that is, recognize their right, to exist and make claims. Central entities of IR (the state, law, UN) remain central because they are *needed* to make sense of natives.

Finally, indigeneity as a concept reflects Northern/Western understandings of private property, land ownership, and relationships to land. On the one hand, the right to private property encapsulated in countries' constitutions and laws and the very construction of sovereignty (Inayatullah and Blaney, 2004: 187–190) does not square with what Chief Seattle of the Suquamish and Duwamish peoples in the Pacific Northwest of the US may have suggested (attributed to an 1854 speech he gave in a somewhat obscure language and translated after the fact several times): no one can *own* the land or the sky.[9] Fenelon and Hall (2008: 1869–70) point out that the Lakota Sioux in North America continue to rebuff US offers of money for land they deem sacred; they want it returned not to be owned but as sacred space for all to use – this despite their deep impoverishment, which might augur acceptance of the money.

On the other hand, land figures prominently in popular perceptions of indigenous people as simple, child-like, ahistorical – particularly as 'land' gets read as 'nature.' Even narratives that acknowledge colonial intrusion can tend to write the indigenous as deeply 'simple' and uncomplicated, in some sense, un(der)developed,[10] but living (happily, at least before the deluge) in accordance with nature and each other in a way the intruders cannot. Fenelon and Hall (*ibid*.: 1895), otherwise sensitive and incisive observers, nonetheless succumb: 'One observation remains true as it has for more than 500 years – indigenous peoples will resist and survive because of their ability to maintain community, find leadership, distribute resources fairly among their people, and above all keep our respect for the land, the earth as our grandmother from which we are born and to which we will return.' There is a surprising (or perhaps not) investment in the supposition that the indigenous are wise, benevolent, simple communities which once lived and hope again to live in harmony amongst themselves and with nature. As our introduction above noted, indigenous people can apparently, with a poof of fairy dust, transport people right out of twenty-first century stress and into timeless harmonious relationships with each other and the world!

This kind of thinking reflects a paternalistic romanticization in which 'life, art forms, food-habits, industries, all become markers of a traditional world that is free from the perils of modernization' (Nair, 2006: 6). 'Otherness' is accentuated in ways that serve no one well and perpetuate a dynamic that is almost certainly damaging, to various degrees, for all concerned (but see *ibid.*: 6–7). The very acknowledgment that people existed in societies 'before' they and their lands were 'discovered' can potentially lead to an assumption that, being *a priori* to the state, they are always already there, one, in 'synch' with each other and the land; they always have been, always will be. And, indeed, a centered IR is about deciding what to do about them, over there . . . those who will always be and always have been in the same local community, without consideration of encounters, changes, resistance, migration, exile, or broken and renewed alliances.

Yes, many communities have long-standing practices, ties to each other and their geographical locations, and profoundly powerful and qualitatively different ways of relating to and respecting land, but these communities change and experience contestation over what they are. It is important to recognize this because 'original' inhabitants may not actually have been the first inhabitants of a place, may themselves have been conquerors and dominators in their context, such as the Inca and the Aztec, and thus may not be able to lay claim to rights if they cannot directly trace their ancestry or historical connection to the land in the same way other groups may. For example, African governments, claiming that all black Africans are 'indigenous,' have been reluctant to recognize the rights of the indigenous San in southern Africa (Mutume, 2007). In effect, indigenous peoples must somehow prove they are the 'original' inhabitants in order to make a claim on territoriality, even though many may not have been 'there' from the beginning (how far back are we going?), while other indigenous groups consider themselves as such because of their own definitions of ethnicity or as a contestation of state-imposed definitions or colonial oppression (Nair, 2006: 8).

We contend that the very dichotomy of settler/indigenous, even when presumably to point to patterns and legacies of brutal colonialism, may not be adequate, because it does not fully capture complicated answers to 'Who was there first?' Systems of domination existed for thousands of years, well before the Europeans sallied forth. The Adivasis who reside in what is now India and the Bedouin of southern Israel, for example (Fenelon and Murguía, 2008: 1669), or, more recently, groups once subsumed under the Incan Empire, all faced such oppression and domination. While European 'white settler societies' are notorious (see Gott, 2007), they were hardly alone. Of course, what is significantly different is the all-encompassing degree to which the North/West actively began to create a narrative in which they were the beneficent and munificent powers come to bring not just civilization but of course 'the word,' for *this* expansion was guided by the hand of God. Valuables acquired, 'open' land claimed, resources 'discovered,' workers bent to the tasks at hand which would somehow benefit them, were simply just recompense or a serendipitous bit of good fortune. Invaders/intruders/interlopers have framed and continue to frame this construct, whether as 'natives' or, more 'benevolently' (a word rife with invidious implications in this context), indigenous peoples, aboriginals, first peoples, first nations, and so on, in ways that are awash with good intentions but bear horrible consequences.

A necessary intrusion: defining a term we want to defy

We are left, then, with a complicated urgency to define and address exploitations and injustices against people who defy categorization. Indigeneity is certainly a deeply Northern/Western concept ultimately redolent of the very sort of Orientalism it is meant to help us avoid. Indeed, don't we all defy categorization? After all, if part of the problem is trying to simplify, or treat as simple, indigenous peoples, it is equally problematic to act as if they are some separate, unknowable entity – mysterious and complicated and otherworldly – as if 'we' know exactly what/whom we are.

Too few scholars explore the inability and unwillingness of IR (and cognate fields such as comparative politics and American political development/thought) to examine its own treatment of indigeneity. However, critical IR theory has uncovered the brutalities of the creation of *indigenous* as a category, how those brutalities were/are in the service of the state, and indigenous politics that challenges and remakes sovereignty. Specifically, Burke (2008: 365) argues that postmodernist IR thought has 'contributed to a more intellectually diverse effort to show how the ontological privilege granted to sovereignty has been used to deny indigenous people full subjectivity and rights within the institutions that govern international relations – a problem that persists and ... gravely undermines the moral legitimacy of "international society."'[11] Such a critique, he notes, 'underpins practical efforts to legitimate the struggles of indigenous peoples against miners, loggers, and security forces ... among a number of injustices that stimulated a deeper challenge to sovereignty as an ontology' (*ibid.*).

Other scholars point out how studying indigenous politics can reveal important lessons for IR. Consider Neta Crawford's analysis of cooperative security within the Iroquois League, consisting of five and later six democratic indigenous nations (Cayuga, Mohawk, Oneida, Onondaga, Seneca, and Tuscarora) from the 1450s to late 1770s. She notes that these nations demonstrated more institutionalized and successful conflict resolution than other examples, such as the nineteenth-century Concert of Europe (Crawford, 1994). As another example, Shaw explores how indigenous struggles (1) reveal unresolved problems about sovereignty (particularly in countries where indigeneity has not been 'resolved' through reservations and citizenship laws); (2) challenge non-indigenous people to consider how their economic and political lives continue violence against indigenous people, particularly through the expropriation of their resources; and (3) highlight how both state sovereignty and international relations are paradoxically enabling yet constraining for indigenous politics (Shaw, 2002, 2008).

Equally compelling is Bruyneel's consideration (2007) of the unique spatial and temporal boundaries that govern relationships between sovereign countries and sovereign tribes. IR, political institutions, and democratic theory are not equipped to understand the ambiguous and uncertain 'space' of sovereignty, at the intersection of tribal sovereignties and state sovereignty. Bruyneel thus examines indigenous responses to the US imposition of citizenship in 1924, attempts to determine the status of treaty rights, the movement for tribal self-determination in the 1960s that distinguished itself from the US civil rights movement and worldwide decolonization, and contemporary tribal political struggles. Finally, consider Beier, who exposes what he terms the 'hegemonologue': 'that decidedly Western voice that speaks to the exclusion of all others, heard by all and yet, paradoxically, seldom noticed, the knowledges it bears having been widely disseminated as "common senses" rather than as politicized claims about the world and our ways of being in it' (2005: 15). He notes that even critical scholars who attempt to contest this hegemonologue participate in this colonial way of speaking.

Indeed, how are 'we' talking *about* natives? Despite the insights we can learn from these authors, the emergence of 'indigeneity' is now a marker of sorts, a sign meant to indicate one's awareness of colonial encounters; we talk about it as if we get it – yes, we know, people's identity and sense of belonging do not derive from formulations of citizenship that performed violence against them. It becomes even more complicated when groups of people identify themselves as indigenous and make legitimate and necessary claims based on indigeneity against the state and for their aspirations and sensibilities. Yet the fundamental dilemma remains: if we subscribe to the notion of indigeneity, no matter how good our intentions, no matter if some of us define ourselves as indigenous, we potentially acquiesce to the particular formulation of the world in the IR story.

Let's spend some time on what indigeneity could be or mean. 'Indigenous' as a term of art, according to Fenelon and Murguía, 'surfaced in the seventeenth century, derived from the Old Latin prefix *indu* which means "within" in combination with *gen* which denotes "root of"' (2008: 1657). In recent years, organizations of indigenous people have rejected efforts to define them ('Concept of Indigenous Peoples,' 2004: 2), not least by others; as the Chairperson and Special Rapporteur for the United Nations Working Group on Indigenous Populations pointed out, 'historically indigenous peoples have suffered, from definitions imposed by others' (Daes, 1997: 3).

Daes's colleague Martínez Cobo[12] produced a working definition which guides many IR discussions of indigeneity and merits quoting:

Indigenous communities, peoples and nations are those which, having a historical continuity with pre-invasion and pre-colonial societies that developed on their territories, consider themselves distinct from other sectors of the societies now prevailing on those territories, or parts of them. They form at present non-dominant sectors of society and are determined to preserve, develop and transmit to future generations their ancestral territories, and their ethnic identity, as the basis of their continued existence as peoples, in accordance with their own cultural patterns, social institutions and legal system. This historical continuity may consist of the continuation, for an extended period reaching into the present of one or more of the following factors: (a) Occupation of ancestral lands, or at least of part of them; (b) Common ancestry with the original occupants of these lands; (c) Culture in general, or in specific manifestations (such as religion, living under a tribal system, membership of an indigenous community, dress, means of livelihood, lifestyle, etc.); (d) Language (whether used as the only language, as mother-tongue, as the habitual means of communication at home or in the family, or as the main, preferred, habitual, general or normal language); (e) Residence on certain parts of the country, or in certain regions of the world; (f) Other relevant factors. ('Concept of Indigenous Peoples,' 2004: 2)

In addition, the definition notes that

> on an individual basis, an indigenous person is one who belongs to these
> indigenous populations through self-identification as indigenous (group
> consciousness) and is recognized and accepted by these populations as one of
> its members (acceptance by the group). This preserves for these communities
> the sovereign right and power to decide who belongs to them, without
> external interference. (*Ibid.*: 2)

If not quite a definition, the 1989 Convention Concerning
Indigenous and Tribal Peoples in Independent Countries adopted by the
International Labour Organization offers an 'understanding' or 'coverage'
(*ibid.*: 1, 3) of who constitute the indigenous:

> (a) tribal peoples in independent countries whose social, cultural and
> economic conditions distinguish them from other sections of the national
> community, and whose status is regulated wholly or partially by their
> own customs or traditions or by special laws or regulations; (b) peoples in
> independent countries who are regarded as indigenous on account of their
> descent from the populations which inhabited the country, or a geographical
> region to which the country belongs, at the time of conquest or colonization
> or the establishment of present state boundaries and who, irrespective of their
> legal status, retain some or all of their own social, economic, cultural and
> political institutions. (*Convention Concerning Indigenous and Tribal Peoples in
> Independent Countries*, 1989: n.p.)

Here again, there is care to recognize that 'self-identification as indigenous
or tribal shall be regarded as a fundamental criterion for determining the
groups' (*ibid.*).

And here too the conventional themes shine through and the basis
for IR theory remains clear. Nair (2006: 7) astutely argues that 'the
category of indigenous peoples ... used by the UN is ahistorical, mirror-
ing the notion of the simple and undifferentiated society in the post-
industrial discourse.' Most problematic, if least surprising, is the obvious
commitment to 'territoriality' that reflects the Northern/Western
obsession with ownership, management, and control of the land;
'a primeval quality of defense of territories against others of the same
species' (*ibid.*: 8).

Nair, then, is holding accountable not just the nation-state but also
other institutions, such as the United Nations, which historically have
legitimized what the state does in the name of sovereignty. Perhaps

most disturbing for Nair (*ibid.*: 17) is that 'scholars, who have expressed concerns about disjunctures in the concept of indigenous peoples, consider such disjunctures as just practical problems, not doubting the theoretical accuracy of the concept,' a concern we share with regard to most relevant academic exercises. In other words, sometimes we think it's about rights for or grievances of 'the peoples,' when it's the definitions of those people that are problematic.

Nair (*ibid.*: 3) goes so far as to argue that 'the popularity of the notion of indigenous peoples is primarily due to the transnational networks that give them a common platform of articulation,' pointing out that the United Nations' International Decade of the World's Indigenous Peoples (1995–2004) sought to generate 'commitment to the "idea" (Béteille, 1998) of indigenous peoples.' Attendant to this, the rights of the indigenous – the indigenous themselves seem to be accepted as a matter of fact – are 'protected by agencies such as the International Labour Organization, the United Nations Working Group on Indigenous Peoples, and the World Council of Indigenous Peoples' (Nair, 2006: 3). But what happens in the transnational/international 'space' of the UN or international law is not without power relations and hegemonic practices and discourses.

Laws and institutions feign (indeed, have a great deal invested in) an objective, neutral, and fair stance, and thus disregard the difficulty that experiences and stories cannot be captured within juridical categories or legal binaries. Furthermore, as many scholars of critical race and postcolonial theory, critical legal studies, and feminist jurisprudence have argued, international law is political, steeped in gendered, racialized, and colonial discourses that mark differences between Europeans and non-Europeans, men and women, different races, civilized and uncivilized (Orford, 2002; Anghie, 2005; Bowden, 2005; Kapur, 2006; Kinsella, 2006; Orford, 2006; Philipose 2009). These authors address how international law legitimizes the juridical foundations of sovereignty, thus participating in the colonial project of the state's denial of so-called natives.

Is there no use, then, for international institutions and law because of the problematic categorization of indigenous? We think the answer is more complicated than that. The gains of using these international institutions are, of course, potentially numerous. It is useful to employ international law to put pressure on the domestic courts system and national/foreign policy so as to disentangle land ownership from ideas of capitalist property rights and eminent domain and from a state's alleged sovereign right to a monopoly on the use of violence to protect its bounded territory.

Consider, for example, the 'Consolidated Indigenous Shadow Report'[13] submitted by the International Indian Treaty Council to the United Nations Committee on the Elimination of Racial Discrimination in early 2008. This report documents apartheid and forced assimilation, calling attention to distinctions between federally and non-federally recognized Indian nations in the US. Disproportionate incarceration, environmental destruction of tribal lands through coal and uranium mining and nuclear dumping, the exportation of banned pesticides from the US to other countries, thus affecting indigenous peoples, and systematized discrimination through US Congressional acts are but a few of the issues raised. The report makes recommendations to the UN committee in ways that strategically deploy international law to call out the US.

Brysk notes that the strategic use of legal institutions is crucial at the international and transnational levels as well:

> Like David battling Goliath, tribal villages unexpectedly challenge the states, markets, and missions that seek to crush them. Even more unexpectedly, their scattered triumphs come from Goliath's own arsenal: from the United Nations to the World Wide Web. Indigenous movements derive much of their impact from an unlikely combination of identity politics and internationalization. In the spaces between power and hegemony, the tribal village builds relationships with the global village. (Brysk, 2000: 2)

Brysk focuses on examples of how indigenous peoples in Brazil, Mexico, Ecuador, Nicaragua, and Bolivia reach out for international support because of persecution by the state (*ibid.*: 9), using 'global symbolic appeals and normative reconstructions of international forces' to engender transformation (*ibid.*: 2). Indigenous resistance has compelled reform within the UN or even evicted corporations from their lands, challenging preconceptions that indigenous/tribal communities are isolated or disconnected from domestic or foreign advocates and state representatives. Brenda Norrell, a journalist covering indigenous issues for close to thirty years and a human rights editor for the *UN Observer and International Report*, also notes the usefulness of transnational activism and international pressure in securing domestic court victories to protect sacred lands or in holding accountable stockholders and corporations responsible for environmental destruction and toxins.[14] Thus, the promise and lure of international law in defining indigenous peoples is that it will eventually lead to the ability to hold states accountable when they, for instance, separate people from their families, livelihoods, and homes through a series of checkpoints, border walls, and virtual fences.

Thus, international arenas, and accompanying transnational activism, are crucial because they bolster the ability of domestic movements to achieve their goals (Keck and Sikkink, 1998; Risse, Ropp, and Sikkink, 1999). In defining and discussing transnational activism, many IR theorists have made distinctions between undemocratic, unaccountable globalization/globalism imposed 'from above' by international institutions, such as the International Monetary Fund (IMF), the World Bank (WB), the World Trade Organization (WTO), and the international trade regime, and globalization 'from below,' encompassing 'global civil society,' worldwide interconnections, and diverse and democratic ideals and dialogues. We will say more about globalization in Chapter 4, but, presumably, indigenous and marginalized communities benefit by engaging in globalization from below: they challenge multinational corporations imposing privatization and trade and capital liberalization. Communities such as the Ogoni of Nigeria and the Confederation of Indigenous Nationalities of Ecuador (CONAIE) use the international NGOs, the UN, and other transnational forums to contest nation-states' participation in suppressing their own populations' rights, while such communities also demand a 'push back' against global financial institutions or more powerful states and corporations.

However, participation in or collaboration with transnational efforts or even large organized domestic movements can affect political struggles problematically because many marginalized communities may not be as politically visible or resourceful as internationally recognized or participatory indigenous movements. Also, doesn't it complicate matters to rely upon the United Nations, which is part of the same institutional framework as the WB and IMF? On the one hand, UN settings invoke indigeneity to promote protection of collective rights; on the other hand, sometimes the same activists point to the harmful effects that international institutions that are fundamentally bound up with the United Nations have on indigenous communities. And so we confront a conundrum of sorts. IR offers the self-serving, even ennobling presentation of 'Others' who need – once again – to be rescued. Setting aside, for the moment, the Otherness inherent in, first time around, their requiring rescue from themselves and their barbaric ways, now *we* are rescuing them from *us* and our colonial ways – or at least those 'uses' 'we' in the North/West think they need rescuing from. For IR, there is no real mess here. If there is any acknowledgment, it is along the lines of 'look, there are indigenous people, they have been wronged, let's help them' – and hence the fuss is confined to the details.

Critical scholars such as Nair perhaps align with the famous admonition of Audre Lorde, the Caribbean-American self-described (Lorde, 2009: 184) 'Black Woman Poet Lesbian Mother Lover Teacher Friend Warrior': 'the master's tools will never dismantle the master's house' (Lorde, 2007: 110). This means that relying upon the very structures – the UN, international law, the state – that have historically enabled the denial, oppression, and displacement of indigenous peoples will have limited and possibly deleterious effects. Crucially, we cannot always separate out the 'state' as the bad guy and the 'UN' as the good guy, because they are all potentially implicated in the oppression and exploitation of indigenous peoples; and, sometimes, in other cases, states will support indigenous rights against the practices of an international actor.

As we have tried to make clear, much damage has been done and there is the potential for considerably more. This is neither to suggest nefarious conspiracy theories nor conscious omissions, though sadly both can be discerned across the years; rather, by and large, it is a sort of unthinking acquiescence to a Northern/Western dominator mode of thought which is impressively insidious. We are aiming to acknowledge social justice struggles and accomplishments while also theorizing the unintended consequences when attempting to 'define' indigenous peoples, or to call upon 'universal norms' to 'help' them. In order to sever all links with the myth of universality, Fenelon and Hall suggest that we 'use specific, grounded examples and discussions of indigenous people' (2008: 1874) rather than 'prepackaged terms such as the "fourth world" or as ethnics in "developing nations" or even hidden in the broader "periphery"' (Fenelon and Murguía, 2008: 1657).

None of this is easy; none of it may even be possible. We must start by rejecting the fundamental presumption that the North/West, particularly the US and Europe, is the primary (even only) reference point and model. We must actively confront the 'usual' ways we question the assumptions and presumptions inherent in our fields and how we form the research questions we pursue. The assumption here is that it is possible and, indeed, desirable to loosen the powerful grip the story of indigeneity has had on not only the academy and the policy world, but the popular imagination of all and sundry. The next few sections sketch out three key ways to do this: (1) strategically using the law to up-end intimate relationships between state sovereignty and the construction of the indigenous; (2) challenging the issue of 'evidence' as it is invoked regarding indigenous peoples; (3) thinking through the concepts of connections and belonging.

Indigeneity as a Site for Decentering International Relations

Subverting the law

As we mentioned above, indigenous groups may find it useful to rely upon international law and institutions to hold states and others accountable, but this tactic is potentially problematic. We therefore propose to look next at how some communities are strategically using *indigenous* law to decenter sovereignty and thus IR. To that end, we find it useful to focus on the work of Christine Zuni Cruz at the University of New Mexico, the first Isleta Pueblo woman to become a tenured law professor. She also serves as the director of the Southwest Indian Law Clinic, which provides hands-on opportunities to practice indigenous law, and as the editor-in-chief of *The Tribal Law Journal.*

Her scholarship implicates Anglocentric law in its inability to account for racial, gendered, tribal, and familial identities and experiences. Her work illuminates her experiences as an Indian lawyer as well as her perspective of witnessing members of her community, including her son, face incarceration and intergenerational trauma (Cruz, 2005). She brings attention to the multitude of differences between tribes, although US federal Indian law glosses over those distinctions. She also highlights and questions the possibilities of intersection between Anglocentric and tribal law – the former focused on burden of proof, legal knowledge, adversarial process, and procedural outcome, and the latter on accountability, narrative, and justice aimed at healing, and rooted in the underlying cause of the issue at hand (Cruz, 2007).

In so doing, she makes clear that traditional (internal to the tribe and oral) and tribal (codes and resolutions adopted under the US Indian Reorganization Act of 1934) laws are distinct (from each other and from US law) and have complicated relationships with each other, which sometimes makes it difficult to determine jurisdiction (Jessepe, 2009). This is particularly so because there is nothing within indigenous legal systems analogous to the law that emanates from nation-states; indigenous legal tradition is 'shared.' 'Land and moveable property are not accumulated for wealth; there is no right to alienate the land itself' (Cruz, 2007). This is a serious challenge to IR theory.

Cruz makes the case for upholding the legitimacy of indigenous legal tradition, which she defines as living, organic, fluid, and operating in the social consciousness and daily lives of indigenous peoples. She notes that it emerges from experience and is transferred through spoken word, memory, and oral narratives. When there is dissent, new traditions are created; at the same time, 'tradition has to be convincing and more persuasive than other ways of living' (*ibid.*).

Understanding the organic nature of indigenous legal tradition is important in the face of the denigration of indigeneity and demands for assimilation from nation-states. As an example, Cruz mentions the role of the US Department of the Interior's Bureau of Indian Affairs in posting signs that said: 'Tradition is the enemy of progress, tradition is the enemy of the people' around Navajo country. Further, Cruz notes that 'modern' legal traditions treat indigenous laws as if they are completely unknowable and can thus be applied unfavorably towards non-Indians who live, work, or enter indigenous territories. In *Duro v. Reina* 496 US 676 (1990), for example, US Supreme Court Justice Kennedy referenced the 'unspoken norms and practices' in Indian territory. In *Nevada v. Hicks* 533 US 353 (2001), Justice Souter lamented indigenous 'unwritten law' and the difficulties for outsiders in sorting out the tenets. Cruz mentions that implicit in these comments is the notion that indigenous communities would actually gain more power if they just assimilated, and if their legal systems would 'evolve' from 'unwritten' and 'confusing,' to a code more like the US system.

It is of course important to have knowledge of Northern/Western systems so that indigenous peoples can be prepared to know at what points to claim rights and self-represent in that system, and when to resist assimilation. So, when indigenous intellectuals are educated in Western schools and universities they must recognize the interplay between Western and indigenous laws: 'Is there complementarity? Conflict? Or do they simply coexist side by side?' (Cruz, 2007). This is particularly crucial when negotiating jurisdictional battles regarding crimes. For example, in cases of sexual assault, coordination among tribal agencies and with federal agencies can aid in obtaining statistical data. However, tribal courts differ in their ability to exercise jurisdiction, particularly because of the varying roles of US federal and state courts and due to the US Supreme Court's 1978 decision *Oliphant v. Suquamish Indian Tribe* 453 US 191, which prevents tribal criminal prosecution of non-indigenous perpetrators (Clairmont, 2008). Furthermore, Deer (2009) highlights that the use of Northern/Western law avoids acknowledgement of the colonial relationship between the US and indigenous people, the significantly higher rates of assault on native women (as compared to other groups of women living in the US), and how US laws and decisions made by the Supreme Court have compromised tribal judicial authority. US rape law historically considered that only white women could be victims of rape (*ibid.*: 151) and that rape was a 'trespass to chattels,' as women were the property of men (*ibid.*: 154). Deer adds that Western trials contradict the emphasis on accountability within tribal nations, particularly when native peoples are not on the juries (*ibid.*: 151). The implications are clear.

At the same time, Cruz (2007) asserts that it does not 'matter what the federal government does or does not do – it's what tribal governments and peoples decide to do with their indigenous legal traditions.' We find compelling Cruz's aim to decenter the Western stranglehold on the rule of law and sovereignty as well as the recognition of multiple, overlapping sovereignties. If it is indeed the case, as Inayatullah and Blaney argue, that property/sovereignty are not governed in 'straight lines,' meaning easy to follow, with clear boundaries (2004: 187), then it is possible that indigenous and marginalized communities can use their own legal traditions subversively to contest the authority of Western legal traditions as well as to disaggregate the very concept of property that underscores modern sovereignty.

Cruz points out that the subversive potential of indigenous law is in the fact that it is not easily understood if one is using 'Western' epistemologies (with their focus on supposed rationality, categories, rules, objectivity). That is precisely because, as she notes, indigenous law is at once 'everywhere,' including places where perhaps law isn't 'supposed' to be, such as people's spiritual practices. Further, indigenous communities may also invoke rules of procedure and evidence to prevent indigenous law from being scrutinized in Western courtrooms. This is important because 'it is through indigenous legal tradition that we as indigenous people know that we have the right to self determination. It is not accorded to us, but it's a right we possess' (Cruz, 2007). Accordingly, because of historical and ongoing attacks on indigenous religions and languages, the imposition of Western political organization on Indian territories, physical removal and displacement, and the imposition of formal Western education, indigenous legal tradition is a site for deflecting and organizing against colonial re-encounters. Furthermore, claiming rights within non-indigenous traditions ends up leading more towards assimilation and further away from rights of self-determination.

To acknowledge the connection between indigenous legal traditions and self-determination of indigenous communities is to start seeing law as potentially open and radically undecided rather than self-enclosed. Indeed, reading Cruz's experiences with her cases is an exercise in suspending desire for closure; she gives none. Instead, she admits that even losing a case can be an opening for better understanding white privilege and, importantly, voicing stories of oppression and resistance, usually not heard in courtrooms. She shows how we can start with struggles to engage with the 'the law "of" Indigenous Peoples, as opposed to the nation-state law "concerning," "about," or "for" Indian tribes' (Cruz, 2008: 631). And she invokes 'shadow wars' of ideas and words, allowing battles over what law is and, through that, a larger struggle to validate multiple epistemologies. This does not mean that indigenous law is immune from critique or dissent; rather, we want to consider the different legal systems that may govern people's lives. For example, Deer argues (2009) that the 'peacemaking' legal model, such as that used in the Navajo Nation Peacemaking Courts, does not go far enough in addressing cases of sexual violence. She thus addresses the problems with 'romanticizing' these alternatives; she deftly argues to connect rape, in particular, explicitly to colonial legacies and to develop new mechanisms, such as 'tribal rape courts,' that combine indigenous law with feminist native perspectives.[15]

Using indigenous law to decenter IR is particularly compelling because it gets us to think about how *all* legal systems could potentially allow us to confront directly what sovereignty is. We tend to treat sovereignty as a given, or theorize it in the context of the nation-state system, rather than explore how people might negotiate what sovereignty means (on this, see Smith and Kauanui, 2008, regarding indigenous feminist participation in 'sovereignty activism'). And, as Shaw points out in her study of indigenous communities in Canada (2008), indigenous struggles with sovereignty are not separate from non-indigenous people's relationships to sovereignty. In other words, these are not battles 'outside' of those of us who might not consider ourselves to be indigenous. The next two sections explore this point further.

The question of evidence: truths and lies

A theme we discussed in the Introduction and one we will revisit throughout the book is the production of knowledge. In mainstream scholarship and discourse, indigenous peoples somehow 'know' (consider the Walkabout commercial discussed above) intuitively ancient, long-standing, immutable truths, thus leading to the extraction, patenting, and commodification of indigenous knowledges for the sake of the pharmaceutical industry (Norchi, 2000), but at the same time they are *also* 'primitive' and untouched by reason, technology, and science. How do we make sense of this convoluted representation? How do we decenter knowledge production about indigenous people, engage with indigenous knowledge claims in less exploitative ways, and reconsider so-called objectivity? Is it possible?

In effect, where does knowledge come from? Much of the scholarly work on indigeneity is informed by ethnographic fieldwork and interviews. In her preface to *From Tribal Village to Global Village*, Brysk mentions in the context of her methodology how 'fellow academics were concerned that [she] would become part of the process [she] was studying and somehow taint the objectivity of the result' (Brysk, 2000: x). In response, Brysk speaks about her normative commitments to social justice and discusses at length some of the connections she made while doing her research. And, we assert, what's wrong with becoming part of the process? Are we not already 'tainting' objectivity by even presuming to write and talk about the issue at hand, by presuming indigenous peoples would not do fieldwork on 'white' peoples? Indeed, critical analysis is actually about unveiling the pretense of 'objectivity,' about discovering how emotional, personal, spiritual, or community-based agendas matter for how we think about the world.

IR as a discipline needs to shatter some of the methodological and epistemological demands of objectivity in order to reflect much more actively upon the possibilities and pitfalls of ethnographic, self-reflexive, and participatory research. Furthermore, we've got to acknowledge overtly how power relationships in the world translate into pedagogical styles in the classroom or political choices professors make as public intellectuals (Shaw, 2003). In fact, does research into indigeneity or the other issues discussed in this book demand deep and enduring connections and consultations with the various communities we write or talk about? This is a crucial question to consider because of the battle lines drawn over issues of 'evidence,' and the simultaneous fascination and distrust by non-indigenous people about what indigenous people 'know.'

Consider the case of indigenous claims about the restoration of human relics removed forcibly (Lalu, 2009: 3). The methods of bringing some sort of authenticity to such attempts are fraught with doubt, ridicule, and the propensity to ask 'What is your forensic and historical evidence?' on the part of 'expert' scientists, governmental officials, scholars, and doctors. Lalu reveals the story of South African healer-diviner Nicholas Tilana Gcaleka who claimed in 1996 to have found the skull of a Xhosa[16] king, Hintsa, murdered by British colonial forces over a century earlier. Eventually disproving Gcaleka's claims, South African scientists employed the very forms of inquiry (such as forensic medicine and phrenology) used during colonialism. All of this occurred in the midst of the Truth and Reconciliation Commission and the concomitant attempts to excavate and return bodies murdered during apartheid. So, while South Africans accepted some truths as crucial to the post-apartheid transition, they contested others as disruptive and unsubstantiated. Lalu artfully explores the role of lies and truth:

> To simply recognize lies as a condition of life is to neglect the structure of the presumed lie that is so crucial to the functioning of social worlds. In other words, it is to ignore the ways in which lies overlap with regimes of truth or, more importantly, how regimes of truth are lodged in the articulation of what are ultimately considered lies. (Lalu, 2009: 5)

In effect, Lalu's analysis forces us to consider the kind of 'proof' we require that oppression happened; do we rely upon the same kinds of questions and standards that enabled that oppression to happen in the first place? A person or group alleging that some type of violence occurred may seem like a quack or charlatan orchestrating a hoax, but the way that scientists and academics treat them reveals a lot about how knowledge about the world is proven. At the same time, we may play along with the falsehoods and contestations at the center of and behind 'truths' about how the world came to be. Think of lies about 'discovery,' 'founding fathers' (the 'mothers,' apparently, all off on holiday), and what 'happened' (industrialization and civilization but not murder and atrocities).

Let us consider another example of the complexities of lies and truths: the controversy around Rigoberta Menchú, who in 1984 published her famous testimony, *I, Rigoberta Menchú: An Indian Woman in Guatemala*, with damning commentary about more than three decades of oppression that Guatemalans, including indigenous communities, suffered during the Guatemalan civil war. Years later, David Stoll, a US anthropologist, challenged the veracity of her testimony in his *Rigoberta Menchú and the Story of All Poor Guatemalans* (1999), proclaiming that Menchú distorted her stories in order to highlight the violence Guatemalans faced. He also criticized Western academics for romanticizing her story in the first place.

Certainly, we can learn about representations, truth-telling, and narratives about war and oppression when we explore the implications of the responses, ranging from the chorus of hyperbole, anger, and disdain for Menchú's apparent lies and Marxism to the many fervent attempts to defend her (ranging from explorations of how multiple truths are conveyed in testimonies to 'Ah, but see, this was a *cultural* response – *we* may tell straightforward facts, but *they* don't/can't'). But what could be lost is an interrogation of the architecture of lies that sustained and extended the civil war. In which cases are people more interested in controversies such as these than in the mundane realities of why the civil war happened, the US's role, or the Guatemalan Commission for Historical Clarification's determination that state violence during 1981 and 1983 constituted genocide? In order for these events in Guatemala, and the civil wars in El Salvador and Nicaragua, to happen, many parties participated in a series of lies, secrets, cover-ups, distortions, and covert operations. Where is the frenzied response to that?

Some scholarly responses to the Menchú controversy are useful as a point of departure to discuss Guatemalan history and politics, the politics of memory, indigenous struggles, and the import of testimonial literature (Arias, 2001). In particular, Pratt recalls the sarcastic treatment by US authors and media of syllabi that included Menchú's book and other non-Western pieces; they either derided or were sincerely confused by the fact that anyone might use such 'multicultural' work (Pratt, 2001: 35–6). In this context of US 'culture wars' about legitimate and worthy perspectives, Pratt points out that it was the frenetic international media response to Stoll's book that elicited attacks on academic freedom and intentional destruction of Menchú's iconic status (*ibid.*: 37–8).

As Lalu puts it, '[w]hen there is mocking laughter there is reason to suspect that a regime of truth is at work' (2009: 9). Indeed, we should follow the sounds of laughter, gasps of horror, pointed fingers of accusation, and biting scorn to see that at issue is not the lies that may or may not have been told but the audacity that non-Western, subaltern people may have something to say that could remind communities of past injustice or that could be used by professors, students, or activists to question government actions. Thus, in order to decenter IR, we might look again at the category of indigeneity and consider when and how we consume indigenous stories, why we are so concerned with whether they are telling the truth and where their knowledge comes from, and, most importantly, why we would never question the veracity of Northern/Western perspectives.

Connections and belonging

Given the discussions thus far on indigenous struggles, epistemologies, and production of knowledge, how can we better use the category of indigeneity in a subversive way? Can we confront how indigeneity is at once denied and complicated in classrooms, think tanks, and international organizations? Can we address how students, professors, and staff have been forced to perform or deflect their indigeneity? In this section, we consider how to rethink the questions of belonging and connections, thus using the category of indigeneity as an entry point for thinking about global issues in new ways.

First, we would like to prevail upon our readers to ask: Who are you? This is a deceptively simple question and one surprisingly difficult to answer meaningfully. What language(s) do you speak? Where did you come from? Where do you live? What is your ethnic or racial identity, and can it be easily defined? What deity/ies (if any) do you worship? Are you indigenous? A '*native*' of your country? Your society? The culture? What are the boundaries of that culture? How do you describe yourself and how do you describe others in your world? And then ask this: What would you give up, who would you stand up for, who would you fight against? Where would IR put you?

Or, try a thought experiment: imagine you are in Puerto Rico or Guam or the US Virgin Islands (a name in and of itself well worthy of interrogation: see Weber, 1999) or even Hawai'i, birthplace of a US president but recently described by an influential US political journalist as 'exotic.'[17] Now, define your identity as an 'American.' What are the core components? The crucial cultural moments and artifacts? How and what does 'America' look like to you? Walt Whitman may have heard varied singing,[18] but he was, however odd, deeply ensconced in the heart of liberal, Lockean, Protestant North America. What does 'America's' singing sound like from south Texas[19] or those places, such as Hawai'i, Guam, and American Samoa, erased from yet crucial to understandings of US colonial history and politics (Hall, 2008)? Have you ever considered that people in Argentina, Jamaica, Cuba, Brazil, Peru, Nicaragua, Mexico, and Canada consider themselves Americans too? Wherever you are, who came before you and how far back can you go? If, for example, you were to find out that you are walking, living, and working on another's sacred grounds, what could your possible responses be?

These questions all get at what it means to belong and how we do or do not connect with each other. Suppose these types of questions were our starting point for understanding global issues, particularly the so-called intractable ones. Here, we sketch out the possibility of using the lens of indigeneity to think about the example of Israel and Palestine. What if we were to consider the issues we examined here: the impossibility of defining indigeneity, overlapping sovereignties, the violence of sovereignty in its founding?

We are drawn to using this complex lens to decenter the way we might usually approach this issue precisely because the 'usual' way is a polemical debate about who belongs, who *deserves* to belong, and who is more wronged. While IR texts may not (sometimes) succumb to such polemics, teaching and talking about the Israeli-Palestinian conflict is fraught with intense difficulties in the US, sometimes more so than many other conflicts, because of the complex politics of US aid and commitments to Israel and the kind of virulent caricatures and accusations that fly forth: denials that Palestinians exist (summed up in the early and still extant Zionist refrain that Israel was founded as a 'land without a people for a people without a land'), dehumanization of Palestinians as terrorists, portrayal of criticism of Israel as anti-Semitism, and sweeping and often dishonest generalizations of Israelis and Jews (with not much distinction among various Israeli and diasporic Jewish positions on this conflict). The battle lines are often raw and clear, particularly considering recent controversies in universities over attempts to censor the academic freedom of professors who are perceived to be pro-Palestinian or do research that critiques Israel's occupation or strategy and tactics, or the campaign to boycott Israeli academic and cultural institutions until Israel recognizes Palestinians' right to self-determination. So, while we could certainly address 'centered' IR scholarship and policies regarding Israel and Palestine, we'd like to emphasize the conversations that surround us in our capacities as professors and US citizens; in that role, we need to repeatedly ask the questions that many have been asking, even if we end up with more questions than answers. Thus far, the answers have been rather unoriginal and not too promising.

Since indigeneity calls up questions of the right to claim one's own existence, it is at the heart of the disavowal of entire histories and subject positions. Certainly a part of what motivates Israelis and Palestinians alike is persistent memories of massacred ancestors and grave injustices, and we can often hear the emotional weight of those genealogies at panels, in classroom discussions, or behind a request to 'uninvite' a particular guest speaker on the issue. We cannot fully grasp what it might mean to decenter IR or the US when we teach or discuss Israel and Palestine until we bring the difficulties of the category of indigeneity to bear on this issue.

More to the point, we must reveal how narratives about the causes of the Israeli-Palestinian conflict often elide the historical relationships between indigenous Palestinian Jews, Muslims, and Christians, and how Zionism, Jewish migrations, the creation of Israel, and wars and displacement reworked categories and classification of Jew, Israeli, Palestinian, and Arab throughout much of the so-called Middle East. We are also intrigued by the possibility of rethinking 'tribal' loyalties[20] as people figure out what they should do as Israelis, Palestinians, Jews, to ensure their self-determination, as it is bound up with that of others. For example, Butler (2004: 111–12) points us to a complex view of a Jewish sense of 'perpetuity,' such that Jewish existence owes more, potentially, to Talmudic traditions of critical thinking than to protecting Israel *from* critique.[21] Hannah Arendt's *Eichmann in Jerusalem* (1963), Tony Kushner and Alisa Solomon's edited volume, *Wrestling with Zion* (2003), and Simona Sharoni's work (2006) participate in difficult questions about Israeli policy towards Palestinians precisely by taking on what Jews do *as* Jews about issues of suffering, theirs and others. Israeli scholar David Shulman, reflecting on Israeli-Palestinian peace work, speaks poignantly about the 'ironic happiness of doing what is right in circumstances of rooted, inherent, unresolvable ambiguity' (2007: 212).[22] Long-standing Jewish connections and traditions still matter, but in a way that decidedly confronts (multiple and diverse) Zionist discourses.

Jews, Israeli or otherwise, who take this approach may struggle mightily with being the dissenting voices who speak about Palestinian dispossession and struggles, in the face of the accusation 'Traitor!' or worse (see Butler, 2004: 101–27). But they are voices that directly confront sovereign violence and ask what it might mean that different answers to 'Who are you?' could and must coexist in the same territorially bounded space, two-state solution or not. Consider the experiences of groups such as the Refuseniks, Yesh Gvul, Courage to Refuse, the Sayeret Matkal (Israeli special forces) dissidents, Soldiers Breaking the Silence (or Shovrim Shtika), and The Pilots Group, who have refused to participate in Israeli political and military offensives in occupied Palestinian territories and against Palestinians. Shulman (2009) notes that historically Israeli courts have argued that a soldier has the right and *duty* not to carry out an order that conflicts with his or her values; those values include a confrontation of what the government is doing in the name of Jewish indigeneity.

Of particular note are the various *shministim* groups dating back to 1970, 1987, and more frequently active since 2001. The *shministim* are Israeli teenagers who reject their conscription into the Israeli Defense Forces (IDF) and declare themselves 'conscientious objectors.' Their claims fundamentally decenter the Israeli state and in essence demand for themselves the right to make and enact policies in accordance with their beliefs. For example, Emelia Markovich first attempted to contact the Israeli special military committee to get out of serving in the IDF by declaring that she was a pacifist, but they rejected her request. She resisted the description of the army as 'sacred' and by definition always morally good. She notes that after the *shministim* letter to the press was published, some Israelis viewed them as traitors but Palestinians welcomed them to the West Bank. Emelia notes that Israeli society 'isn't ready for the kind of change necessary but what's crucial is to get Israelis to rethink their actions as well as to give a sense of hope to Palestinians.'[23]

Another *shministim,* Or Ben David, responds specifically to the issue of Palestinian use of violence: 'if we want to make a happier world, we can't use the weapons we are against. But it's a complicated question, because I don't know what I would do in their shoes.'[24] While she faces resistance from even close family and friends, she supposes that 'Palestinians get hope especially from a girl that is from the "other side," the side that harms them.' And Efi Brenner points out, 'I am Israeli, but I don't believe in Zionism. . . . People in Tel Aviv live in a bubble. They don't know there are people living 30 minutes from them whose lives are not "life." The positive effects are that Palestinians see that Israelis refuse to enlist in the army. A lot of Palestinians protesting nonviolently are sent to jail.'[25] So too are the *shministim.*

These examples prompt important questions, given that these particular *shministim* do not invest too much into how their actions might change Israeli policies; rather, they consider the kind of connectivity other Israelis and Palestinians might experience in response. These students espouse fundamentally different views from Zionist youths who live in or support settlements, or US Jewish students who travel with Birthright or go to Israel after graduation to serve in the Israeli army or government precisely because of their connection – historic, ancient, enduring – to Israel. And, while they may seem marginalized or a small percentage of what Israelis do, looking at examples of students, youth, or, frankly, anyone, who do 'something else' about conflict or their own sense of belonging is simply a start in figuring out that there are much deeper complexities and contradictions underlying global issues than we might like to admit.

For example, what kinds of possibilities are Israelis and Palestinians forging through peace work, as illustrated by Shulman's *Dark Hope* (2007), an examination of the efforts of the Israeli-Palestinian Ta'ayush (meaning 'living together,' in Arabic) coalition? As Shulman suggests, what might it mean to give up having a monopoly on what's right (or wrong)? If indigeneity, as we discussed above, defies categorization and definition, how does the impossibility of the category matter for this conflict? How might we explore Palestinian visions for citizenship and statehood in the context of paradox? For example, Palestinian Israeli citizens (about 20 per cent of Israeli citizens) may push for liberal equality with Jewish Israelis while Palestinians, both those with Israeli citizenship and those living in the Occupied Territories, might invoke the right of return or militate against occupation on the basis of collectivist indigeneity.[26] What contradictions emerge in calls for civic equality and Palestinian self-determination, as well as in the secular and religious nationalist aspects of resistance, both of which pose various problems and possibilities for Palestinian women's organizations (see Abdulhadi, 1998)? Is state sovereignty necessarily exclusionary, and how do people hoping for statehood confront the limits of state sovereignty in delivering justice? Or consider the weight of Yiftachel's (2006) claims that in confronting the Zionist-Palestine 'dialectic' (between Israeli expansionist, 'ethnocratic' claims and resulting resistance, counter-mobilization, and counter-narratives about indigeneity and territory by Palestinians), we must not forget the recognition and rights of Bedouin and Arab-Druze village communities as well as alienated Mizrahi and Haredi Jews, and immigrant workers.

Consider also how people grappling with their indigeneity in the US have responded. Groups of youth who identify themselves with various tribes in the US traveled in August 2009 as part of an unprecedented 'Indigenous Youth Delegation to Palestine' to make connections between common experiences of dispossession and self-determination struggles. They aimed, in a sense, to displace the US and Israeli states as the starting point for how they define their lives, politics, and sensibilities. Organizations and institutions such as the grassroots Seventh Native American Generation (SNAG) Magazine, the Brooklyn-based Palestine Education Project, and Seventh Generation Indigenous Visionaries (at Haskell Indian Nations University) sponsored and supported the trip to meet with Palestinians involved with and living in various refugee camps in Nablus, Bethlehem, and Jerusalem, as well as with other organizations, such as Women for Life/Flowers Against Occupation.

Ora Wise, a co-founder of the Palestine Education Project, one of the sponsors of the trip, points us towards thinking about the connection of struggles through resistance art and popular education, but also towards carving out moments to be teenagers – to dance, love, write, heal, and jam. She notes the importance of this delegation in showing marginalized young adults that others wanted to hear from them.[27] Indeed, this is not a case of uncritical parallels made between different indigenous communities. Tribal nations in the US are varied and diverse and can't easily be compared to Palestinians; Palestinians vary in their experiences as well, particularly if one considers the experiences of, for example, Bedouins, Palestinian Israeli citizens, and Gazans. Rather, young people talked about strategies of empowerment in the context of restrictions on movement, agricultural destruction, and surveillance. How do people who feel 'left out' of IR identify with the prospect that transnational connections are made among people who similarly feel that policy makers don't care about their voices? How do they, together, see what it means to define themselves through the lens of indigeneity?

We will not easily solve the contestations over who belongs, and where. But, Nathalie Handal, Palestinian American poet, playwright, and writer, notes that beyond the 'facts' (however construed and produced) about Israel and Palestine, students should 'inform themselves of . . . a people's spirit. . . . We need to go to that *withinness* and *beyondness*. We have to allow ourselves to see and be seen, listen and be heard. . . . We can be so-called enemies, and secretly read and enjoy each other's poems.'[28]

Chapter Three / Human Rights

A night without a blanket, a blanket
belonging to someone else, someone
else living in our homes.
All I want is the quietness of blame to leave,
the words from dying tongues to fall,
all I want is to see a row of olive trees,
a field of tulips, to forget
the maze of intestines, the dried corners
of a soldier's mouth, all I want is for
the small black eyed child to stop
wondering when the fever will stop
the noise will stop, all I want is
a loaf of bread, some water
and help for the stranger's torn arm,
all I want is what we have inherited
from the doves, a perfect line of white,
but a question still haunts me at night:
where are the bodies?
(Nathalie Handal, 'Jenin,' 2005.)

Introduction

This chapter examines the way human rights as a category centers IR narratives about 'us,' 'them,' and 'over there.' In particular, we ask: (1) Where did the category of human rights come from, and what are human rights? (2) How do we respond to human rights? (3) Which stories of human rights violation matter? We discover an overarching human rights 'narrative' with its Western protagonists and selective interpretation of events; types of responses to human rights violations that inevitably center the North/West as the repository of morality; and the privileging of institutionalized, professionalized human rights narratives over different types of storytelling. But we also examine how IR can be decentered through creative, informed, and contextualized engagement with social justice struggles. Handal, author of the poem that opens this chapter, explains that her words allow 'bodies to have a conversation with the world . . . [to get] readers to be conscious of the fact that even if they can't see these corpses or even know about them, they exist, and remain *unrested*.'[1] Her words motivate the following discussions.

The 'Origins' of Human Rights

IR tells a story about the origins of the human rights category that may have little to do with how various communities experience and talk about human rights. The events, institutions, and states memorialized in this story 'center' IR and, perhaps inevitably, measure the world against a somewhat mythical Northern/Western standard against which they are inevitably found wanting. While the 1948 United Nation's Universal Declaration of Human Rights is the most obvious starting point, human rights *qua* human rights did not simply spring fully formed from the foreheads of the delegates in Paris that December.

Reading backwards, a somewhat troubling but inevitable tendency of historians and social scientists alike, some have identified nascent conceptions of what we would now consider human rights in various compendiums of human knowledge. For example, those in the North/West, inclined to see the ancient Greeks and Romans as the font of all that is good in the world (democracy, accurately or not, is perhaps the most notable example),[2] see early glimmers of concern with human rights in Greece (Aristotle) and among Rome's Stoics and invoke England's Magna Carta (1215 CE) as a critical statement. More commonly, John Locke and other 'Enlightenment' thinkers associated with the rise of liberalism and capitalism are summoned and presumed to lay some sort of ground work, the fruition of which is seen in the 'twin' liberal democratic revolutions in the United States of America (1776) and in France (1789).[3]

What the human rights story often ignores is equally long and arguably more storied (albeit contradictory and oppressive in their own right) texts and practices outside of the North/West, such as the Hindu laws of Manu, Confucianism, the Quran, the Ten Commandments, early formulations in the early years of the Persian Empire (539 BCE), the edicts of Ashoka (272–231 BCE), the Constitution or Charter of Medina (622), early forms of welfare (such as free hospitals and education) in early empires in South Asia, and the intersubjectivity of *ubuntu*, most recently articulated by Archbishop Desmond Tutu.[4] The somewhat self-congratulatory story that we are following focuses instead on the US's Declaration of Independence and France's Declaration of the Rights of Man and of the Citizen – often, though less so in recent years, eliding the fact that those documents left out the great majority of people (women, the 'indigenous,' minorities, children). Nonetheless, the early nineteenth century witnessed an increased interest in the North/West in what we would undeniably construe as 'human rights,' particularly in the debates around slavery, the subjugation of women in various forms, and the treatment of working children. Still, it was an attenuated notion of human rights, one that was defined by the North/West.[5]

Then, the twentieth-century emergence of 'Wilsonian ideals' (abroad if not at home in the US), the defeat of fascism, and responses to the suffering during the world wars (particularly in the Holocaust)[6] gave rise to the modern human rights movement. United Nations documents and agencies and international legal regimes eventually institutionalized this movement, to the point that countries increasingly consider human rights issues in the creation of their foreign policies.[7] As such, the human rights story draws a neat line from early Western conceptions to the present moment, where Western states, activists, and the UN have the tools to call out human rights violations and press for change. Thus, communities can respond when they notice something happening in the world that offends their (and, by extension, all people's) basic moral sensibilities, then form or call up norms that say as much, and ultimately create, rely upon, strengthen, or encourage compliance with laws, principles, and institutions that end impunity and enforce accountability, hoping all the while that perhaps with more education, democracy, rule of law, good governance, and economic development will come deterrence of and an end to human rights violations.

But we tend to simplify the complexities of tragedy because we filter what we 'know' and 'learn' about the multiple kinds of experiences these victims underwent, leaving out many other tragedies (a point we address below). We reduce nuances into a 'perpetrator versus victim' binary instead of understanding better what makes human rights atrocities possible. Uncritically, we may celebrate international legal institutions as preferred forms of justice (more on this in Chapter 5). The atrocities of the Jewish Holocaust, the Bosnia and Kosovo wars, and the Rwandan genocide are particular *sites* for the articulation of human rights in ways that affirm the narrative discussed thus far, and the turn to certain Northern/Western states, institutions, and international law for 'solutions.'

For example, regarding the Holocaust, we contest the profoundly pervasive hero narrative that the US and its allies saved some Jews and indeed 'the world' (or at least Europe) from 'fascism' (everywhere) and set about creating the institutional framework, including the United Nations and, importantly, the Universal Declaration of Human Rights, which would powerfully shape discourse on human rights; aren't there other relevant lessons and implications of the Holocaust, besides those having to do with universalism and US power? IR textbooks tend to represent the Holocaust as a quintessential, defining moment of wanton killing of innocents. Imagine instead that, sadly, rather than a unique moment of shame and depravity never to be forgotten, the Jewish Holocaust was one among a deeply disturbing number of instances of brutal repressions, withering oppression, mass displacements, and intentional elimination of groups of people.

In particular, Jews were historically rejected as 'European,' and it would not have been unusual during colonialism and fascist movements to attempt ethnic cleansing of such a racialized group within Western Europe. However impressive in scope and scale, so too were the sufferings of indigenous Americans, ravaged Africa, colonized Asia, Semites – Arab and Jew – in western Asia (see Mills, 1997). Why was King Leopold's Congo not shocking enough to prompt the emergence of the modern human rights movement? Was the genocide of the Armenians or the 'slow genocides' of indigenous peoples insufficient? To be sure, colonialism was different from European fascism, but we have to ask about the timing, purpose, and political expediency of responding to systematic ethnic cleansing. While we have collectively gotten better at acknowledging these crimes and also understanding the rise of Nazism, we would do well to see postwar responses to this genocide as a site for the US and its allies to create powerful institutions and to shape international criminal law. For example, the Nuremberg Trials, the Tokyo Tribunal,[8] and Israel's trial of German Nazi leader Adolf Eichmann importantly established that victors of wars and conflict determine the parameters of justice and the discourses about 'good' and 'evil' (see Arendt, 1963). Because these trials served, in some ways, as precedents for the development of international criminal tribunals, it is crucial to understand the political choices made before and at these trials (see Minow, 1998). Are we left with better answers about why the Holocaust and other atrocities (see note 8) during World War Two occurred, and how to prevent genocidal actions?

Also consider the Bosnia and Kosovo wars, which facilitated the 1990s *de jure* and *de facto* acceptance of international intervention in conflicts, and witnessed the 'moralizing' role of international lawyers and the increased use of international law as an explicit tool of powerful governments (Koskenniemi, 2002). Indeed, the Bosnia war, from about 1992 to 1995, and the Kosovo war, soon thereafter,[9] raised questions about the role of the North Atlantic Treaty Organization (NATO) and prompted the creation of an *ad hoc* tribunal, the International Criminal Tribunal for the former Yugoslavia. During both wars, Northern/Western narratives elided the very complex context in favor of pathologizing Slobodan Milosevic's nationalism and comparing him to Hitler (Kozol, 2004: 9–10). Particularly key was representing, through both text and photojournalism, Bosnian Muslim prisoners of war in Serb detention camps or Kosovar refugees on trains, calling up the very familiar images of emaciated Jews in Nazi concentration camps. The US public relied upon war-time photojournalism and its aura of objectivity, particularly important in the face of NATO's exaggerations of statistics and of Serbian and Yugoslav cover-ups of crimes (*ibid.*). In the case of Kosovo, the visual representations of mainly women and children rendered them 'without' ethnicity or religion, so that they were read as white, domesticated, supplicant (*ibid.*).

This is not to say that depictions of those in war zones should 'play up' or purposely exoticize the subjects of the photograph, as photojournalists certainly do this as well; rather, we should ask questions about how we could represent war and suffering, and why we need to see victimized bodies, posed in certain ways that indicate their innocence (rather than, say, their resistance or material resources) (*ibid.*). In addition, these photographs and narratives distracted from understanding how the intricacies and tragedies of these particular wars did not so easily compare to the rise of Nazism or the persecution of Jews. Nor did they illuminate the role of the NATO countries in contributing to instability in the region in the first place (through the support of destabilizing IMF or World Bank policies, by demanding access to new political economies as the region splintered, and by pursuing oil corporation imperatives to secure pipelines through the region). We also need to explain NATO's need to legitimize itself in a post-Cold War context, particularly by reducing the complexities to a simple story about the inevitable failures of socialist Yugoslavia. We must ask why there was such a dearth of critical analysis when it came to the role of (and violence by) the NATO-backed Kosovo Liberation Army (*ibid.*: 4–5, 6; see also Dauphinee, 2007; Campbell, 1998a; Zizek, 2000).

In the case of Rwanda, many have written at length about the colonial legacy that made possible divisions between the Hutus and Tutsis, the Western indifference to and collective failure to prevent and intervene in the Rwandan genocide, and the complicity of Rwandan citizens, particularly in the role of radio propaganda (Barnett, 1999; Gourevitch, 1998; Wibben, 2009). A 'centered' human rights narrative typically writes the genocide as an example of Hutu revenge against Tutsis, a revenge that somehow culminated in the shocking rampage (killing at a rate faster than the Nazis and in a period of 100 days) that 'should have' elicited calls of 'never again.' Because it did not, the US and Europeans played a role in setting up and supporting the International Criminal Tribunal for Rwanda (ICTR), and Security Council-mandated United Nations peacekeeping missions are now able to use certain types of force due to the new 'robust peacekeeping' doctrine, in ways they could not during the Rwandan genocide (United Nations, 2008). Human rights activists further point to Rwanda as the 'obvious' reason as to why there should be militarized intervention in Darfur and other sites of genocide and crimes against humanity (see below).

But Mamdani (2002) contests the human rights discourse of evil perpetrators versus innocent victims by contextualizing the naturalization of identities during colonialism and in the postcolonial period, particularly as the 1959 revolution further entrenched those very identities. He also explores how the colonized, constructed as natives, rebelled against colonial alien outsiders and then proceeded to attack others constructed as outsiders; in this case, a significant number of Hutu government officials and citizens increasingly coded the Tutsi citizens as settlers. It is also important in our examinations of human rights violations in Rwanda to consider how the North/West initially saw this country as a success story during the 1960s and 1970s, due to the coffee economy, which colonial officials had directed (Kamola, 2007). However, the coffee plantations also exacerbated class conflicts, as Tutsi chiefs forced Hutus to pay taxes and provide the labor during colonialism (*ibid.*: 578). Then, the collapse of international coffee prices in the late 1980s precipitated a crisis to which the World Bank and IMF responded with austerity measures, which heightened the conflicts. The Rwandan government used the funds as well as foreign loans to purchase arms, which eventually ended up in the hands of Interahamwe and rural supporters of Habyarimana's Mouvement Revolutionaire National pour Développement (MRND) (*ibid.*). At the same time, outside countries played a role in the conflict, particularly in the civil war that preceded the genocide; France, Belgium, and Zaïre (now the Democratic Republic of the Congo) supported the regime of Hutu President Habyarimana (whose assassination later served as the catalyst for the massacres) during an attempted coup by the Rwandan Patriotic Front, formed by Tutsi refugees in Uganda, supported by the US, and eventually responsible for ending the genocide.

We will say more about institutions and humanitarian intervention in Chapter 5. For our purposes here, we assert that human rights stories, discourses, and instruments are formulated by deploying and representing, perhaps inaccurately or too simplistically, the very victims for whom the human rights regime exists. The binary of evil perpetrator and innocent victim is often the easiest and seemingly most accurate way to describe events that are incomprehensible. But these events did not appear out of thin air; there are always contexts, the historical roles of multiple players, and multiple narratives about what made *possible* what most can never imagine.

Further, we claim that human rights emanate within and among communities as much as any advocacy movement, international organization, or state, and they would appear to have been around for at least as long as we have been recording history and presumably for quite a bit longer. Recognizing this, we also assert that there are multiple ways in which to unpack and decenter the human rights narrative, while drawing attention to justice activism that merits more debate, engagement, and solidarity. In addition to complicating the narrative, as we have done above, we explore in the next two sections how the still little-appreciated Haitian Revolution and anti-colonial and anti-racism movements throughout the twentieth century provide particularly powerful entry points for understanding what counts as human rights, how to define human rights, and who is addressing human rights violations.

Beyond mountains, more mountains

The Haitian Revolution (1791–1804) has been rendered a 'non-event' in the annals of human rights movements and revolutions, even though it directly challenged the incompatibility of equality and slavery. African slaves, 'illiterate' by Northern/Western standards but inspired by the revolution their colonial taskmasters in France had made, promised *liberté, égalité, fraternité* and rose up to win their independence, the first victorious slave revolt in the Western Hemisphere; they became 'the first free nation of free men to arise within, and in resistance to, the emerging constellation of Western European empire [France, Great Britain, Spain]' (Lowenthal, 1976: 657). The only black independent state in the world was both 'a spiritual heir to the French Revolution [and] . . . a serious challenge as the first non-European postcolonial state in the modern world' (Fauriol, 1996: 520). Perhaps Haiti's 'disappearance' was (and is) no accident.

The 1791 slave revolt was initially focused primarily on taking seriously the Declaration of the Rights of Man and of the Citizen, claiming the fruits of the French Revolution for slaves themselves. The Haitian revolutionaries articulated challenges against modern racial slavery at a time when American revolutionaries and European philosophers spoke of slavery only as it applied to *white* men in their relationship with nobility, the church, and government, as if historical slavery did not exist.[10] Furthermore, Haitians constructed slaves as agents and makers of history (instead of unfortunate by-products or background scenery), so as to place racial liberation on par with national sovereignty as the goal of modern societies. In other words, it was a revolution with a dual focus on 'the sustained development of both liberty *and* social equality' (Nesbitt, 2008: 23; emphasis in the original), a rather daunting 'twofer' under any circumstances.

Haiti's import could not be entirely erased. Haiti's revolution had a profound impact, as 'a radically heterogeneous, transnational cultural network emerged whose political imaginary mirrored the global scope of the slave trade and whose projects and fantasies of emancipation converged, at least for a few years, around Haiti' (Fischer, 2004: 1). The impact in Latin America, particularly in Cuba and the Dominican Republic, ranged from fervent hopes for emulation to questions about Haiti's significance to the region and African lineages, to race and class tensions that manifested in literature and art, to the rewriting of Haitians as black barbarian 'Others' who traumatized their neighbors (*ibid.*).[11]

Furthermore, Knight contends that, in the nascent US, it affected the 'language, religion, politics, culture, cuisine, architecture, medicine, and the conflict over slavery' (2000: 113–14). Radical black abolitionists and their allies in the US carefully and strategically valorized the revolutionary, Toussaint Louverture, particularly his violent tactics, while others presented him as gentle, compassionate, and emblematic of the romanticized, domesticated slave many white reformers insisted upon (Clavin, 2008). And it merits mention that just prior to World War Two, Afro-Trinidadian social theorist C. L. R. James (1989) argued that Haiti offered a powerful story for the decolonization of Africa, the story of African slaves standing up to and defeating their European masters.

For all these reasons and more, the political currency of these events must be forgotten in order for the North/West to claim modernity for itself (Fischer, 2004). And so, we let slip from our minds that a combination of French ex-slave owners' demands for reparations from their former slaves (essentially, payment for freedom), a series of US occupations and interference, and the imposition of IMF austerity programs have created the 'neighbor nobody wants,' 'a basket case,' 'the most wretched place on the earth,' the 'backwaters' of the Caribbean, and, most recently, the 'worst' place for an earthquake.[12] It is crucial to understand Haiti's relationship with Western countries, particularly after its liberation; indeed, the promulgation of paradigmatic '"Western values," hallmarks of its civilizational superiority, [occurred] at the very moment when Western nations were engaged in slavery, colonization, expropriation, and the denial of liberty and equality not only to the colonized but to large segments of Western subjects, including women' (Narayan, 2000: 83–4).

Furthermore, Western and non-Western societies were and are not too different with regards to 'hierarchical social systems, huge economic disparities between members, and the mistreatment and inequality of women' (*ibid.*: 84). Thus, we are *not* saying that the Haitian Revolution, anti-slavery, or anti-colonial movements were free of the problems of inequality in Western societies, or have a moral upper hand in the realm of 'human rights.' If we are to challenge Northern/Western claims to defining and defending human rights, we should also contest any romanticized claims that Haiti stood as the 'perfect' example of a slave uprising. Haitian revolutionaries participated in variants of ethnocentric pride, Jean-Jacques Dessalines crowned himself emperor, and Haitian leaders struggled to figure out how to address the class issues remaining after the revolution. In the end, militarized agriculture replaced plantation slavery, and the country was not able to consolidate the dual focus on individualistic liberalism and social equality (Nesbitt, 2008: 23). Not surprisingly, the Haitians struggled to transcend the lessons they had learned from themselves. The same could be said of any revolution – regardless of where and when it happened or among whom.

Essentially we are arguing that we must find multiple locations where the concepts attributed to the North/West – liberty, equality, self-determination – and the problems attributed to the South/East – violence, injustice, suffering – are articulated, debated, and negotiated simultaneously. Doing so will create a more complex, contextualized, and global (and, yes, decentered) discussion of the concept of 'human rights.' Specifically, Haiti offers a remarkable point of entry for understanding simultaneously (1) how the very *fact* of a slave revolt reverberated across the world and inspired other revolts, art, stories, and narratives about black liberation; (2) how attempts to gain rights are fraught with contradictions – with the descent into Robespierre's terror in France, salutary intentions aside, being as telling as Haiti's post-revolutionary experiments with tyranny and forced labor; and (3) how to recognize the politics of framing some revolts, uprisings, and other attempts for justice as excessive, savage, unspeakable, and barbaric (such were European and white settler accounts of Haiti's uprising), and others as noble, brave, historical, and pivotal, even providential (such as white settler anointing of the US). If we can reveal how projects of Northern/Western modernity marginalized the stories of Haiti in order to privilege national sovereignty over questions of racial equality, to valorize the French and American revolutions but consign Haiti's revolution to the margins of history, then it becomes impossible to tell the story that human rights are the gift of (enlightened) Northern/Western modernity to the dark oppressed masses of the world. Instead, we decenter that story and start to uncover how 'forgotten' players in various moments in history indubitably took on forces of domination.

Anti-imperialism and anti-racism

Decentering the human rights story by restoring the places and stories erased from the mainstream narratives is a start, but we also need to dig deeper into the kinds of definitions of human rights often ignored in many of the textbooks on IR or conversations among professional human rights activists. The recently departed twentieth century alone, for example, was awash in incredibly diverse anti-racism and anti-imperialism movements – but we would not know this if we examined only the kind of mainstream human rights discourse that enfolds human rights within capitalism or considers private property rights as a 'human right.' Historically and in the present, social movements that have articulated claims to personhood, group rights, equality, and liberty – core human rights tenets – have married their demands to significant critiques of (neo-)imperialism and global capitalism. Ishay argues (2008: 117–72) that the struggles for universal suffrage, workers' rights, education, and forms of social justice originated in nineteenth-century socialism. While we contend that those Euro-American socialists had a mixed record on examining the particular intersection of race, capitalism, and colonialism, our point is that we must complicate our examination of human rights.

Take, for instance, a key but systematically understated part of the struggle for 'human rights': the civil rights movement(s) in the US. The mainstream narrative of the civil rights movement in the popular US imagination is surreal, presented as a nice, neat (male) linear progression in which a good and well-intentioned society communally struggled with difficulty to overcome a sordid legacy of a confused past. This reassuring fairy tale dehistoricizes race and strips the struggles of class content, transnational solidarity with anti-colonial movements, and extended explorations of the legacy of slavery (von Eschen, 1997). We think that decentering IR requires challenges to the types of stories the beneficiaries of North/West power tell themselves and each other about social justice struggles. This is particularly crucial, given the paranoid response to the civil rights movement in the context of the Cold War as well as the implications of US support for South Africa's apartheid regime well after the 'achievement' of civil rights; both bear upon questions of social movements, foreign policy, and security interests in IR.

We could deepen our analyses by seeing how the African, Caribbean, South Asian, and Southeast Asian diasporas and communities became focal points for resistance and, increasingly, the reformulation of human rights (although it might be more aptly named social justice). The many examples include the role of the American Negro Labor Congress in protesting and developing a political position on the US occupation of Haiti from 1915 to 1934 (Plummer, 1982; Suggs, 2002).[13] We also point to the role of radical US black leftist organizations and activists forced into hiding or exile, and their employment of Marxist and Leninist critiques of imperialism, particularly through the Council on African Affairs and black presses such as the *West Indian Gazette* (see Boyce Davies, 2007). Consider also the work of the Pan-African Congress in the Manchester meeting of 1945, the 1955 Africa-Asia Conference in Bandung, Indonesia, the 1956 International Congress of Black Writers and Artists (bringing together Aimé Césaire, Frantz Fanon, Richard Wright, and others), and Dr Martin Luther King, Jr's careful attention to Ghana's independence. Indeed, King's 'Birth of a New Nation' speech[14] at Dexter Avenue Baptist Church in Montgomery, Alabama on 7 April 1957 began with a celebration of Ghana's independence and proceeded to critique the Suez Canal crisis of 1956, particularly for the 'imperialistic' and oppressive intentions and actions of the 'great powers' of US, France, and England. This speech also sought to establish the 'Asian-African' bloc, rather than the North/West, as the court of world opinion.

Thus, IR should rethink the potentially diverse and sometimes contradictory contributions of anti-colonial, anti-racism, anti-imperial thinkers, such as Achille Mbembe, Audre Lorde, Aimé Césaire, Frantz Fanon, Claudia Jones, and Andrea Smith, who shaped radical discourse about rights and justice and explored how racism, misogyny, empire, homophobia, and other forms of oppression intertwined, and still do. At what point were they written *out* of human rights analysis,[15] and why? If self-proclaimed human rights scholars and advocates were to recuperate some of these writings and events, we might be able to respond to the question: 'What happened to the dissidence and rebellious spirit of human rights?' (Kapur, 2006: 666). It's there when we look for it.

Indeed, between and among these various movements and moments was the powerful sense that finally, as said in Grenada during their brief revolutionary experiment, it was 'freedom we making here now' (cited in Hodge and Searle, 1981: 82 and Searle, 1984: 118). Of course, this does not preclude a critique of how these various movements could be reactionary, misogynistic, or caught up in the trappings of nationalism. Instead, we are proffering *a starting point* that could build on significant work in this area. What did these solidarities engender and make invisible? What did visions of diaspora, nation-building, anti-racism, anti-imperialism, homeland memories mean, and how do they continue to reverberate in comparison to the salience of 'rights' talk? These are relevant questions in the context of the endless possibilities of human rights, such as framing the right to water as a human right, encompassing for many an abiding right to *not* privatize water services. As we noted in Chapter 2, a centered IR would not take seriously the conversations and struggles people experience as they try to articulate what human rights and social justice might mean for them. There are missteps with aiming to figure out human rights, as well as deeper consequences, such as being kicked out of one's country or being driven underground to write 'subversive' material; but these are the lived experiences of the very people for whom the human rights promises also matter.

Where is (Y)Our Moral Outrage?

It is not only the definitions and 'story' of human rights that center IR; it is also our own reactions, in our capacity as students, scholars, or activists, to what we label as human rights violations. In particular, human rights discourse centers IR through an often-distorted and misinformed focus on human rights violations *elsewhere*. Human rights are an issue or a problem among *those* people over *there*; human rights are not an issue or a problem *here*. In any case, if by chance there are human rights violations – almost certainly an accident, misunderstanding, or confusion – we have the appropriate infrastructure, means, and methods to handle them in ways that protect (or even extend) the human rights of all concerned. When those in the centers of power do violate human rights, they may justify it or even reject the very premise; 'We do not torture people,' US President Bush flatly declared in 2007, at a time when the US was doing exactly that. No harm, at least to anyone who mattered, and thus no foul.[16]

As more than a few scholars from multiple disciplines have pointed out, human rights discourse is problematic and contradictory, in terms of its focus on the 'universal,' its challenging of states' roles in human rights violations while simultaneously requiring them to reinforce human rights, and its reliance on international law (see Chapter 2). We are certainly not arguing, however, to dismiss the category of human rights. As we mentioned in the previous section, there are multiple starting points that can help us rewrite and see better how human rights are subversive: human rights can be used to challenge whether racially unequal liberal democracies are 'civilized,' thus disrupting assumptions about what kinds of processes lead to human rights.[17] But there's more to be done.

A significant step would be actually to decenter ourselves precisely when we wish to comment on 'horrors' and inadvertently parrot the ubiquitous universalizing human rights 'talk' which academics, activists, and politicians of all stripes have adopted. This means we recognize the seduction of human rights; even with our best efforts to unravel, reveal, theorize, dig through what happened, sometimes we cannot resist commenting on *our* surprise, shock, disbelief – and, yes, outrage. 'How *could* they?' The moment we do, we should ask ourselves several questions: Is there another way to register solidarity, compassion, or empathy? What is this outrage about? Is it about sensationalism or a sense that such a thing would never happen here or to me? Do we try to downplay our own reactions by adopting a putatively neutral, antiseptic, analytical stance? Do we wonder if *our* rights are at stake and whether someone else could theorize about *our* loss, *our* pain? Consider the numerous Human Rights Watch and Amnesty International reports on human rights violations within US borders. Could someone else help us? Consider, for example, Venezuelan President Chavez supplying free or discounted home heating oil (through Venezuela's oil subsidiary Citgo) to the working class, the poor, homeless shelters, and over 160 indigenous tribes in the US.[18]

In many ways, then, this section is our attempt to decenter the alluring 'moral outrage' rhetoric while simultaneously unraveling the very presumptions of those who continue to be 'outraged.' This is our attempt to seriously engage with social justice advocates while swatting away the insistent buzzwords and cutting through the slogans. It is our attempt to negotiate the need to intervene in human rights discourses about 'us' and 'them,' while recognizing how distracting and soul-sucking it can be to do so, again and again. We want to note, as clearly as possible, that we support and fight for human rights, and we spend considerable time documenting and researching different types of injustices, but we must do so in ways that do not replicate pervasive destructive patterns or misread people's experiences.

For this chapter and this book, we considered the *New York Times* and Northern/Western journalistic sources and essays as much as the major academic journals and books; both reflect and constitute Northern/

Western responses to human rights violations. After all, for many of us, our students and colleagues outside of or interested in IR are much more likely to pick up the *New York Times* than they are *International Studies Quarterly* or *Review of International Studies* to learn more. The casual conversations in faculty dining rooms, dorm hallways, or cafeterias in organizations matter as much as panel discussions at political science conferences; they all show that we may be responding more because of the way we think than because of the actual suffering.

'Human rights' and other phraseologies such as 'violence against women,' 'women and children,' 'genocide,' and 'terrorism' have tremendous leverage in IR and beyond, and we find them to be useful to talk about certain issues in a 'common' language. But (and this is why we interrogate it so stringently) 'human rights' becomes the central, even only, referent for understanding pain. We contend that more than other concepts, such as democracy or freedom, human rights has a powerful ability to center IR because it allows us all to 'care' about 'real people.' This feels good and it feels 'right.' Even those who say we can't impose democracy on others seem to be okay with encouraging human rights. What could be bad about studying 'human rights,' much less defending, maintaining, and seeking to extend them? Indeed, the subject of human rights has been part of both of our research agendas, because it seems to fulfill some of the responsibilities and sensibilities we have better than would, say, studying nuclear weapons or game theory.

We have two main points in response. First, we are concerned with the web of meanings that haunt our analyses. Both academic scholarship and popular political commentary have asked: 'How do we help them?' or 'Why do they hate us?' or 'Why are they doing that to their own women?' in response to human rights violations. These questions are asked without really desiring an answer. The ability to ask those questions, after all, is the answer. For example, 'Why do they hate us?' – a popular question in the US after the September 11 attacks – was '[m]ore than a rhetorical question, it was a ritual act: to insist on its unanswerability was a magical attempt to ward off this lethal attack against an American "innocence" that never did exist' (Buck-Morss, 2003: 24). Our very assumption that 'we' are the (only) ones to formulate and ask these questions is part of the problem.

Even reasonable discussions about 'regions' and 'issues' find ways to veer quickly into the spectacular and absurd. For example, consider how a query about news reports morphs into an overarching concern about 'Islam' (Muslims in Africa, Muslims in the developing world, Muslims 'inside' Western borders, and especially Muslim women and children). Invoking 'Islam,' often dramatically, can often obviate the need for analysis, explanation, or accuracy. 'After' 9/11, we wondered why so many said that we now need to know about Islam when knowledge about Muslims was quite certainly produced and circulated *before* 9/11. Moreover, this knowledge sutured together Muslims and Arabs, with little attention to the complexities of either category, or the different kinds of political positions Muslims offered as Indonesians, Persians, Bosnians, Kurds, Chechens, Bangladeshis, and so on. How was it that, suddenly (it seemed), Osama bin Laden and the Taliban, our former allies in Afghanistan, had something to do with teach-ins to 'understand' Islam? The North/West's new 'Other,' new enemy, seemingly lost after the end of the Cold War, was written as strange and otherworldly as possible, almost a welcome relief. We've got to recognize how these desires for an enemy, for a strict us–them division, underscore our analyses.

Our second point is to call attention to how some professors, students, and practitioners of IR are forced to 'perform' IR because of what they look like or the countries from which they hail. Who precisely is responding to human rights, and who is forced to speak about them? When we might be questioned by professors, students, neighbors, or colleagues about 'barbaric' practices from 'over there' (where our immigrant families might be from), such as 'lynching gays,' 'stoning women,' 'dowry deaths,' 'fatwas,' 'acid burning,' 'burqas,' 'child marriage,' 'child labor,' 'repressive and corrupt governments,' and the list goes on, we find ourselves trapped. On the one hand, we struggle to be in solidarity with social movements, and we see practices that we fundamentally oppose; on the other hand, we know that if we don't talk about it carefully, we will feed into more problematic discourses about our 'backward' cultures. Omer Shah, a social justice advocate based in Brooklyn, NY, notes that he attempts to organize his identity as a Muslim while also aiming to hold Northern/Western, non-Muslim, and Muslim journalists accountable for 'addressing us as [a] whole.'[19] But 'by stressing our positions, are we somehow still stressing the West and [its] centrality?'[20] As Said (1979) so aptly posited, the ideology of 'knowing' the Other is really a reflection of what the Self thinks about itself.

How did we get trapped in such a tiresome script (and did Samuel Huntington offer himself as a leading playwright)? It all seems narcissistic, but if you bear with us for the next several paragraphs, we invite you to consider some recent myths and responses, critical to the construction of human rights claims about Islam, the developing world, and 'over there.' We do not want to indulge what has become a seemingly endless, dramatically misinformed, and at times puerile obsession with Islam. However, this discussion is particularly important as we see more and more IR textbooks with at least one obligatory chapter on terrorism, and, invariably, this includes a discussion of Islamic fundamentalism (sometimes with a marginal interest in other religious practices that have been politicized), how 9/11 created an urgent interest in the Islamic world (thus deflecting attention from the way power struggles during the Cold War helped to create the very networks that eventually sponsored and cultivated the hijackers), and non-state terrorists (without exploring how states also use terror (Krishna, 2002)), with the requisite disclaimer: 'Oh, and by the way, of course we know that not all Muslims are terrorists.' The three prototypical human rights 'responses' to certain events, now theaters of 'outrage,' demonstrate how easily human rights, as a category, can center or decenter IR. So let us turn now to responses about (1) the expectations of others to protest human rights violations in the way we expect; (2) the feeling that we should rise up, since they can't or won't; and (3) the specific role of feminist interventions.

Response 1: Where are the Muslims?

The first type of response is based on a presumption that those living in the North/West are not only outraged at human rights violations but know how to respond, just as any other civilized society should. That's why we hear questions such as 'Why don't they see what they're doing to themselves?' and 'Why don't they stand up and say "not in our name"?' We respond that we should catch the moments 'we' expect 'them' to do what we want them to. Instead, as we noted in the previous section, perhaps we can do a better job at looking for and understanding the responses that are happening, and why people respond the way they do. In other words, can we engage, listen, and dialogue instead of judging, presuming, and classifying?

Let's consider the following example. Soon after the terrorist attacks in Mumbai (formerly called Bombay),[21] India, in November 2008,

New York Times columnist Thomas Friedman, whom we will meet again in the chapter on globalization, asked, with great concern, about all the missing and silent Pakistani Muslims: Shouldn't they, 'at least once,' rise up and call for an end to terrorism in 'their name'? A healthy society, he determined, cannot emerge in Pakistan without such an outcry (Friedman, 2008). This is a common trope, the heartfelt query after the 'good Muslims' who share our ideas and horror at what has happened: 'Where are the Muslims protesting violence against non-Muslims?' Putting aside the way that an onus is put on Muslims in a way that it is not on other religious communities, we should ask: Would anything that Pakistanis or Muslims 'at large' do be 'enough' to convince Friedman or anyone else about the legitimacy of their protest? Further, why is it presumed that it is protest, rather than different geopolitical strategies on the parts of Pakistan, India, and others, that would effect a reduction in random violence (Shah, 2008)?

Shah joins others in calling out a Northern/Western desire for 'some deranged liberal political pornography.' He chides Friedman: 'You want it to be big and colorful. You want to see veils, beards, and banners. Certainly, Mr Friedman, people know when to resist and how and they do in their own ways and on their own terms' (*ibid.*). The problem with Friedman's assumption, then, is that it ultimately forces a particular type of agency onto Pakistanis and, ultimately, Muslims as a whole so as to render a particular kind of outcome. Friedman is a reminder of the ease with which one can fall into the kind of stance that exerts judgment and scrutiny on resistance or the presumed lack of it.

The specter of terrorism has centered discourses about the relationship between India, Pakistan, and the US. A decentered response would recognize that people have the agency to mourn, mobilize, and engage as they see fit; they do not have to show 'enough' moral outrage. Writer Arundhati Roy (2008) calls attention to how '[w]e've forfeited rights to our own tragedies.'

Interestingly enough, there *was* a spectacular uprising in Pakistan, both preceding and continuing after the terrorist attacks – but not in the form that Friedman and others wanted, or in response to what people expected. Consider the historical and unprecedented Pakistani Lawyers' Movement (Malik, 2007; Munir, 2009). Pakistani lawyers and other members of civil society protested in 2007 when then-President Pervez Musharraf dismissed Chief Justice of Pakistan Iftikhar Muhammad

Chaudhry on the heels of a series of cases that indicated both critique of and potential challenge to Musharraf's eligibility for re-election (Kalhan, 2009). The Supreme Court of Pakistan eventually restored the chief justice, which prompted Musharraf's declaration of a state of emergency and the re-dismissal of Chaudhry as well as the dismissal of more than sixty judges. Another set of uprisings eventually resulted in the lifting of emergency rule, the reinstatement of Chaudhry, and the resignation of Musharraf. The significance of the Lawyers' Movement over a period of two years cannot be understated and would probably be the best example of the kind of accountability and attempts to strengthen the rule of law and the judiciary that Western journalists, commentators, and pundits demanded from Pakistani civil society after the Mumbai/Bombay attacks. Indeed, lawyers and law associations around the world, including the International Commission of Jurists, the International Bar Association, and the Law Association for Asia and the Pacific, called for restoration of the rule of law and offered symbolic support to Pakistani protestors.[22]

In effect, if the concern really is for Pakistan's civil society and the importance of human rights and the rule of law, then an investigation of the Lawyers' Movement and the complex roles of the constitution and judiciary (see Kalhan, 2009), civil society, and politicians such as Musharraf, Nawaz Sharif, Asif Ali Zardari, Benazir Bhutto, and others, would presumably be key. People mourn loss, due to terrorism as well as other factors; they resist, are fearful or defiant, may be violent or non-violent. But we don't seem to be interested in what people actually *do*; we're more interested in the perception that peoples and communities are complicit with the violence members of their states, cultures, and religions perpetrate. Perhaps sometimes they are; but so are we and every other community we can think of. If we want to use human rights to decenter IR, we have to challenge our own desires for what we want others to do when seeking justice. As we discuss in the next section, those desires can lead us to decide to advocate 'on behalf' of putatively voiceless, oppressed populations.

Response 2: We've got to do it

There's a fine line between solidarity and speaking 'for' those we imagine can't or won't speak up for themselves. How does one tell the difference between human rights activism that is engaged in a mutually respectful attempt to address and connect injustices and that which is self-serving and myopic? We tackle that question in this section.

First, 'centered' human rights work parrots easy, and often distorted, explanations, even and especially in attempts to be 'culturally sensitive.' The first line of analysis should be about one's own self-serving attachment to both the issue and being the one who gets to 'help' (and thus, perhaps, gets the gratitude), but without due attention to one's complicity, in various ways and particularly through such help, in enabling the injustice in question. Second, it is problematic when human rights activists fail to investigate, or acknowledge, the kinds of actions and efforts that are *already* occurring. There are a considerable number of nongovernmental organizations, intellectuals, activists, regional organizations, and some humanitarian advocates much closer to the conflict that are rarely part of the conversation the way they should be.

The responses to the conflict in Darfur, Sudan are relevant to both points. Mahmood Mamdani's critique (2007; 2009b) traces the work of movements, particularly the inter-religious US-based Save Darfur Coalition, and journalists primarily located in the North/West, specifically the US, in claiming that since the crisis is a genocide, militarized humanitarian intervention is warranted. In particular, he demonstrates that the knowledge produced about Darfur is unapologetically error-filled. But this is to be expected, for, as Mamdani asserts, '[r]eporting from Africa is a low-risk job: not only are mistakes expected and tolerated, but often they are not even noticed' (2009b: 20). Specifically, he points to (1) the manipulation of the numbers of dead and dying; (2) the construction of the crisis as yet another example of 'Arab jihadists'; (3) the silence on other conflicts that are as egregious; and (4) the neglect of the role of the African Union in addressing the conflict. We take each point in turn.

Mamdani's book on the politicization of the Darfur conflict, *Saviors and Survivors*, spends considerable time dissecting the inexplicable rise, fall, and rise (again) in the reported numbers, particularly as described by *New York Times* op-ed columnist Nicholas Kristof; the steady refusal to examine that a significant percentage of the deaths are due to lack of 'environmental sanitation'; and the lack of analysis, particularly in the US, of why various organizations, including the US State Department, reported different estimates of the number of deaths from those trumpeted by the US media (*ibid.*: 25, 26). The idea of quibbling over the number of dead may seem particularly obscene in and of itself. However, the overarching point is that numbers are politicized. Numbers and statistics are conveniently marshaled to support mainstream narratives about what is happening; they can thus reveal political agendas. Why, Mamdani asks (*ibid.*: 33), did international activism and then-Senator Hillary Clinton's call for a 'no flight zone' occur around the time the violence de-escalated to the point that it was no longer a humanitarian emergency?

In this case, the 'agenda' is to frame Darfur within the larger context of the US 'war' against terrorism. Indeed, consider Kristof's description of Darfur, particularly in relationship to the Democratic Republic of the Congo (referred to as Congo by many):

> Darfur is a case of genocide, while Congo is a tragedy of war and poverty. And now that I'm here in Congo, I think that's exactly right. It's terrible to see kids dying here in eastern Congo of malaria, malnutrition and simple ailments like diarrhea. It's appalling that Western governments haven't tried harder to end the war here (e.g. by putting more pressure on Rwanda to stop supporting militias here and to take back more of its Hutu exiles). But there is still a big difference. Congo is essentially a tale of chaos and poverty and civil war. Militias slaughter each other, but it's not about an ethnic group in the government using its military force to kill other groups. And that is what Darfur has been about: an Arab government in Khartoum arming Arab militias to kill members of black African tribes. We all have within us a moral compass, and that is moved partly by the level of human suffering. I grant that the suffering is greater in Congo. But our compass is also moved by human evil, and that is greater in Darfur. There's no greater crime than genocide, and that is Sudan's specialty. (Kristof, 2007)

But Darfur is actually not so simple: there are war crimes, crimes against humanity, environmental disasters, and struggles that indicate that power matters more than 'evil.' Mamdani (2009b) contextualizes the Darfur conflict in three ways. First, he draws our attention to the two civil wars in which colonial-era racial, ethnic, and religious divisions played out between the North and South of Sudan after independence. Second, he reviews the overall conflict between President Omar al-Bashir (and his support of the Janjaweed) and political leader Hassan al-Turabi (and his support for the Sudan People's Liberation Army/Movement's southern-based insurgency and the Darfur-based Justice and Equality Movement) as this power contest played into the struggles between nomadic and sedentary tribes in Darfur (and, indeed, the atrocities in Darfur have more to do with who has land and who does not, than with 'Arab' versus 'black'). Finally, he adduces the specific, historical, complex understandings of 'Arab,' 'African,' and Muslims (see also de Waal, 2004b). In addition, Mamdani shows that even progressive and critical human rights advocates sometimes employ the overarching analysis of 'Arabs' (now popularly associated with terrorism and definitionally anti-Northern/Western) killing 'Africans,' in a horrendous 'Muslim-on-Muslim' violence (Mamdani, 2009b: 58–62). While this is a simplistic way of understanding the conflict, these are the same kinds of categorizations deployed in the US 'war on terror.'

As such, as evidenced by the intricacies of the civil wars in Sudan as well as the various power struggles, politics in Darfur is as complex as anywhere else. There is also considerable debate about whether genocide is occurring/has occurred. According to the 1948 UN Convention Against Genocide, evidence of genocidal intent should compel action. The United Nations Commission of Inquiry (2005) found no evidence of genocidal intent,[23] and in 2009 the International Criminal Court, despite the recommendation of the ICC special prosecutor, Luis Moreno-Ocampo, found evidence of war crimes and crimes against humanity but not genocide (Mamdani, 2009b: 42–3). Then, on 3 February 2010, the ICC appeals judges found that there was evidence of intent to commit genocide. We need to investigate the politics and implications of these various findings to better analyze Darfur.

As to the Democratic Republic of the Congo, while we think that calling certain events 'evil' and others 'human suffering' is fundamentally unproductive, there are clear issues around which human rights activists could mobilize. The Second Congo War (from 1998 to 2005, involving eight countries and over twenty armed groups) is officially over but the ramifications, particularly ongoing and rampant sexual violence in the eastern part of the Democratic Republic of the Congo, continue. Activism is so muted that Northern/Western media outlets routinely (ironically enough) call it the 'forgotten war.' Recently US Secretary of State Hillary Clinton has started to discuss gender violence in Congo, and Eve Ensler's *Vagina Monologues* includes scenes regarding rapes there. But any sustained Congo activism that occurs is often in conjunction with Darfur activism, as evidenced by the 'Enough' campaigns. Again, while we do not recommend simplistic activism, or uncritical analysis of the sexual violence, we are left asking: if Northern/Western activists can mobilize so well around Darfur, why not Congo?

Interestingly, Kristof (2007) recommends Western pressure on the Rwandan Tutsi government as a response to its role in the Congo conflict. But Rwanda's history, too, has been simplified into the evil Hutu genocidaires versus the victimized Tutsi allies of the US (Mamdani, 2002). Thus the US would have to consider its options if it were to respond forcefully to Tutsi leadership, both in terms of the violence inflicted on Hutus in Congo and in the export of coltan, a mineral used in cell phones and electronics, from Congo.[24] All of this is to say that when we ask why here and not there, we start to see the answers about which violations get politicized, and how.

Accordingly, Mamdani (2009b) asks about the 'silences' in Northern/Western human rights activism. Specifically, he contrasts the passionate Darfur activism with comparative lack of sustained attention to Iraq. Mamdani's claim is that activists have read Darfur in a simplistic way, whereas Iraq is 'messy,' particularly as Americans would be likely to feel more *responsible* for US actions there (Mamdani, 2007). Compare the activism on many US college campuses around Darfur with that regarding Iraq or other issues. The differences can be stunning, particularly because the US military actively recruits college students, sometimes as they're coming out of classes. Is the difference in activism because we've decided Darfur is a simple, clear-cut case of evil, whereas with Iraq, although Iraqis are indeed *suffering* (per Kristof's dichotomy), we should probably support the troops or 'finish the job,' or – well, we're just not sure? How are anti-genocide activism and anti-war/anti-occupation activism coded and accepted in different ways?

Finally, as Mamdani points out, human rights activism around this issue has largely ignored the significant role of the African Union (AU) in negotiating the conflict, understanding the power struggles, and helping to reduce the number of deaths. Mamdani (2009b), who participated in the Darfur–Darfur Dialogue and Consultation process, and Alex de Waal (2006), who worked on AU peace negotiations in his capacity as a member of AU mediator Salim Ahmed Salim's staff, both detail the complexities of the AU process and the importance of non-violence-related deaths, particularly regarding food (de Waal, 2004a) and water. They both draw attention to the ineffectiveness and potentially disastrous consequences of military intervention. But activists, often within or bolstered by the Save Darfur Coalition, continue to claim the need for (militarized) intervention by the US, NATO, *somebody*, *anybody* to stop the genocide. Even those who are against US military intervention and are in favor of UN-led peacekeeping troops would do well to ask why the UN Security Council (resolutions 1706 and 1769) was in favor of a (limited) UN peacekeeping force and transfer of authority from AMIS (the African Union Mission in Sudan) to UNAMID (the United Nations-African Union Mission in Darfur) rather than directly funding AU peacekeepers (Mamdani, 2009b: 44–7). In other words, what are the politics of Security Council resolutions, the appropriate role of UN peacekeeping forces, and the reasons for the inadequacies of AMIS? What are the complications of using any types of peacekeeping forces (more on this in Chapter 5)?

Potentially, literature on social movements and transnational advocacy networks could highlight why and when certain issues are framed in particular ways and the concomitant problems with representation, funding, and strategies. But we need more on the actual activists themselves, what they do with complexities in the quest to build a movement, and their motivations for aligning with certain organizations and groups but ignoring others (see Carpenter, 2007; Watson, 2007). To that end, Eichler-Levine and Hicks (2007) examine the internal dynamics of the Save Darfur Coalition, with more than 150 national and regional groups, including Amnesty International and the National Association for the Advancement of Colored People.

The Coalition draws heavily and publicly on a Jewish-black alliance and evangelical Christians (who were involved prior to the Darfur conflict on behalf of Christians in the south of Sudan), all of whom buy into some notion of Arab/Muslim militias destroying Sudan and participate actively in American nationalist narratives of redemption, wherein victims of atrocities can now stand up for other 'silent' victims (*ibid.*: 715, 718–19). The idea, particularly after 9/11, that Americans 'together' can do anything, from defeating terrorists to ending genocide, features prominently in an array of activism. In fact, speakers at a 2006 Darfur rally in Washington, DC explicitly evoked both the Americans 'together' trope and Al Qaeda (*ibid.*: 719–20). But as Eichler-Levine and Hicks demonstrate (*ibid.*: 724), the DC rally left out mainstream Muslim organizations who are actually part of the Coalition, and there were contentious politics in terms of which Muslim and Sudanese immigrant (including non-Darfuri) voices to include. What are the motivations here?

Why is there a persistent *need* to say 'Not enough is being done,' or 'Nobody understands how bad this is,' in the face of massive, messy complexities? Perhaps part of it is genuine fear that those who stood by and did nothing will have blood on their hands. But the people pointing out the nuances could hardly be accused of either holing up in their offices or recommending complete denial. Rather, they point to how the very desire to 'save' is possibly about a deeper compulsion to sidestep any questions or interrogations of power, for doing so implicates the structures and entities of which one might be a beneficiary (see also Campbell, 2007).

In effect, what are the ways we deploy our identities and forge alliances for *particular* victims, but not others (see Aidi, 2005)? What are we to make of Kristof's impassioned claim that 'if you believe that Sudan is so wretched that it can't get worse, just wait' (2009), or his retort that Mamdani did not seem to have access to primary sources, 'ordinary Darfuris,' and, essentially, the 'facts,' as much as Kristof presumably did?[25] Mamdani (2009a) responds to Kristof's claims by pointing out that Kristof mistakenly thinks that understanding history and power translates into apologias for perpetrators of violence. But already we can see that any subtlety, any nuance, any attention to the complexities aswirl has been lost. It is a familiar script laden with defensiveness, misunderstandings (real and imagined), and little that is new or useful. Again, we are emphasizing how to decenter ourselves; surely, this is difficult to do at the very moment we want our students, colleagues, or friends to stop being so apathetic. But responsibility, accountability, and engagement do not necessitate quick and easy answers.

Response 3: Pitfalls of feminist interventions[26]

The third response presents a particular challenge, because it usually emerges out of the kind of thoughtful and activist work we support and draw upon. Typically, feminist theorizing and research is critical in revealing the experiences of marginalized people due to the abuse of power, or how misogyny, homophobia, or essentialized norms about gender, sex, and sexuality figure in global politics. But the fact that we may actively look for power relationships, or the traces of colonialism, imperialism, heteronormativity, or masculinity, does not mean that we are immune from critique or that we do not have political agendas. The reason *why* this particular type of activism can be problematic is precisely because feminist theory is not singular: it includes or intersects with postcolonial, queer, liberal, standpoint, socialist, and other theories. As Ang notes,

> Feminism must stop conceiving itself as a nation, a 'natural' political destination for all women, no matter how multicultural. Rather than adopting a politics of inclusion (which is always ultimately based on a notion of commonality and community), it will have to develop a self-conscious politics of partiality, and imagine itself as a *limited* political home, which does not absorb difference within a pre-given and predefined space but leaves room for ambivalence and ambiguity. (Ang, 2003: 191)

In other words, if we act as though we are necessarily speaking *from* a readily understandable, given position, for example, one that prioritizes gender or queer solidarity over and against race and class, we will 'center' ourselves in the conversation. This is, of course, terribly difficult. We mobilize around connections with others who share our position. But the very movements and theorists that claim to challenge and, indeed, decenter power structures can participate in exclusionary politics; Smith (2008), for example, points out the tendency to try to 'include' non-white feminisms, often to address the limits of white Western feminisms, thus presuming that feminism necessarily 'started' in the global North/West and emanated outwards (much like the narrative of the human rights story).

In this section, we focus on feminists' unwitting and intentional collusion with hegemonic discourses. Various political actors can easily appropriate feminist activism and rhetoric for aims other than those intended by the activists and scholars. This happens when the issue, such as gender violence, is particularly salient and serves as a site for articulating certain political agendas and world views (Nayak and Suchland, 2006). Gender violence, in particular, is a thorny issue because 'addressing violence requires resistance to and/or advocacy for what men and women should be and do' and offers ways to promote political agendas in the name of 'helping' the people being targeted (Nayak, 2003: 72).[27] We are particularly curious about how those who label themselves as feminist theorists and activists avail themselves of the appropriation.

As postcolonial feminist theorists have documented, colonial empires co-opted the issue of women's rights, mobilizing campaigns to end 'harmful customs' against women in the colonies; colonial feminists and officials participated in targeting a variety of practices while feminist movements were suppressed 'at home' (Ahmed, 1992; 'Saving Amina Lawal,' 2004: 2374). In turn, predominantly male anti-colonial nationalists often focused on legitimizing these particular practices as a way to paint women as nobly upholding 'cultural traditions,' but, in effect, used women's bodies as terrains for articulating self-determination struggles (Mani, 1998; Spivak, 1988; Kapur, 2002). The multiple feminist responses and women's claims *within* the countries or territories in question seem(ed) to matter little in the battles to deploy brown and black female bodies as cultural symbols, either for the North/West, in terms of their alleged brutalization, disfigurement, and mutilation (supposedly indicative of the backwardness of the colonized), or for colonial/postcolonial nationalists, as key to the survival of the nation.

Furthermore, this kind of politics has continued 'after' colonialism, particularly with the tendency of some Northern/Western feminist responses to human rights issues *there* to reproduce us–them divisiveness or to demonize the very states that the North/West happens to construct as rogue, adversarial, enemy, or unintelligible. As Krishna pointed out a decade ago in his analysis of postcolonial India, Pakistan, and Sri Lanka, 'foreign policy [is a] discursive practice that, far from being the actions of an always recognizeable "us" on a "them," is historically emergent and produces and reproduces the very antinomies critical to identify itself: us/them, domestic/foreign, self/other, inside/outside' (Krishna, 1999: 4). The same should be said of social movement activism that sustains and uncritically upholds foreign policy imperatives. This is not to say that anyone should fear to critique the misogyny, homophobia, or other forms of repression at the hands of any leader, regime, or entity; rather, we should question whether and how responses depend upon and sustain the power relationships and us–them binaries that enable forms of oppression in the first place. Otherwise, we'll know very little about issues of violence, but we will perform other levels of violence by misrepresenting both these issues and the contexts in question; we will miss how global political phenomena, such as neoliberalism, military intervention, and IMF or World Bank structural adjustment programs, and local patriarchal and class structures make possible such violence; we will continue to Other countries – and the dictatorial, deranged, uncivilized people we imagine live there – which opens the way for international conflict and the justification of militarized intervention, and thus more suffering and violence.

As postcolonial feminist theory points out, we get far away from the ability to analyze how religion, nationalism, or state-making play out on people's bodies when the premise of the argument is that a particular religion, nationalism, or state is *bad* and that citizens, particularly women, are perpetual victims (Yegenoglu, 1998; Abu-Lughod, 2001; Bahramitash, 2008). We can see this in some campaigns explicitly framed as 'feminist' or 'queer' for the sake of standing up for women, sexual minorities, or marginalized populations who are being targeted in specifically sexualized or gendered ways. We concur that 'the human rights promise of progress, emancipation and universalism, has been exposed as myopic, exclusive and informed by a series of global panics, especially a panic over national security, sexual morality, and cultural survival in the contemporary period' (Kapur, 2006: 665–6). Activists, institutions, and states sanitize and depoliticize human rights when they bring this category into the fold of neoliberalism and Western liberal democracy, and inconsistently and problematically invoke human rights in ways that ultimately support military interventions, feed into 'us versus them' notions about so-called cultural practices, and uncritically view issues such as sex work, dowry deaths, *sati*, or female genital cutting (Kapur, 2002).

For example, consider when feminists focus primarily on 'honor killings' (rather than more broadly on gender violence) or other crimes allegedly due to 'cultural practices,' without taking into account that such practices are political, contested, and changing rather than ancient, inherent, and static. Their discussions reduce complex situations to matters of culture, religion, and tradition in the global South/East and posit these factors against the freedom, empowerment, and feminism allegedly espoused in the North/West (Narayan, 1997). Furthermore, it is difficult to separate claims to 'save' women from the Taliban or governments or men 'over there' from the colonial history of the very regions in question; these are the same societies in which colonizers used 'backward' treatment of women to justify occupation and intervention (Abu-Lughod, 2002: 784–5). Why are we more likely to leverage feminist theory and activism to address women's rights when the alleged perpetrators are men with 'Other' religions and backgrounds than when they are men from culturally similar backgrounds or from countries that are allied with our countries? Why are we less likely to critique what is done in the name of secular humanism than so-called religious movements (*ibid.*: 788)?

By the same token, it is not useful to lump together all Western feminism as complicit with (neo)colonialism. We should instead politicize what feminism is used for. Consider the trope that feminism can 'save' us all, perhaps a variation of the 'if women ruled the world, there would be no war' claim. For example, the US Feminist Majority had a role in disrupting a secret plan between the Taliban and the US corporation Unocal to build an oil pipeline through Afghanistan (*ibid.*: 787); however, its program to 'Stop Gender Apartheid in Afghanistan,' often singularly focused on the burqa, was disconnected from the concerns articulated by Afghani women's organizations, and cohered with the Bush Administration's military imperatives there (Nayak and Suchland, 2006: 477; Russo, 2006). A singular fixation on globally sensationalized cases of gender violence can obscure multiple types of gender and political violence. For example, in the case of international human rights activism around Amina Lawal, sentenced to death by stoning in Nigeria for adultery, the focus on sexual repression elided a focus on how men are victims of sexual mores as well, or the internal flaws of the legal system itself ('Saving Amina Lawal,' 2004: 2366, 2370–1). Furthermore, the international community has been unable to simultaneously 'hold' together multiple struggles, such as both Nigerian women's fight for legal rights and the indigenous Ogoni resistance to oil companies' exploitation (*ibid.*: 2365, fn. 7).

In such cases, self-proclaimed feminists fail to listen to the stories of the Revolutionary Association of the Women of Afghanistan (RAWA), or BAOBAB, a women's human rights organization in Nigeria, or Women Living Under Muslim Laws (see Sunder, 2003). To be sure, there are tensions and questions about privilege, strategies, and dissent within those organizations and regarding their relationships with other, less globally recognized, organizations and networks. We are certainly not claiming that activists *from* or living there are innocent; they may not be attentive to their own privileges, or may purposely speak to Western audiences to represent an 'insider' view of their communities.[28] However, the existence of these different narratives belies the image of the monolithic mass of muted women living in these countries.

Even feminist solidarity with dissidents can become an indictment of a country that may not result in pressure for that country to change its behavior. For example, we noticed an overheated response to the post-election uprisings in Iran in summer 2009, with the 'We are all Iranians now' placards, the fetishization of hijabi-clad women running from teargas, and the presumption that it was 'Westernized' upper-class youth who formed the basis of the resistance to the theocracy.[29] We should ask: Are we using oppression of women in other countries to justify policies such as racial profiling, armed attack, or sanctions, thus leading to more conflict in and between both the US and other countries (Bahramitash, 2008)? Further, how does well-meaning solidarity feed into the rhetoric that the uprisings, protest, and dissent are fueled by a Western conspiracy (see the response by several members of Iran's Guardian Council) rather than a homegrown event? When Northern/Western activism uncritically takes on issues 'elsewhere,' they can potentially damage the ability of various feminist groups to maneuver against governments and political actors who would like to dismiss their work as crude Westernization.

Thus Puar (2007) compels an examination of how both feminist and queer activism can elide critical analysis of power and, willfully or not, cohere with US nationalist projects. She looks directly at organizations that participated in the International Day of Action Against Homophobic Persecution in Iran on July 19, 2006. Certainly, many argued, Iran deserved such outrage, given its alleged stances on nuclear weapons, Israel, women, and 'the West' in general; its homophobia was yet another example of its rogue ways. Yet, the very people who might protest an invasion of or military action against Iran relied upon the problematic discourses that set up Iran as a pariah in order to claim solidarity with gay communities within Iran; this aligned all too well with US political anti-Iran rhetoric. Why Iran and why then? We could ask this question both of President Bush, when he declared Iran as part of the 'Axis of Evil,' and of queer activists, when they failed to react in the same way to other high-profile persecutions of gays and lesbians in other parts of the world (*ibid.*: xi). Accordingly, Puar essentially asks: When we redress human rights, how do we play into militaristic, colonial, racist, and heteronormative imperatives in our very attempts to be 'sensitive,' globally inclusive and aware, and outraged at examples of violence that reveal misogyny, homophobia, or fascism? What is this activism missing, and will its form actually make the situation better or more *complicated* for the persecuted groups? We think there are multiple ways to support and draw attention to struggles, but as we noted in the previous section, we simultaneously have to ask careful questions about what we're doing, why, and to what end.

Feminist responses can thus be problematic when they try to be 'sensitive,' perhaps hoping to avoid mistakes and misunderstandings, about oppression caused by so-called cultural issues *there*, rarely *here* (Narayan, 1997). Ehrenreich's 'To Defeat Terrorists, Try Listening to Feminists' (2004) is a combination of the 'feminism saves' and 'feminism understands' themes. She proposes that in order to combat terrorism, US politicians must consider a litany of feminist topics we appreciate: the US should support financially girls' education in Pakistan, expand gender-based asylum, lead the attempt to end trafficking of women, ratify the Convention on the Elimination of Discrimination Against Women, increase the number of US women in political office, and allow family planning. It is, obviously, hard to take issue with any of these; many would agree that these are 'good' things that would increase the human rights of women. But these are also the topics that will surely let the North/West do all the acting – and all the saving. It is even more ironic that she seems to be writing this letter to John Kerry (then running for president of the US), because the kind of feminism a political candidate would/could take on, even seriously, would not be very disruptive to the neoliberalism and militarism underlying state and non-state terrorism.

Regardless of the lack of critique in her piece, Ehrenreich ventures right into the territory of asserting her authority, knowledge, and understandings. Referencing Carmen bin Laden's *Inside the Kingdom*, which addresses how the Saudi royal family treats women, Ehrenreich says, 'I'm not expecting these measures alone to incite feminist insurgency within the Islamist one. Carmen bin Laden found her rich Saudi sisters-in-law sunk in bovine passivity, and some of the more spirited young women in the Muslim world have been adopting the head scarf as a gesture of defiance toward American imperialism' (*ibid.*). Immediately we wonder: What does it mean that the US would (or could) 'incite' a feminist insurgency? And, why does she assume or need to say that the head scarf is a gesture of 'defiance'? Are some women doing something (veiling) so *obviously* 'backward' that it makes Ehrenreich and others feel better if they say that, surely, they must be doing it in some sort of grand political protest? In Ehrenreich's case, it becomes difficult to read subtlety, nuance, or historical context in her statements, particularly given her casual attribution of 'bovine' to Arab women, a colonial trope.[30] 'Sensitive' feminism, alleging that it really 'gets' how Othering works and understands the 'spirited' women elsewhere, is mightily dangerous.

Another example that is important here is the reaction to the release of the pictures of US soldiers torturing Iraqi prisoners in Abu Ghraib. Many, including progressive feminists, dismissed the events as the actions of a 'few bad apples'; others remarked that such events were likely in the context of the Bush Administration's rejection of multilateralism and international law. But several of those critical of militarization and the occupation of Iraq often reduced the complexity to (some version of): 'Abu Ghraib was especially horrible because of the humiliation and shame those Muslim men must feel because of sexuality taboos in Islam.' The focus of the outrage in the North/West quickly skipped over anger or discussion about the US war and occupation that enabled such acts. It shifted deftly from anger at the US soldiers in the pictures to shock that female soldiers were participating in the violence and to intrigue about the outrage that conservative Muslim society must be experiencing.

This problematically assumed the following: (1) any other men in the world wouldn't be equally humiliated (can we really compare or measure humiliation, shame, and rage?); (2) the Iraqi men in Abu Ghraib identified primarily as Muslim and thus singularly experienced some static *Muslim* taboo about homosexuality; (3) if the US military only understood 'Muslim culture,' no one would have participated in such acts; and (4) gay, lesbian, queer, bisexual, and transgendered communities in the US don't experience state-sponsored or systemic exclusion, terror, oppression, or discrimination that is dehumanizing in its own right (Puar, 2007: 82–8; Richter-Montpetit, 2007: 47). US male soldiers involved female soldiers in staging the male prisoners in sexual positions with each other for specific reasons, especially in positing supposedly free, sexual US women against backward, repressed Iraqi men; such a heteronormative, racialized, and sexualized script was useful during colonialism to mark colonized men as perverts but simultaneously impotent in the face of stronger Western forces (Richter-Montpetit, 2007). But various people, particularly Northern/Western feminists, who responded, horrified, to Abu Ghraib, did not go far enough in making these connections, naming the acts in Abu Ghraib not as sodomy but as forcible rape or highlighting how the soldiers treated the prisoners as *animals*, literally (with the leash) and figuratively through their words and the staged positions (Richter-Montpetit, 2007: 48–9).

This particular form of feminist silence, relatively speaking, may be connected to how and why Euro-American feminists in particular were unable to face, comprehend, or make intelligible the scene enacted in the photos – of *women* torturing and tormenting Iraqi men; unable to figure out what this meant for *American* feminism; and consequently were mourning the ostensible 'loss' to feminism (Puar, 2007: 90). Puar quotes Zillah Eisenstein:

> When I first saw the pictures of the torture at Abu Ghraib I felt destroyed. Simply heart-broken. I thought 'we' are the fanatics, the extremists; not them. By the next day as I continued to think about Abu Ghraib I wondered how there could be so many women involved in the atrocities. (Quoted in Puar, 2007: 89)

And Barbara Ehrenreich:

> Secretly, I hoped that the presence of women would over time change the military, making it more respectful of other people and cultures, more capable of genuine peacekeeping. . . . A certain kind of feminism, or perhaps I should say a certain kind of feminist naivete, died in Abu Ghraib. (Quoted in Puar, 2007: 89)

Eisenstein and Ehrenreich have provided us with several powerful pieces on capitalism, race, and gender. But their interjections about Abu Ghraib are all too familiar, because so many of us found ourselves similarly surprised, shocked, or outraged, and probably said the same thing. But, as Puar notes, US public and feminist 'reaction of rage, while to some extent laudable, misses the point entirely, or perhaps more generously, upstages a denial of culpability' (*ibid*.: 80). It's easier to be shocked about graphic details of 'deviant' sex (if 'sex' is even the right word in this context) than to recognize that torture and attempted humiliation are part of, rather than aberrations from, state violence, than to theorize gender violence, misogyny, and homophobia as *necessary* to hegemonic power (Nayak and Suchland, 2006); what is war but violent? As such, in trying to be *with* the Iraqis, in calling out the US, feminist responses might inadvertently fail to examine the relationship between state violence and bodies, a connection that historically feminists have been particularly adept at pointing out. Why are the connections so hard to see, to make, 'elsewhere'?

There are alternatives to the supposed distinctions between us and them, Islam and the West, fundamentalism and feminism (Abu-Lughod, 2001). For example, Alina Sajed astutely comments that attempts to 'rescue' women from the image of an oppressed class and to insert the possibility of freedom/autonomy reduces the complexity of veiling, for instance, to a reductivist binary of oppression versus autonomy (2008: 8). Veiling functions differently in different political contexts and historical periods – and women participating in it might hold contradictory and multiple meanings rather than 'choosing' between oppression and autonomy. Sajed further notes that attempts to critique, reveal, and discredit Orientalist representations of Arabs and Muslims in the context of the war on terror may just reinscribe the boundaries of those very stereotypes, thereby 'discount[ing] the political richness that emerges from the concept of the "Arab" and the manner in which it has operated, shifted and metamorphosed historically' (*ibid.*).

Indeed, some of us are so tired of combating stereotypes that we no longer want to talk about veils, burqas, or other issues. Abu-Lughod's article 'Do Muslim Women Really Need Saving?' (2002) interrogates why universities and reporters asked her to speak about 'women and Islam' immediately following 9/11; she wondered what that topic had to do with the complex and messy factors that caused those attacks or with Al Qaeda, and why similar questions about women and religion were not asked after attacks and crises in other regions of the world (*ibid.*: 784). As such, it's hard to speak critically about human rights violations because of the onslaught of judgment, pity, revulsion, sadness, and grave concern for 'those women,' for that persecuted group.

However, the disruption of these problematic narratives does not mean that we're left with the inability to speak, political paralysis, or endless disclaimers anytime we want to say anything. Actually, it's an amazing opportunity to do something different in IR, to politicize what we do and say in order to be more uncomfortable and honest about our activism. The challenge, laid down in Chapter 2, to perceptions of the happy, simple, undeniably good, and harmonious native accords with Sajed's point (2008) that it is not helpful to confront or replace harmful stereotypes with 'good' ones. Perhaps, then, we can use sarcasm, irony, farce, humor, and paradox, interrogating how we can play *with* stereotypes, rather than trying so damn hard to *confront* or replace them with 'positive' images (*ibid.*). This could entail some engagement with performance art, cinema, novels, and other 'aesthetic narratives,' which have been somewhat better at using modes of speech and literary devices to sketch out the interplay of identities, colonial and postcolonial contexts, and various forms of oppression (*ibid.*).

What exactly is the purpose of your activism? What myths and responses can you dismantle? What responses can you not bear to deconstruct? Just as human rights advocates encourage 'fact finding' to eventually advocate for a particular policy, we encourage 'myth finding' to understand the stories we eagerly believe, to question why, and to stumble across resistance, rewriting, rethinking, and lived experiences of those attempting to craft sustainable communities. Decentering, then, requires using human rights as a site to subvert dominant discourses about justice and to reveal social justice struggles that are occurring in worlds and communities.

Stories and Storytellers

We have to recognize that stories of IR must be performed, heard, and told in a different way. We're so focused on more laws, institutions, and mechanisms and in professionalizing and institutionalizing human rights because we believe that the testimonies and documented violence we've seen and heard demand coordinated strategic responses. In a sense, this approach has its successes. But our focus here is to question what would happen if we could imagine/find different ways to represent pain and suffering and struggles, because it's not just the advocacy network, the UN resolution, the *ad hoc* tribunal that circumscribe human rights – it's also the stories that matter. We forget that all too often. In her engaging and challenging work on the body and pain, pointedly subtitled *The Making and Unmaking of the World*, Elaine Scarry notes how the reality of the physical pain of violating people 'seems to confer its quality of "incontestable reality" on that power that has brought it into being. It is, of course, precisely because the reality of that power is so highly contestable, the regime so unstable, that torture is being used' (1985: 27). For the person in pain, there is no reality besides pain; if it hurts, it must be real, making the pain useful politically. Scarry notes that 'physical pain has no voice, but when it at last finds a voice, it begins to tell a story' (*ibid.*: 3).

Centered IR, as we know it, has often missed what that story is. Human rights discourse fails to deal with the deflections of some acts of violence and the consumption of others – because human rights believes more in itself as a discourse than in anything else. It believes so much in its universality that it doesn't ask which stories are left out, which are glamorized, which are already known but ignored, which are not known, and whose utterance would be disturbing. Are human rights only for those who deserve it, those who don't piss off the wrong people and forfeit their 'inalienable' rights because they are on the wrong side of history and power? As Muppidi notes, in *The Colonial Signs of International Relations*, there are those who are 'always already dead within the world of IR ... [and] their deaths don't raise a stink' (2010: 172).

Accordingly, if we really are to call ourselves human rights activists, we should think about three types of stories. First, there are stories we have to recover from the distortions or dismissals. Second, purposeful silence tells stories about what cannot yet find words. Third, there are forms of stories that we aren't used to seeing in IR: spoken word, poetry, music, performance.

As to the first point, Muppidi notes: '[r]igor and precision define theory in IR. But the stuffiness of dead bodies, their unpleasing decomposition, their stench, rarely comes through our fields' (*ibid.*: 8). Muppidi asks:

> What'd it mean for IR to enter into conversations with . . . bodies? What self-referential and sole/soul-pleasuring fantasies of power, beauty and excitement about world politics and about the nature of knowledge must we relinquish for such conversations to happen, for the stench of corpses and the smells of bodies to permeate and be part of our understandings? What body languages do we need to be literate about? (2010: 10)

Indeed a significant part of what we are trying to accomplish in this book is to ask how easily we accept distorted narratives rather than really *engaging* with ugly stories that may well implicate us, leaving us troubled, disturbed, angry, and more than a bit nervous. Think of times we look at pictures of burned, charred, and broken bodies and explain how they really did it to themselves (they shouldn't have used human shields, they should have supported occupying forces, they should have agreed to the terms of the peace treaty, etc.).

Think of mass losses due to earthquakes, tsunamis, or other disasters anywhere in the world, and think about what happens when the US military, food packages, or volunteers show up. Inevitably a US president, politician, or diplomat will say something about everyone's common humanity, but he or she will also note that the relief efforts showcased US values 'in action.' Condoleezza Rice spoke about the tsunami as an 'opportunity' to witness 'American generosity' (see Muppidi, 2010: 55); President Obama's State of the Union address, January 2010, spoke about the 'decency' of Americans volunteering in Haitian earthquake relief efforts and one occasion of Haitians chanting 'USA! USA! USA!' Sure, any politician needs to talk about the greatness of his or her country and citizens. But what's wrong with us? We either need the spectacle of the gory details, or skip over the suffering and death to make a political point.

Some stories are not told, because there are reasons to keep secrets, be in denial, or lie flat out. We saw in Chapter 2 that some stories might be fictionalized or imagined or (sur)real but still offer testimony. Consider events we don't know much about. For example, the long event of the India–Pakistan Partition of 1947,[31] and the concomitant widespread sexual violence against women in public spaces, places of worship, and their homes, are still shrouded in silence and shame. Both countries were more invested in nation-making than in wanting to know the stories of how people suffered. Shortly after Partition, the passage of India's Abducted Persons Recovery and Restoration Ordinance Act No. LXV of 1949 set off a massive 'rescue, recovery, and rehabilitation' cooperative Indo-Pakistan campaign, replete with camps and transportation, to 'return' Muslim, Sikh, and Hindu people displaced during the Partition to their 'proper' countries (Bacchetta, 2000: 574).

The collaboration between the two countries was remarkable, considering that India used the issue of recovery of women to express the 'dishonor' of the allegedly less civil, unsecular, intolerant Pakistan – a constant reminder of betrayal, of the cutting up of the body of India (Butalia, 1998: 134). However, Indian officials could not explain why they could not recover as many women from Pakistan as Pakistan did from India. The recovery operation lasted until 1956, with approximately 22,000 Muslim women 'recovered' from India and 8,000 Hindu and Sikh women 'recovered' from Pakistan (*ibid.*: 123). The lives of the homeless, women who committed suicide, and women rejected by their families have not been included in these estimates. Nor do these numbers tell the stories of police participation with abductors to prevent the voluntary return of women to their families. In response to the anxiety India experienced about having the proper inhabitants within the proper space of its territory, India, despite being secular, emphatically promoted religion as defining home – Hindus and Sikhs were to live in India. As Butalia documents in her narrative study of women during Partition, 'women living with men of the other religion had to be brought back, if necessary by force, to their "own" homes – in other words, the place of their religion' (*ibid.*: 105). At the same time, many women, including Dalits, on both sides of the border used unexpected mobility to work, to get educated, or to challenge caste and class boundaries (Bhasin and Menon, 1998; Butalia, 1998; Bacchetta, 2000: 576).

Many survivors still cannot or will not speak about their experiences, and they do not participate in rituals of mourning; rather 'than bearing witness to the disorder that they had been subjected to, the metaphor that they used was a woman drinking poison and keeping it within her' (Das, 1997: 85). The Partition narratives continue to unfold in ways that recognize the silences, figurative language, and fragmented stories, as indicative of the incompleteness of our 'pasts' and the impossibility of history ever being fully recorded (Menon and Bhasin, 1996; Bhasin and Menon, 1998; Butalia, 1998; Kumar, 1999; Bacchetta, 2000; Didur, 2000). The question of silence is relevant for the so-called comfort women, and in many cleansings, partitions, displacements, occupations, wars, and migrations around the world. Thus, we encourage a recognition and acceptance of perhaps not knowing.

As to the third type of stories, we are mindful of Doty's (2004: 378) concern about the sanitized, authorial academic voice that dominates much of IR literature. She asks, 'Where is the soul in our academic writing? Where is the humanity in our prose? Where are *we* as writers?' Or, as Mary Louise Pratt asks, 'How ... could such interesting people doing such interesting things produce such dull books? What did they have to do to themselves?' (Pratt, 1986: 33, quoted in Doty, 2004: 378, fn. 2) Indeed, even in IR's attempt to include 'real' voices, the voice we use to talk about what's going on is completely devoid of blood, energy, sound, feelings. To be sure, this is not about writing in our outrage; as we have noted, this is an all-too-common and problematic practice. Rather, this is about reading/writing our own work aesthetically, responsibly, and meaningfully, instead of in an antiseptic yet authoritative way.

We should listen to, talk with, and learn from poets, writers, musicians, artists, dancers, and performers telling stories about the world, because they offer useful and provocative correctives to the drudgery in IR. Tehila Wise, a social justice advocate and poet in Brooklyn, NY comments:

> It's frustrating that in classrooms, history is presented as something detached and separate from us. Like our story told through someone else's lens. And they told it wrong. On purpose. And wrote us out of it. On different scales and in different ways [what we learn] is just our stories as people, and the majority of people do not have printing presses and books to bind their knowledge in . . . so, it makes sense that poetry would serve as a powerful means of educating ourselves and others, excavating the emotion involved in our collective . . . experiences.[32]

So as to further explain, Tehila notes that her performances as a poet are not just about resistance to power but also about creativity, movement, love, and solidarity. Decentering, particularly when trying to understand issues commonly coded as human rights, might involve a recognition that, as Tehila notes, '[w]e are who we are whether or not they despise us, are confused by us, are afraid or in awe of us. We are beautiful whether or not they think we are horrendous.'[33] We think a decentered IR would open up and legitimize access to stories of pain and triumph. Do we dare?

> It's a lie if they tell you Darfur is genocide and sit silently watching Iraqis die
> While the funding gets bigger to back triggers that turn people into
> numbers and figures
> Blinded
> But then I'm narrow-minded
> When I expose that, though it's been a while, for a black man on trial today
> the gavel can be the same as a rope
> Each time I wrote I soaked up the hope
> The vision, the precision of quiet riots to get someone to listen
> Of movement
> After being kept from walking so long realizing you have legs is an
> improvement
> So many voices I gotta spit fast to avoid getting choked
> Each time I wrote I soaked up
> And now I spill
> Over their borders, onto my pages
>
> And like Columbus
> They did not discover me

Their lines on maps and railroad tracks will never cover me
I won't be left standing with some beads in my palm and my land is gone
Cuz they won't steal my name, reduce me to a Disney movie or song
But
I wasn't born strong
I was made
Path paved by others who have walked this way.

(excerpted from Tehila Wise, 'Spill,' 2009)[34]

Chapter Four / Globalization

Grappling with Globalization

If hardly a new concept, globalization is certainly a promiscuous one these days. The term is used frequently and loosely with a surprising degree of shared meaning. But, '[d]oes it mean we exist in a "global village" where a few get to have all the comforts and riches on the basis of their geographical location and race, while the rest literally clean their toilets? Or does it mean seizing opportunities to ensure equal access to the benefits of trade and investment, and to fairness, equity, and justice?' (Adeleye-Fayemi, 2005: 39). Certainly, a 'centered' IR rarely looks at bathrooms and who is cleaning them, even though we all use them. Chances are, 'someone else' is doing the labor that allows 'us' to do our labor – which might include writing about class relations and the global flows of migration.

We – those of us writing, doing, learning IR – all love, eat, travel, work, study. Who lets us do this? Who might be harvesting or cooking our food or taking care of members of our family? Who is benefiting from our labor? Who, as we mentioned in the Introduction, do we presume could not 'do' IR and are instead the subjects of studies? These questions inspire our discussion in this chapter. We explore how the category of globalization centers IR in three ways: (1) positing a so-called borderless world that ignores the realities of 'borders and bodies'; (2) the production of knowledge in universities and journalistic media; (3) imagining a putatively 'global' economy that ignores the existence of multiple, overlapping economies.

Before we proceed, a few points. For good or ill, globalization as a term enjoys great currency in both popular and academic usage. Unpacking the incarnations, permutations, and peregrinations here would distract from our purpose, but allow us to proffer a working definition of sorts drawing on common usage of the word. Generally, globalization reflects three familiar facets: *economically*, it presumes the triumph of neoliberalism, denoted primarily by efforts to increase the flow of goods, services, and especially capital across borders with little or no restrictions; *politically*, it accepts the superiority of 'Western liberal democracy';[1] *socio-culturally*, it assumes the denationalization of 'policies, capital, political subjectivities, urban spaces, temporal frames, or any other of a variety of dynamics and domains,' such that these things are no longer just the domain of the state (Sassen, 2006: 1). It is this last aspect which leads proponents such as Friedman (2005) to see a 'flattening' of the world, which purportedly bodes well for the world's immense majority. Globalization thus reflects in part Northern/Western triumphalism, captured in some measure by former British Prime Minister Margaret Thatcher's (in)famous formulation that with the end of the Cold War 'there is no alternative.' While the sun may have set on the British Empire or, dare some suggest, even on US dominance, breakfast, lunch, dinner, and more is always available at a McDonald's near you somewhere in McWorld (Barber, 1992).

Thus we recognize, with no little discomfort, that globalization is the metanarrative of our age, having subsumed Enlightenment and rationalist thinking as well as the various and sundry spawn of international capitalism: colonialism, imperialism, modernization, development, and dependency – all of these flow *from* the center to the margins, the periphery. Whether it is multinational corporations that operate worldwide, international financial institutions, the governments of 'developed' ('advanced industrialized' or 'post-industrialized')[2] countries, or some combination of these and more (perhaps reflected in something such as the so-called Washington Consensus),[3] globalization is most often simply presented as a done deal: it's here, it's clear, get used to it. Yet while we might reasonably construe ours as an age of globalization, much about that claim remains unclear: the issues, the dynamics, the limits, the possibilities; in short, what globalization means on the ground. Nowhere is this more evident than with regard to the relationship between the narrative(s) we call globalization and the material and ideological conditions of people's everyday lives. The devastating consequences of global capitalism and neoliberalism in every region of the world are increasingly apparent – even to some of globalization's supporters. In classic centered fashion, we can point to current and former champions, such as Joseph Stiglitz, Nobel Prize winner and former senior vice-president and chief economist of the World Bank, international financier George Soros, and economist Jeffrey Sachs, special advisor to the UN Secretary-General, co-president of the Millennium Promise Alliance, and former director of the United Nations Millennium Project; they have all cautioned us about both the potential and the consequences of globalization.

In this chapter, we draw upon the very rich and dense literature on both the socio-political forces that ensure and maintain hegemonic norms, regimes, and institutions of globalization, and the multiple normative and empirical forms of resistance and alternatives to neoliberalism (see Rupert, 2000; Harvey, 2005). Thus both globalization and responses to it are actually political projects (rather than inevitable). Our main focus is on how this category of globalization centers IR but can also serve as a site of resistance when interrogated.

Bodies and Borders

As is so often the case with so many things heralded as 'new' and 'distinctive' and 'unlike anything which has come before,' globalization, *per se*, is not particularly novel. Yet the refrain persists: 'globalization has ushered in a borderless world.' This would seem to imply that anyone who wishes to can go wherever they want at whatever time. Microsoft, an epitome of globalization at an array of levels, ran an advert for several years with the tagline 'Where do you want to go today?' with the clear implication that thanks to Microsoft and its global access, you could go anywhere at any time. This is hardly the case, and the 'lines' in the North/West are drawn particularly tightly for those from the Global South who wish to relocate or those who do not have the resources to move within the South or North, or anywhere for that matter. In this 'new' globalized world, it would seem that the only thing flowing free and easy is capital, which does so 24/7 and is increasingly detached from any one or even any few states. To some extent commodities share this ease of movement – especially when it is people who are the commodities (sex slaves, domestic servants, 'mail order' brides).

Actually, people, empires, conquerors, trading families, corporations, and others have been buying, selling, and moving goods (and, for that matter, services and people) around the globe for millennia. Consider the 'Silk Road,' which has linked disparate parts of Asia (East, South, and West) with the Mediterranean world and hence Africa and Europe for thousands of years; the trans-Saharan trade between Mediterranean countries and sub-Saharan Africa from the eighth century until the late sixteenth century; or the sailors, slaves, pirates, laborers, market women, and indentured servants who helped to create and service the economy of the Atlantic during the sixteenth, seventeenth, and eighteenth centuries. Today, globalization is undoubtedly 'farther, faster, cheaper, and deeper' (Friedman, 2000: xviii), thanks to phones, computers, jet planes, and the like, but it is not, in the end, *so* new that power relationships no longer matter.

The insistence on a flattened, borderless world that many uphold has two problems. First, it ignores but also feeds into commitments to *borders* as if they are real. Second, it ignores that *bodies* do not cross borders easily; they may be abused, criminalized, commodified, categorized, or immobile. And, the ones who do cross might have certain desires and resources that are intimately connected with borders.[4]

With all the globalization talk of the questionable 'relevance' of the nation-state *vis-à-vis* transnational corporations, the Internet's speed, global governance institutions, international law, and non-state actors, we miss that 'borders' of states still do matter. And, thus, the category of globalization ends up centering IR by creating, ironically enough, an added emphasis on boundaries. This is a story about territory, once again. Thus, we are concerned not only with whether countries still have political and economic sovereignty in the face of trade and financial liberalization and the role of international financial institutions; certainly, many scholars and political leaders have pointed out that even though some paint a picture of trade liberalization breaking down hostilities and antagonisms, international trade and financial regimes can challenge the decision-making abilities of poorer countries. But we also point out that in response to whatever is understood to be globalization, states and political actors such as nationalist movements use the opportunity to *commit* to the securitization of boundaries. Maybe the globe is shrinking, but the borders seem to be bigger.

IR takes for granted that the territory is ontologically prior to the state, rather than being an *effect* of state (or empire) practices as it produces its identity (cf. Edney, 1997); '[b]oundaries form indispensable protections against violation and violence, but the divisions they sustain in doing so also carry cruelty and violence' (Connolly, 1996: 141). As Campbell points out, 'the drive to fix the state's identity and contain challenges to the state's representation cannot finally or absolutely succeed' (1998b: 12). If it did succeed, the state's conception of itself, poised and authorized to regulate and control its territory and what happens in it, would no longer be real or intelligible or necessary. Accordingly, states must produce and name something as dangerous in order to justify disciplinary actions while guarding their borders. The more a country can say 'we've got to protect you from x or y,' the better it can reaffirm its national security objectives, allocate money for war-making and militarization, and galvanize citizens to support these actions. Thus, we are required to believe in and treat borders as if they are real divisions. We are supposed to know exactly what is meant by the terms Canadian, Russian, Chilean, Jamaican, Swedish, or Indian; that 'something,' the Canadian-ness that is supposed to be that distinct, stabilized identity inscribed within the geographical space of Canada, is so important that true patriots would go to war over any perceived assault on that identity. A state without anxiety – an anxiety we assert is evident in response to features of globalization such as international financial institutions, private global corporations, states that might own parts of another state's debts, or the 'threat' economic migrants pose – would have no reason to limit what people can be or do on, near, or across territorial borders. Indeed, the modern state system we discussed in Chapters 1 and 2 made possible international commerce among European countries and empires, particularly in 'protect[ing] traveling merchants from undue taxation, piracy, or confiscation by local authorities' (Ling, 2010: 101). Globalization and borders have been tied together for a long time.

A state must continuously demarcate and politicize borders in the process of producing its territorial integrity and deciding what counts as a threat to it, what/who gets to enter (multinational corporations, peacekeepers, etc.), and who/what gets to leave (even money – if you think about capital controls). In various ways, other actors, such as domestic movements, paramilitary forces, or vigilante groups invest in the political project of territory as well, thereby also participating in disciplining who belongs 'inside' the territory, and who is an 'outsider.' Consider also border conflicts in the context of recent forms of political interaction that are a direct consequence of global capitalism and the concomitant reconstitution of territorial borders. Examples include the ever-expanding types of legal, economic, and security regimes (national, regional, international, private/corporate) that cohere and clash on borders and make it difficult to trace who is accountable for the violence that occurs. Also consider the uprisings, protests, and undocumented migration in response to free trade zones, such as NAFTA (North American Free Trade Agreement) or CAFTA (Central American Free Trade Agreement).

One might argue that the emergence of the European Union (EU) was one of the great transformations of the twentieth century – from disintegrating empires in the midst of two wars to a single market, a single currency, internal cooperation, and a common security policy (Lebow, 1994; Adler, 1997). But this image of 'peaceful,' 'unified,' and, importantly, borderless Europe contrasts with, for example, how European integration can affect borders and conflicts over territorial claims (Diez, Stetter, and Albert, 2006). For example, the legacy of the partition of Ireland – the conflict between the Republic of Ireland and the United Kingdom of Great Britain and Northern Ireland, and the Troubles, lasting from the late 1960s to 1998 – is deeply significant in the context of European integration, not least because the seeds of these conflicts originated during an earlier phase of globalization, via British imperial expansion. In this case, even when violence abated, non-violent conflicts persisted, particularly *within* Northern Ireland. EU initiatives have in some ways eased border tensions between the Republic of Ireland and Northern Ireland; at the same time, EU integration's economic successes have merely highlighted the deprivation of some of the border cities while attempts to bring together 'old' enemies have sometimes only reified sectarian violence within state borders (Diez and Hayward, 2008: 59–60).

The relationship between neoliberalism and militarization is also important. As Enloe notes, 'globalization can become militarized' – national security, surveillance, weapons industries, and war-making are pivotal to certain international and transnational relationships, and corporations hire militarized security to ensure that workers in offshore factories do not organize (Enloe, 2000; Enloe, 2007: 6). Conversely, 'militarization can be globalized,' specifically when one considers global sales and flows of arms (Enloe, 2007: 6). The still unsolved serial rapes and murders of *maquiladora* workers in Ciudad Juarez, Mexico, along the highly militarized US–Mexico border, illustrate the confluence of offshore factories, security, NAFTA, territory, and militarism. In other instances, political leaders might leverage their citizens' resistance to international financial actors to push their own political agendas, drum up support for militarization, or push forward certain kinds of territorial nationalism. In other words, we should challenge the notion that the state is 'on the side' of those protesting, or has lost interest in its borders, even and especially when it joins citizens in calls to keep Nike, Monsanto, foreign troops, the International Criminal Court, or other political actors out. And, of course, militarized suppression of protests against globalization reinscribes the state's control.

The second problem with the insistence on the borderless world that accompanies globalization talk is the disavowal of what happens to *bodies*. Once again, decentering IR requires us to ask the question: Where are the bodies? Whose bodies matter and why (Butler, 1993: xii; Agathangelou, 2006; Doty, 2004, 2007; Muppidi, 2010; Biswas and Nair, 2009)? Neoliberal globalization has been in no small part predicated on the discipline and domestication of individual bodies – as slaves, as sex objects, as entertainment. Countless scholars have documented the violent effects of globalization on people's lives (Aguilar and Lacsamana, 2004; Kuokkanen, 2008). Further, bodies that are not able to 'move' (perhaps lacking the resources or desire) are also made disposable, particularly as governments do more about servicing a debt or building a middle class, in the context of neoliberal restructuring, than providing access to clean drinking water or anti-retrovirals, or allowing people with HIV or AIDS to travel, or investigating why farmers in some areas are killing themselves *en masse*. Building on the work of these scholars, we emphasize that globalization as a category tends to neglect these 'immobile' bodies – as well as the migration, movement, displacement, and trafficking across borders that is made at once possible and necessary by neoliberal globalization, but also reaffirms the role of borders in people's lives.

For example, despite promises to the contrary, many women, particularly those who have left their home for employment in various capacities – legal or not – in the North/West, find themselves in much worse straits than had they remained at home. They arrive in countries that have outsourced the care of family members because neoliberal adjustments have ended state subsidies for child care and assistance for the elderly (Misra, Woodring, and Merz, 2006). In the context of neoliberal globalization, states simultaneously desire and criminalize undocumented labor and economic migrants (Entzinger, Martiniello, and Wihtol de Wenden, 2004), and Northern/Western countries classify these people as 'economic migrants' so as to deny them asylum and refugee status (Ganguly-Scrase, Vogl, and Julian, 2005).

Also, hypocrisy abounds when we start to trace how and when countries selectively link labor standards to trade agreements, as is the case for an increasing number. Kang (2009), for instance, explores how a memorandum of understanding between China and the US allows the latter to investigate any suspected prison labor in the creation of the products that flood US supermarkets and homes; indeed, the word 'gulag' is applied freely and frequently to Chinese prison labor. Congressional debates suggest a US desire to encourage the free flow of goods without brutalizing the people who create those products. However, as Kang notes, the US's startlingly high incarceration rate (the highest in the world), coupled with both labor within US privatized prisons and prison labor for private for-profit corporations, reveal both US double standards and its violations of the International Labour Organization's 'core labor standards.'[5] Kang's analysis shows that the anger over Chinese private labor was effectively more about US political posturing domestically (evidenced by its lax implementation of policies regarding Chinese goods) and forcing trade conditionality (regarding labor standards in *other* countries) with China and other trading partners. The US, then, is using what happens to bodies in the context of globalization to create certain kinds of economic and political advantages.

Despite their familiarity with such issues, IR scholars and policymakers don't get the complexities, like why migrants may end up in guestworker programs in some cases, but in detention centers in others. States reduce people with varying political sensibilities and identities to the category of 'migrant.' These migrant bodies not only come up against but sometimes *become* borders. This happens when they are neither 'let into' a country, nor allowed to enter a third country, nor willing to return to their home country. In such cases, 'their lives of perpetual mobility are rendered into an existence of petrifying immobility' (Raj, 2006: 517–18). As Raj notes in his examination of the temporary center in Sangatte, France for refugees – some of whom may have been trying to reach the UK to apply for asylum, some of whom somehow ended up there during their various journeys – such descents into limbo do not only occur in refugee centers. They may also be experienced in public housing, markets, police stations, or any location where people are forced to stand as a bodily border between legal, 'good' citizens (see Chapter 5) and outsiders (Raj, 2006: 518).

On the other hand, some bodies are indeed celebrated when they migrate, often when they reaffirm classic 'going from worse to better' migration stories. This story works for many on all sides, including the family members and loved ones of the authors. In addition, states hail *particular* diasporic bodies (which wouldn't include the trafficked, undocumented, exiled, or others) as part of their nationalist projects, treating diasporas in a celebratory fashion, as they serve as sites through which state and national authorities (re)inscribe their commitment to borders. India, for example, since 2003 has sponsored an annual *Pravasi Bharatiya Divas* event, at which the national government actively constitutes non-resident Indians and people of Indian origin as singularly *national* subjects, thus eliding the class and political differences of migrants and writing out stories of partition-related displacement (Mani and Varadarajan, 2005: 51–2); the event also enables the state to perform its sovereign power and to call upon diasporic Indians to 'contribute' via political and economic investments in India's decidedly neoliberal development, and acquire a stake in India as a brand (*ibid.*: 47, 68). Thus, countering the image of diasporas transcending the state, Mani and Varadarajan point to this global phenomenon of states courting diasporas. In some cases, they even count on them for remittances (cash) sent back home, often to rural communities. In this frame, diasporas are or can take advantage of one more of the many benefits globalization brings, ignoring the broader and deeper implications.

What kinds of politics do diasporic communities support, and why? The complex politics of diasporas underscores deep and abiding attachments to articulations of sovereign power. Kamat and Mathew (2003), for example, outline how many Indian communities in the US supported or actively dismissed the ethnocidal violence perpetrated by Hindu nationalists, with the complicity of government leaders, against Muslims in Gujarat, India, in 2002.[6] At what point do diasporic communities (inclusive of exiles, migrants, and refugees), ranging from Tamils to Armenians, Palestinians, Jews, Kurds, Croats, Eritreans, Colombians, Cubans, and many others, choose militarized patriotism to support violence at the hands of the state or to intervene in peace processes (Wayland, 2004; Smith and Stares, 2007)? Why do others, such as Indians who joined the Coalition Against

Genocide, or other groups who have called out state-sponsored terror and oppression, hail themselves as part of the state or nation precisely *because* they wish to challenge political violence?[7] Racism and exclusion in the 'host' country, as well as the desire to belong to a 'home' country/ nation that values and needs diasporic support, tell us about longings for territorial attachment (Kamat and Mathew, 2003).

Roohi Choudhry is a writer who grew up in Pakistan and South Africa and migrated to the US in 1999. When we asked her about resisting and challenging the West's centrality and narratives about the world, Choudhry responded:

> All four of my grandparents migrated during the Partition and had strong ties to their places of origin – they very much considered themselves in diaspora, without using the word. Almost every family member I have challenges the West's centrality and politics *constantly* – we can hardly ever have a dinner without it. My grandfather was in the Communist Party in Pakistan in the 60s and sent my uncle to the Soviet Union to study, so that was another diasporic connection that was quite independent of this East–West narrative. The 'going to America' narrative has never been particularly strong in my family and I never knew anyone who wanted to go. I was the first one who did. (Emphasis in original.)[8]

Choudhry joins others in pushing back certain assertions about traveling bodies in globalization discourse; she, for example, claims the descriptive 'nomad' as 'a way of owning the peripatetic life I had had and making it a positive identity rather than a source of angst.'[9] She also reminds us that IR must look at novels, which re-imagine the 'bodies' in IR as not necessarily rootless and hopeless, even when they must actively resist serving state hegemonic projects or mainstream diasporic activities. Instead, one response may be to take control of the material and ideological conditions of one's daily life through fiction writing. This counters the notion of an all-oppressive globalized economy that will necessarily result, either through neoliberal interference or resistance, in more border conflicts and more violence.

In effect, borders matter but in a paradoxical way, because they are both porous and impermeable, both violently disciplinary and imaginatively remade, both oppressive and sites for radical transformation (Brown, 1995; Honig, 2001). We will revisit the issue below, but allow us to emphasize the point now: borders – violent, restrictive, naturalized as they are – do not necessarily 'contain' the politics and economics of the people within, near, or crossing these lines. Consider radical Mexican

American feminist, writer, and activist Gloria Anzaldúa's concept of *la frontera*, 'the border' (1999). Anzaldúa's deft and nuanced rendering of borders refers to gender, ethnicity, class, spirituality, and more, including the physical boundary that 'exists' between the US and Mexico, which is a cartographic and political fiction that enables modern political sovereignty.

She imagines the lands immediately on either side of this artificial border as part of a whole, a space 'betwixt and between' (Turner, 1967). This is a liminal space; in it, people are not violently forced to be immobile, 'inside' or 'outside.' Something else is possible. This is not a call for pretending borders don't exist. It is impossible to act as if borders did not exist when so many people's lives are thoroughly inscribed by them. But tracing the political activism and networking of so-called irregular migrants, who are under the constant threat of deportation and undetermined citizenship status, reveals a variety of possible attempts to challenge what borders do. They can, for example, make it clear that their presence enables states and 'safe' citizens (see Chapter 5) to do what they want because of what those 'in between' do (from performing labor to serving as a danger against which states can push forward certain legislation – see Raj, 2006). Recognizing such liminality opens up the potential to decenter traditional conceptions literally – why not talk about Kurdistan (eastern Turkey, northern Iraq, northwestern Iran, and small parts of Armenia, Azerbaijan, and northern Syria – see Mojab and Gorman, 2007), Euskal Herria (the Basque Homeland on the Atlantic coast of northwestern Spain and southwestern France), or a multitude of indigenous groups. But liminality decenters figuratively, too, with regard to community and equality, ethnicity, gender, class, and other aspects that would open up other ways of seeing.[10] In effect, our point is that we can use globalization to recognize, trace, and unsettle experiences with borders – these borders center IR, but understanding *how* they do so is simultaneously an attempt to decenter IR. We revisit this point in the last section of this chapter.

The Production of Knowledge

When someone browses through UN or think tank reports, takes a class on global politics, or studies abroad, they are engaging in a production of knowledge (or least a certain kind of knowledge) that has the potential to center or decenter IR. A crucial way the category of globalization centers

IR is through the production of knowledge about how to define and achieve development, thus centering as well the political actors involved in researching, disseminating, and acting upon the 'facts' about social, economic, and political changes in the so-called underdeveloped and developing countries. The 'road' to development is controversial, with debates over the role of foreign aid, microfinance, education, structural adjustment programs, foreign direct investment, governance, and the role of outside governments, NGOs, and institutions. There are also considerable debates over the various goals of development, such as economic growth, standards of living, material conditions, health, educational attainment, life expectancy, and quality of infrastructure.

Arturo Escobar's work has revealed the production of power and knowledge through development discourse, which narrates a particular set of problems with solutions; there are 'rules that must be followed for this or that problem, theory, or object to emerge and be named, analysed, and eventually transformed into a policy or a plan' (1995: 41). The main point is that those narrating, defining, and categorizing the problem are located in particular power relationships with those who are being problematized. Certain people located in particular agencies, foundations, countries, and institutions get to decide what the problem is, what it means about the people/countries that are problematic, and what to do about it. Consider the compelling contention of Vijay Prasad (2007: 13): 'The Third World was not a place. It was a project.' Prasad sketches how the 'Third World' emerged as an important player in the early 1960s, seemed to offer a challenge to the powerful, and by the end of the century was pushed out, 'assassinated' by 'a debt crisis and a policy of planetary reorganization' (*ibid.*: 216) – in a word, globalization. This powerful reminder that not everyone agrees to or acquiesces in the roles ascribed to them in Northern/Western stories about globalization demonstrates how the North/West constructed the concept of a so-called underdeveloped or developing world as the obverse of its successes (Escobar, 1988). Typically, these stories neglect the role of the now-developed world in contributing to the underdevelopment of formerly colonized or enslaved populations (Rodney, 1981).

Following Prasad, we locate the production of the 'Third World' project not just in international institutions, think tanks, and development agencies but also in the production of knowledge in academia and journalistic media. Let's consider the perspectives of three of the most influential IR scholars of the past fifty years. In their view, the Third World was/is not even acknowledged as a set of players but rather a problem to be handled – if, even, the 'rest of the world' had any visibility at all. In *Politics among Nations*, a foundational IR text, Hans Morgenthau suggests that prior to World War Two, Africa – the entire continent – was a 'politically empty space' (1948: 369). Kenneth Waltz, in his highly influential *Theory of International Politics* (1979), could not have been clearer: 'the theory of international politics is written in terms of the great powers of an era. It would be . . . ridiculous to construct a theory of international politics based on Malaysia and Costa Rica. . . . A general theory of international politics is necessarily based on the great powers' (1979: 72–3). Finally, for Samuel Huntington, an ardent supporter of US saturation bombing efforts (a war crime) during the Vietnam War and latterly a proponent of the 'clash of civilizations' thesis (1996), the end of the Cold War witnessed that 'the people and governments of non-Western civilizations no longer remain the objects of history as targets of Western colonialism but join the West as movers and shapers of history' (1993: 23; see also 1996). Presumably prior to this they had simply been irrelevant or, perhaps, in language also made famous by the Vietnam War, little more than 'collateral damage' as the big events that mattered in the world unfolded.

On the face of it, with all due respect, this would seem to be so much nonsense. Critical IR theory has spent considerable time discrediting and challenging the Morgenthaus, Waltzs, and Huntingtons of IR. As Rai (2008) puts it in the conclusions of her assessment of the impact of state-building on development: 'Not only should we ask: "can the subaltern speak,"[11] but can the metropolis hear?' In its eagerness to construct the world and bring its gifts, the metropole has proved itself stunningly obtuse, all too often unable to hear or see the people whom they purport to be there to 'help' (whether they want it or not – which raises an interesting question little remarked upon in the North/West: Is it 'help' if you do not want it?). This dynamic derives from many sources, but no small part of the problem is how we write and teach about globalization in classes with texts called Global Political Economy or International Political Economy and with theories about development and modernization,[12] which begin from 'here' (the US) and assume the world is 'ours' to be improved as we see fit.

Grovogui points out that IR theory, when invoking globalization, employs 'Africa' to substitute for all possible ills, such as collapsing and failed states, AIDS, poverty, gender violence, catastrophe, ethnically motivated outbursts, and corruption (2001: 426; see also Mbembe, 2001; Ferguson, 2006). IR engages in this sort of theorizing and exploration even as it shrouds itself in innocent talk of institutions and structures or takes vague notice of poverty's connection to 'culture' and 'race.' What is thus required, Grovogui suggests, is to ask 'how the "West" became "white"'[13] and how it exemplifies cultural adaptability, political competency, and ethical sophistication, while 'Africa became "black" and the symbol of international dysfunction' (2001: 427). Interestingly, we would note, when it is not Africa the other common stand-in is Haiti, an Afro-Caribbean state known (by which we mean defined by the North/ West) in part for its 'blackness.' To the 'center,' apparently, the 'world' is participating in a 'universally' recognized project of globalization; Africa and the most remote areas of the world must be brought up to speed and hence worthy of our time and attention.

As we mentioned in Chapter 3, academic writings should be considered in concert with journalism, as they both constitute knowledge that professors assign, students discuss, decision makers utilize, and various others depend on for information about international and global issues. *New York Times* columnist, public intellectual, and globalization's pre-eminent cheerleader Thomas Friedman (2000; 2005; 2008), self-styled international relations pundit and *maven*, is a case in point. While he is not an IR scholar *per se*, Friedman's work has had an enormous influence, not least among students, since so many in the field assign his work as class readings. The following excerpt is long but worth the read. While some of you may find it funny or even respond with recognition ('this is so true'), the racialized talk is (disconcertingly) evident.

> What if regions of the world were like the neighborhoods of a city? What would the world look like? I'd describe it like this: Western Europe would be an assisted-living facility, with an aging population lavishly attended to by Turkish nurses. The United States would be a gated community, with a metal detector at the front gate and a lot of people sitting in their front yards complaining about how lazy everyone else was, even though out back there was a small opening in the fence for Mexican labor and other energetic immigrants who helped to make the gated community function. Latin America would be the fun part of town,

the club district, where the workday doesn't begin until ten p.m. and everyone sleeps until midmorning. It's definitely the place to hang out, but in between the clubs, you don't see a lot of new businesses opening up, except on the street where the Chileans live. The landlords in this neighborhood almost never reinvest their profits here, but keep them in a bank across town. The Arab street would be a dark alley where outsiders fear to tread, except for a few side streets called Dubai, Jordan, Bahrain, Qatar, and Morocco. The only new businesses are gas stations, whose owners, like the elites in the Latin neighborhood, rarely reinvest their funds in the neighborhood. Many people on the Arab street have their curtains closed, their shutters drawn, and signs on their front lawn that say, 'No Trespassing. Beware of Dog.' India, China, and East Asia would be 'the other side of the tracks.' Their neighborhood is a big teeming market, made up of small shops and one-room factories, interspersed with Stanley Kaplan SAT prep schools and engineering colleges. Nobody ever sleeps in this neighborhood, everyone lives in extended families, and everyone is working and saving to get to 'the right side of the tracks.' On the Chinese streets, there's no rule of law, but the roads are well paved; there are no potholes, and the streetlights all work. On the Indian streets, by contrast, no one ever repairs the streetlights, the roads are full of ruts, but the police are sticklers for the rules. You need a license to open a lemonade stand on the Indian streets. Luckily, the local cops can be bribed, and the successful entrepreneurs all have their own generators to run their factories and the latest cell phones to get around the fact that the local telephone poles are all down. Africa, sadly, is that part of town where the businesses are boarded up, life expectancy is declining, and the only new buildings are health-care clinics. (Friedman, 2005: 316–17)

Who will play these countries and their people in the film or TV mini-series that Friedman's agent almost surely has in the offing? Our point is that such depictions and descriptions are common ways of thinking about and theorizing the 'problems' of development, poverty, or entire regions: the Middle East, the Global South, the Third World, Africa, the Muslim world, the Arab world, Eastern Europe (and no distinctions among Western European countries). We've already decided what we are going to find when we look 'over there.' And, because of such descriptions and easy access on the Internet to stories, pictures, blogs, and organizations around the world, we've lulled ourselves into thinking that, if we want to, we really can understand anyplace, anywhere. We may still register our outrage or befuddlement at how others can act the way we think they do, but, in the end, knowledge about the world is taken for granted as much more accessible now than it ever was. If a columnist can explain it all in a few hundred words, how hard can it be?

But when we decide to read such work carefully and critically, as an example of popular Northern/Western 'journalism' and all too much social science research about the world, we begin to see how the 'Over There' movie is made. We start to see and connect and understand how it is that international financial institutions and Northern/Western policy makers and technocrats around the world 'juxtapose the ingenuity and charitable dispositions of the West with the discipline and dexterity of Asian states for the purpose of contrasting them with the absence of foresight in Latin America and the cultural deficiency of Africa and the black world beyond it' (Grovogui, 2001: 428). A reduction to soundbites or the 'known' are based on centering the North/West's understanding, with itself as the 'knower,' and sidelining those to be known.

We assert the need to contest, challenge, and politicize the kind of knowledge production that enables the continuation of globalization as a cohesive, totalizing process. In an analysis of 'the social production of globalization's facticity,' Kamola examines how the very writing and theorizing about globalization renders it a 'serviceable term' that produces '*the global imaginary*,' the global as a 'discrete and observable *thing*' (2009: 2, italics in original). What this means is that instead of examining the multiple worlds that are unmade and made concurrently and endlessly, books and articles assert and confer a singular totality on 'the global' that ostensibly has a 'single meaning' and is located in a single, uniform, universal space (*ibid.*: 6). Like us, and the scholars we discussed in the introductory chapter, Kamola believes and performs the possibility of 're-worlding' the global, meaning that the world is not an entity 'out there,' to which peoples and communities must 'adapt,' but rather lives in and through us – our world views, our daily lives, our practices as thinkers, writers, and readers (*ibid.*: 9).

Accordingly, Kamola conducts a nuanced contrapuntal reading of US and South African academies as sites that 'produce' the global but also enable us to study material relations, gender, race, power, subjectivity, and difference (*ibid.*: 13). Specifically, Kamola examines interdisciplinary programs, business schools' attention to world markets, area studies programs, study abroad programs, and internationalized/globalized curricula in US universities as particular locations for producing Northern/ Western knowledge about 'them' (*ibid.*: Chapter 4). With reference to South African universities, Kamola studies the relationship to the World Bank's programs, post-apartheid economic and higher education policy, and philanthropic support, as significant for 'incorporating South Africa into a "global knowledge economy"' (*ibid.*: Chapter 5, 146). Kamola's analysis is too complex and in-depth to discuss here; suffice it to say that it offers much-needed insights into how precisely the 'global' is produced, and it convinces us that students and professors should participate in responding to, analysing, and reshaping a notion of the 'global' that fails to represent the multiple worlds people make and experience.

Instead, students are being prepped to be 'ready' to meet the challenges, and to take advantage of the benefits, of globalization. After all, universities around the world construct students as 'consumers' (and potential donors). As universities increasingly attempt to adapt themselves to a putative neoliberal global economy, they focus on professionalization, internationalization, and other methods of cranking out 'productive,' 'global' citizens. These are citizens well able to 'handle' the constant changes engendered by information technologies and to function in any 'cultural' situation. In other words, changes in the borderless world shouldn't slow them down, and the supposedly static 'cultural ways' that are entrenched in other parts of the world can be easily learned and managed. This way of thinking directly aligns with private corporations seeking to maximize profits on a global scale and with countries seeking to increase their security by knowing more about other cultures (Rosow, 2003: 6).

But shouldn't students, as part of intellectual communities, be questioning how the knowledge created at universities might serve the interests of various governmental institutions, militaries, and corporations (Currie and Newson, 1998; Aronowitz, 2001; McKinley, 2004; Newson, 2004; Sidhu, 2006)? Shouldn't we focus on critical thinking skills to understand why political changes occur, to see countries one may travel to or work in as more than a set of truisms, to understand that negotiating one's place in the world is fluid, changing, and a mutually constitutive process – we interact with and shape each other and other worlds, just as they shape us? Shouldn't students be aware of how their professors engage in the policy-making worlds, perhaps by serving as consultants at the World Bank or protesting particular foreign policies? That way, students would understand that what they know and how they know it matters. These are the questions that we think should be key in decentering the type of knowledge production in universities about the world 'out there.'

From International Political Economy to Local, Sustainable Communities of Possibility/ies

The third way globalization centers IR, as we've suggested throughout this chapter, is through a notion of 'one' global economy that structures the decisions of countries and shapes everyone's lives. But we can decenter globalization by investigating how countries, communities, and people experience economic realities that do not necessarily match the singularity accorded to the international political economy in which they supposedly live. We have encountered a number of protests to such a claim: first, some might say that there is no choice but to participate in the global economy, which is a real thing that is all-pervasive (just ask countries that have defaulted on loans or have resisted the Washington Consensus; or ask the people who are suffering in informal labor markets or have lost jobs due to outsourcing; or consider the way catastrophes, financial or otherwise, reverberate across regions); second, the problems with globalization notwithstanding, those concerned about poverty might say we have to address the needs of the 'bottom billion,' those poverty-stricken people who are entirely disregarded by the global economy, or even by the world (see Collier, 2007). We consider each point in turn.

As to the first issue, if we are to take seriously some mainstream political economists, countries and people are, apparently, either part of the global economy or risk losing the ever-fleeting benefits. Even when discussing countries' reluctant agreements to World Bank or International Monetary Fund loans and programs, the conclusion seems to be that these states are in a difficult position because they *must* attract foreign direct investment, or be deemed creditworthy, and cannot possibly opt for protectionism or isolationism. The only two options, it seems, are the kind of inward-looking focus on domestic industries (at which point many might highlight the abject failures of import-substitution industrialization in Latin America) or outward-looking opening up of borders for unfettered access of corporations and other states. We contend that this choice is a false one, because we see evidence of alternatives and thus a real fracturing of the 'global' economy.

You have undoubtedly encountered stories documenting resistance to globalization that challenges and takes on, in various ways, international financial institutions and more powerful states and corporations. As we will outline below, these are important examples of resistance, but many of them are a marked response *to* the center. Our main concern is with examples of concerted attempts to *displace* the centers of globalization in ways that are not easily classified as global or local. In effect, we push for an understanding of overlapping political economies. To consider how radical it might be to confront the notion of a singular global economy, review the numerous arguments that, unless the 'center' fundamentally changes certain policies, particularly in the context of climate change, the rest of the world must remain crucially anchored to the West. Specifically, the North/West has created a climate change, food, and water 'debt,' wherein the South/East pays, in currency and lives, for the conveniences; the twenty-seven Principles of Climate Justice articulated at the United Nations World Summit on Sustainable Development in 2002 certainly emphasize this point. In the context of global warming, we understand that changes in sea levels and ecosystems are fundamentally interlinked, particularly in terms of the rising costs of fertilizers, transportation, and fuel. We are all connected, so we are told.

Sometimes, the idea of this overwhelming globalization is reinforced by the way we look at resistance. We usually classify documented resistance to neoliberal global capitalism in the following three ways. First, we see examples of 'contestation and reform,' or attempts to 'restrain' globalization by recapturing the nation-state's ability and authority to impose regulations and deliver benefits to citizens (Peet, 2003: 195–6). Advocates involved in these movements would push for nationalization, the roll-back of structural adjustment programs, and state accountability. Second, movements involved in 'globalization from below' aim to democratize global governance institutions (*ibid.*: 196). Advocates and theorists involved in these movements might articulate these struggles as becoming part of 'global civil society.' Transnational, solidarity-based attempts for self-determination and environmentalism, social democracy, and labor rights would be included in these movements. Finally, resistance may take the form of 'delinking' or local 'cutting off' from global markets – a strategy, with the emphasis on rejecting the global, whose advocates include anarchists, religious nationalist movements, and some sustainable movements (*ibid.*: 197).

These mechanisms are very important and we should understand them, but they do not capture everything. Even critical international political economy scholars are reluctant to consider the ability and power of local cooperative initiatives to rethink and remake the conditions of people's lives without being 'squashed' or subsumed by more powerful forces

(Gibson-Graham, 2002: 25). Indeed, '[t]he disavowal or denunciation of attempts to elaborate a localized economic politics seems to emanate from a bodily state, not simply a reasoned intellectual position. For many, it seems, recourse to the obviousness of global power provides a form of comfort, one that we find difficult to replicate or displace' (*ibid.*: 25–6). Gibson-Graham draws attention to a false global/local binary, wherein '[t]he global is represented as sufficient, whole, powerful, and transformative in relation to which the local is deficient, fragmented, weak and acted upon' (*ibid.*: 29–30). For example, Gibson-Graham contends that local struggles need not necessarily build connections or be replicated in other places across the world in order to be relevant or powerful.

We shouldn't deny that promising attempts to address the quality of people's lives have been and continue to be built across different interests and transnational solidarity in different locations: the Indonesian-based Urban Poor Consortium, Focus on the Global South (in Thailand, the Philippines, and India), the South African *Abahlali baseMjondolo* (shack-dwellers') movement, Via Campesina, the global farmers' movement, and the Brazilian-based but worldwide World Social Forum, which presents itself (and its numerous regional and country-specific affiliates) as the alternative to the capitalist and globalization-friendly World Economic Forum, based in Switzerland. Consider also the indigenous-based movements described in Chapter 2, groups in the Global South demanding Northern/Western accountability for 'climate justice,' or the possibility of citizenship involvement in the Bolivarian Alternative for the Americas (ALBA), Venezuela's vision for an alternative to neoliberalism. At the same time, bigger and better is not necessarily the way to go in empowering *all* forms of labor. But more than a few critical scholars writing about global capitalism and empire have explicitly argued for alternatives at the global level; their ability to look outside of themselves *at* globalization indicates how entrenched globalization talk is. After all, the non-capitalist Mondragon Co-operative Corporation (MCC) throughout the Basque region of Spain successfully created possibilities for exchange, research, education, health, and various types of production *before* it extended its model to various places in North Africa, Europe, and Thailand. Surely such models are powerful without being 'replicable' (Gibson-Graham, 2002: 26)? Indeed, perhaps the 'one-size-fits-all' approach of international financial institutions has effectively lulled us into thinking that we've got to 'emulate' what happens in one place everywhere else. Why do we have this 'copy-and-paste' approach to social science research and policy recommendations?

Accordingly, it is not helpful to consider resistance or alternatives to neoliberal globalization if we think of the global economy as this 'thing' that doesn't have its own contradictions and fissures, if we don't believe that contestation, protests, reform, and delinking *transform what the global is*. If we don't try to correct our assumptions about the stark 'global versus state versus local' distinctions (and we've probably made this error several times in this book), we're not really decentering globalization. So, because we reject, as we noted earlier, the 'flattening' of the world, in which all spaces and places are ostensibly equally interconnected and able to access resources, we also reject the demarcation between global, state, and local spaces. There are, of course, conceptual distinctions between one's home, one's state, and the United Nations, for example, but what we're saying is that the 'locations' and politics of these entities are complex. For instance, the World Bank has physical addresses;[14] the people who work there have citizenship and residence in various parts of the world and were trained in particular institutions and universities; Master's degree students in the US work with the World Bank and NGOs on projects in various locations as part of their degrees. The World Bank's employees may hire documented or undocumented migrants to clean their homes and watch their children; there are multiple places, spaces, and connections.

Thus, Gibson-Graham (2002) challenges the global–local binary by deconstructing both what is supposed to be global (more powerful, singular space) and local (less powerful, multiple spaces). This is not a romantic view of the local. 'Delinking' does not imply that we are all essentially and inevitably 'local.' We start where we are, in terms of how we see and act in relation to worlds around us. We walk down the street to the store; take a train or drive to our place of work; get on the phone in our homes to fight with insurance companies; go *with* our neighbors, at least those in our zip code, to marches and rallies; visit a friend to chat and eat dinner. And in each of those actions is some 'globalness' in terms of other locales, regions, and places – or perhaps goods exchanged. Gibson-Graham (2002) admits the difficulties in breaking through the alleged impenetrability of the global economy, particularly because the most critical and radical of theorists and activists are always talking about top-down globalization, emanating from the US and its Western allies, that is seeking profits in every nook and cranny, or corporatizing, privatizing, commodifying every living entity that can be made into a thing with value assigned to it. You can run, but you can't hide. In a sense, the 'center' seems powerful, but so-called global power is but one form. Global resistance to that global power is just one way of thinking about activism. So, in what follows, we will try to sketch out some thoughts about overlapping diverse economies and markets (also see Gibson-Graham, 2002: 38–9).

First, even in seemingly clear-cut examples of resistance to globalization, questions abound, as do experiments, dissent, plans, and visions. It may seem obvious, but there's a lot going on in each of these examples. Those who study democracy and social movements would readily come up with the examples of the democratic 'pink tide' in Latin America and the Caribbean, the reverberating rejection by that region's voters in democratic elections of many of the most fundamental tenets and precepts of neoliberal globalization as they struggle for everyday or ordinary democracy in the material and ideological conditions of their everyday lives. Consider Mexico's modern-day Zapatistas, anti-capitalist and anti-globalization rebels who surveyed their society and, in the face of the globalizing North American Free Trade Agreement, asked: 'Is this the democracy you wanted?' Accordingly, many outside of Chiapas, Mexico have latched onto the Zapatistas because of their resistance to NAFTA (and thus neoliberal globalization writ large) and the possibility of counter-hegemonic transnational publics that they have inspired. That's certainly part of the story; but, as we discuss in Chapter 6, we shouldn't read the Zapatista uprising and resistance as singular. The Zapatista maxim, *Caminando preguntamos* (as we walk, we ask questions), is instructive because it compels us to think about the multiple perspectives and subcultures that are part of even well known or strongly connected movements.

In addition, consider the case of the industrialization of food, a systematic process that certainly seems to tie the world together. In October 2008, Michael Pollan addressed then-US presidential candidate Barack Obama in a letter entitled 'Farmer in Chief' (2008). This editorial note, published in the *New York Times*, looks at the inequities and dangers of the global food production system that heavily favors the needs of US corporations and consumers. Agricultural systems which survived (and worked well) for thousands of years have been re-engineered to produce maximum commodity crops, such as corn, soybeans, wheat, and rice, at a profit for agribusiness. These seemingly small resulting shifts in what is grown when, how, and where have had an enormous impact on health care, energy dependence, and climate change.

Meanwhile, excess commodity crops are dumped in the Global South. Consider the context of one example: when Mexico joined NAFTA it was forced to alter its constitution and eliminate the historic protection of small farmers enshrined in Article 27, thus ending a guaranteed price for them that functioned similarly to minimum wage laws for workers. Weakened by a sudden influx of imported corn from their neighbors and no price supports, the bottom fell out of the market and an estimated 15 million Mexicans (Becker, 2003: C4) – almost one-sixth of the population – lost their livelihood and migrated to Mexico's already overcrowded cities or to the US. Meanwhile, the price of corn tortillas in Mexico – a food staple – went up. In a few short years, a self-sufficient staple that was the backbone of the rural and poor Mexican food economy has been replaced by foreign suppliers whose first (and only) priority is profits. When there are better prices elsewhere or, as happened in the mid-1990s, a corn shortage due to poor crops in the US, Mexico faces a food crisis. The drive to patent, genetically modify, and homogenize corn seeds has also severely affected the long-standing diversity of Mexican corn. In an assessment seven years after NAFTA took effect, Global Trade Watch noted that '[p]ost-NAFTA Mexico no longer has policies to ensure it can feed itself' (Global Trade Watch, 2001: 25). The implications of this are staggering, particularly as we consider how this pattern is repeating elsewhere (Shiva, 2000; Patel, 2008; Pringle, 2005).

So, how is it possible *not* to remain anchored to what the US/Global North does or does not do? The example of Cuba serves as a possible point of departure. Cuba entered an extended economic crisis, known as the 'Special Period', upon the collapse of the former Soviet Union and US actions to strengthen its embargo (the Torricelli/Cuban Democracy Act of 1992 and the 1996 US Helms-Burton Act). In order to shift from large-scale, chemical-dependent farming and agriculture to horticulture, Cubans also used techniques of permaculture, or 'consciously designed landscapes which mimic the patterns and relationships found in nature, while yielding an abundance of food, fiber, and energy for provision of local needs' (Holmgren, 2002: xix) using sources like mulching, rainwater capture, and composting.

The Cuban government also organized volunteer agricultural work brigades, converted state farms into self-managing cooperatives, distributed state land to producers, pushed urban agriculture, created agricultural markets that allowed private farmers and neighborhood organizations to sell produce, emphasized organic farming and crop diversification, and leveraged the country's research institutes to develop biopesticides and biofertilizers (Rosset and Benjamin, 1994; Gonzalez, 2003). As noted in the film *The Power of Community: How Cuba Survived Peak Oil*, widespread blackouts sometimes lasted the entire day and the average Cuban lost around 20 pounds; Cuba responded with the development of small-scale solar energy (Quinn, 2006) and wind farms ('Off the Grid,' 2008). Faced with hunger and a strained social safety net, Cubans focused on food subsistence, energy-saving mass transit, co-housing, walking, hitch-hiking, and car-pooling (Quinn, 2006). Forced by circumstances to redefine what they did and how, Cuba provided an example of what is possible.

But Cuba's experiment is not a simple story of the triumph of a country over global capitalism, or the 'greening' of the revolution. Cuba faced such severe food insecurity after the Soviet Union's collapse in part because of its sugar monoculture, one that persisted from pre-revolutionary US dependency through Soviet dependency, as well as the chemical- and capital-intensive, heavily mechanized agricultural reforms initiated in the 1960s (ironically, *after* the revolution); these factors led to lasting 'environmental degradation, including soil erosion, water pollution, and loss of biodiversity' (Gonzalez, 2003: 707). Cuba's growth and diversification of food production and increased food security during the Special Period was due not just to the Cuban state's decisions but also to the local practices of its citizens. The effects and successes of these policies and citizen actions are still up for debate, particularly considering the continued use of chemically based methods for sugar and tobacco crops (*ibid.*) and political discussions about the continued meaning of the revolution.

What we *can* learn from the Cuba example is how a decentered IR would consider not only international financial institutions, currency and trade regimes, and the other so-called global issues we usually find in international political economy textbooks, but also permaculture, transition towns, food systems, solidarity economy movements (which explore how people participate in non-capitalist exchanges and relationships), place-based activism, and political ecology (see, for example, Escobar, 2008). This, we believe, would be the kind of 're-worlding' Kamola (2009) references regarding knowledge production about the social and economic realities of people's lives. That is why we are less interested in what Cuba *as a state* did (particularly because there are numerous examples of countries negotiating and maneuvering their sovereignty in the face of international financial institutions and other global pressures) than in what *Cubans* did – with each other and with non-Cubans, such as Australian permaculturalists.

There are, in effect, non-exploitative exchanges all around us that involve multiple markets rather than 'the' global marketplace – gifts, comfort, care, community, barter, volunteer projects, youth centers, music circles, rituals, an endless list – and that are not necessarily in the service of neoliberalism (Gibson-Graham, 2002). This is not to set up some utopian 'locale' that glamorizes/romanticizes what people do in their day-to-day lives in ways that are magically untouched by commodification and power, but rather to point to the fragility of such domination. Decentering globalization does not necessarily mean a 'global' alternative that takes down the 'centers' of globalization, because not all people participate in such protests or movements. Instead, it might mean that we rethink 'where' political economies operate – and they are not always inside or facing down a WTO ministerial meeting, or at a McDonald's, or in the halls of the institutions.

Nor does this mean that the 'local' carries all the answers. Sometimes, 'local' may not be the best solution. For example, the response of many Northern/Western consumers to the industrialization of food and to as the carbon footprint of transporting food over hundreds of miles is to 'eat local,' or buy food produced as close to their homes as possible. But what if the way the food imported from thousands of miles away is made in a more sustainable manner than that produced nearby (McKie, 2008)?[15] Universalist solutions and platitudes, such as 'eat local' or 'clean coal,' will not be enough because it is never so simple, and they inevitably underestimate the multiple reasons why seemingly singular problems, such as global warming, are happening and escalating.

In a more radical vein, Chatterton (2006) suggests that we might consider 'giving up' the agenda of activism, at least in order to seek the 'common ground' with others that emerges spontaneously or unexpectedly during the use of various tactics. In his account of participating in solidarity direct action against a meeting of the Group of 8 (Canada, France, Italy, US, UK, Russia, Germany, Japan), aimed specifically at the oil industry, Chatterton discusses the anger, apathy, hostility, and hopelessness those living in the town expressed. He thus urges readers to rethink the supposed divide between activists and non-activists in order to allow different and sometimes contradictory types of strategies to emerge, as well as to get activists to see 'beyond' their own convictions of their agenda, knowledge, and goals to include their daily interactions with people.

Political economies are operating between the activist chained in front of the coal plant and the curious citizen driving by; between a logger with a family to feed and an activist hoping to alert politicians about the dangers of logging; between a consumer hoping to buy a product that says 'fair trade,' the consumer insisting on becoming a 'locavore,' and the farmers producing and harvesting these products. What we are suggesting, in effect, is to challenge the received wisdom about our own positions in the global economy and to start looking at unexpected connections around us.

The second point in this section considers the notion that 'poor' people must be brought into the global economy. We have often heard the familiar refrain that we somehow have to bring the most desperate, wretched, primitive people in the world 'into' advanced society, so that they can benefit – with literacy, education, food, water, shelter, and, quite interestingly, the option for class mobility. 'Just educate them,' is what we're told, never mind how, to what end, or what it means to say that. The very question, 'Does more development necessarily mean that everybody has the Internet or goes to college?' elicits a shock, particularly from students whose families migrated to the US for the very opportunities they were told would make the difference between happiness and poverty. Some of our colleagues have begun to question some of the assumptions about class mobility, often in the face of withering criticism. Pointing out, for example, the futility of sending laptop computers with wifi to remote Honduran villages which lack electricity and have much more dire needs opens one up to charges of racism and, somewhat more bizarrely, ethnocentrism. Apparently this is read as a desire to keep all the laptops for ourselves and not share our bounty with those less fortunate – even if they serve little or no purpose. Is it, perhaps, the principle?

The question of helping poor people is fraught with difficulty, particularly because not enough thought is given to the intricacies, details, and nuances of where 'these people' are located. For example, why do we find among our students or neighbors empathy for a poor person in a 'hut' in a tropical country but scorn and crass stereotypes ('the welfare queen') applied to poor people in the US? And, as discussed earlier, the development project is less about people affected by poverty and why different forms of poverty exist than about imagining a monolithic place where stagnation and underdevelopment are apparently endemic. Strangely, Africa is both a massive, dark, possibly lost continent but also a nameless rural village; it is the lowest common denominator on the global scale and reducible to the most 'local' – as in isolated, disconnected, apart, before time. Gibson-Graham's caution about global and local is relevant here. This is why Wanjiru Kamau-Rutenberg, Assistant Professor of Politics at the University of San Francisco and founder of Akili Dada, an international non-profit organization providing scholarships and mentoring opportunities to girls from impoverished families, is working on a project to figure out what it means to 'save' or 'help' Africa.[16] Kamau-Rutenberg asks who is working to address issues in Africa and why; what a 'saved' Africa would look like and whether that goal will ever be accomplished; and what 'Africa' means in development, philanthropy, and humanitarian discourse.[17]

To illustrate why Kamau-Rutenberg's project is so necessary, some examples are in order. Alice Walker, a key figure in US black feminist thought, and Pratibha Parmar, a British filmmaker of Indian descent who lived in Kenya as a child, were filming *Warrior Marks,* their 1993 documentary about female genital cutting in Senegal, Gambia, Burkina Faso, the US, and the UK, when they were confronted with the issue of poverty in the Senegambian region. Walker was surprised that their host asked for a refrigerated truck to help transport produce of women's gardens to the markets, though the film's budget wouldn't allow such an expenditure (Walker and Parmar, 1993: 73, quoted in Obiora, 1997: 213). Walker and Parmar, then, failed to read the realities of the economy or why many of the women were not interested in discussing female genital cutting when they could talk about other things (Nnaemeka, 2005). Obiora (1997) argues that Walker did not recognize the underlying connections between practices, such as genital cutting and circumcision, and development (in so much as there is access to clean instruments in hospitals, or circumcision might ensure marriageability and thus assurance of shelter). Here are classic examples of a centered IR, distinguished by defiant resistance to understanding that local complexities of poverty cannot easily be solved or treated with computers and gadgets, or even through a proposition for education or ending certain practices. Walker and Parmar are examples of feminists, who, much like the ones we discussed in Chapter 3, have written and produced influential, pioneering work that has deeply connected with many aspects of our lives – as well as those of our students, friends, and colleagues. Their problematic experiences in Africa only go to show how powerful and dangerous the concept of helping is.

In addition to examples of individuals or smaller organizations bringing the 'forgotten' and voiceless into the global economy are larger initiatives, such as the Millennium Development Goals and the United Nations Development Programme's various projects. A vast literature in IR and other disciplines discusses the politics of these initiatives in the context of the global economy, global capitalism, global governance, or resistance to globalization. Our concern here is the mechanisms, such as remittances and microfinance, that are supposedly a part of globalization with a 'human' face, because they link non-state actors with each other, treat previously neglected groups, such as poor women, as financial actors, democratize access to financial products, and enable people to improve their lives even when their own countries are not able or willing to leverage the benefits of liberalization (Weber, 2002).

We focus here primarily on microfinance, particularly because of its promise, via donors and professionals in the microfinance industry, to 'bring in' the poor. Microcredit initiatives lend money, usually at subsidized interest rates, and often provide additional training and support to small-scale entrepreneurs. As microfinance institutions admit, the aim is to draw poor people into the global economy and allegedly 'bring assistance from the haves to the have-nots, constitut[ing] a point of intersection between the world's bourgeoisie and the world's poor' (Anderson, 2002: 87). Microfinance at once utilizes 'market incentives,' such as 'readily available funds and repayment requirements' (*ibid.*), potentially illustrating how markets 'work' for the poor, or at least offer ways effectively and practically to address being 'left out' of or 'behind' globalization. Proponents of microfinance, including international NGOs working very closely with the World Bank, argue that small loans may help poor entrepreneurs and allow some to stop the generational cycle of poverty (Banerjee, Duflo, Glennerster, and Kinnan, 2009; Karlan and Zinman, 2009; but see Morduch, 1998; Roodman and Morduch, 2009).

The problematic assumptions of the alleged 'connection' between the so-called haves and have nots notwithstanding, analysts and economists who travel to the villages and towns where people are using microcredit report significant changes in the quality of people's lived experiences, including confidence, family dynamics, ability to send children to school, and meeting basic needs. Microfinance disproportionately targets women for loans and assistance on the grounds of high female repayment rates and the demonstrable contribution of women's economic activity to economic growth. The premise that the 'poor' are both 'credit-worthy' and trustworthy is new and interesting, as is the appreciation and acceptance of informal and local political economies and the recognition of multiple ways of saving, forms of social capital, and manners of community engagement.

By now, you will rightly predict that we'd like to complicate this issue, as such matters are rarely so simple. The profound empowerment of women, and poor women at that, would run counter to many of the fundamental precepts that undergird the globalization construct. Thus, the 'successes' and 'failures' are complex, as

> poor women are getting access to a much-valued financial service and they are finding room for manoeuvre within the model to pursue their chosen objectives. [At the same time] high loan volumes and repayment rates conceal the failure of the model to consistently spawn new, enterprising rural subjectivities, as well as the extent to which the whole system rests on ever-expanding cycles of debt. (Shakya and Rankin, 2008: 1231)[18]

In effect, an investigation of microfinance reveals a need to understand the complex multiple economies at work.

Let's look more at this concept of a 'model,' neoliberalism, and the debt issue. To that end, Kamau-Rutenberg argues that activities geared towards poor populations tend to globalize specificities: for example, because the Grameen Bank worked in Bangladesh, some in the microfinance industry operate on the assumption that what works for poor people in the poor part of one poor country could work for all poor people everywhere.[19] That model has now become an industry. And as diverse as the microfinance industry is, as Kamau-Rutenberg put it, 'the loans are small; the donors are not necessarily.'[20] In other words, microfinance accompanies, in most cases, other institutions and agencies (the World Bank, regional development banks, development agencies, the United Nations) that come with their own sets of effects. Microfinance then becomes more about 'facilitat[ing] financial sector liberalization as well as extending the policy of trade in financial services to the local level' and 'dampen[ing] and contain[ing] resistance to the implementation of neoliberalism' (Weber, 2002: 541). Thus, microfinance is potentially about managing the poor in ways that legitimate and consolidate neoliberalism and the role of certain players in it (*ibid.*). Microfinance, even when helping a woman sell a product, cannot be understood without also examining how these other political actors interact with various political economies. We should understand how at least some portion of the microfinance industry is about 'banking' on the poor; banks and financial institutions can potentially profit from tapping into the approximately 'two-thirds of the world's adults [who] do not have a basic bank account' (Consultative Group to Assist the Poor, 2006, quoted in Hudson, 2008: 324).

There are also specific challenges that reveal the microfinance industry's difficulty in understanding the root causes of poverty and the issue of debt. Thus, analyses of microfinance should ask: Are the loans low-interest, and if not, why not? How does the community in question think about debt, and what does it mean to introduce new forms of debt? What are the different implications of microloans and microgrants? What are the socio-political consequences of being indebted? How do 'micro-entrepreneurs' see themselves in the context of multiple political economies, including various systems of debt (of their family, communities, cities, and countries)? What's the difference between individual and group responsibility? This last question is crucial because if there's group responsibility, there are better chances of repayment, but there are reports that people are also threatening to kill themselves when they can't.[21]

Microfinance can lead to greater impoverishment because of high interest rates and the transaction costs of some commercial microfinance institutions (Wanyeki, 2007). It can also create enormous pressure and shame when the debt burden is public knowledge, as it becomes with group lending, a common practice valued by the microfinance industry because of high repayment rates. Sometimes, people end up hiding from microfinance *lenders* in fear (Gokhale, 2009). Kamau-Rutenberg also mentions examples of a sort of 'loan sharking,' where grassroots organizations provide commissions to people, in many cases local college students, for every micro-loan processed.[22] While anecdotal stories note that, despite initial resistance by men to women's economic empowerment (when they successfully pay off debt and actually profit), more egalitarian relationships are being built over time, and in cases of severe backlash, such as violence or beating, other women involved in microfinance groups are joining in solidarity to stand up for each other, other stories do reveal that the backlash *can* persist.[23] All of these examples should point to the necessity of understanding the vastly different kinds of effects on microfinance 'clients.'

Furthermore, even in the context of group lending, the microfinance industry can emphasize individual responsibility, rationality, and 'self-help' in the context of a heavily capitalist system, ultimately empowering Northern/Western decision-making designed to alleviate the structural adjustment programs and excesses of capitalism wrought by globalization (Rankin, 2001). So, if neoliberalism disadvantages the poor, and micro-finance initiatives presume that market-based neoliberalism is the best economic model, how do beneficiaries of microfinance examine this paradox? Is microfinance simply 'tweaking' neoliberalism? Could it ever offer direct challenges? Is it meant to, and, if not, what are the effects? As to these questions, Kamau-Rutenberg asserts that it's important to understand desires for capitalism in the conversations about ending poverty.[24] Like Hernando de Soto in *The Mystery of Capital* (2000), we should ask who owns idea and property, and the translation of ownership (particularly in the Global West) into visible and legal forms (mortgage deeds and so on). Accordingly, what precisely are people 'owning' when they become entrepreneurs via the microfinance industry?

Underscoring this tool is the neoliberal assumption that markets help those who help themselves; thus, presumably poverty can be solved when 'the poor . . . work harder, get educated, have fewer children, and act more responsibly' (Feiner and Barker, 2007). But what is actually happening in many cases is that microfinance recipients are transgressing protocols, regulations, and entrepreneurial norms, through illicit investments, innovatively borrowing and managing risk, and resisting, sometimes through humor and mocking, mandatory meetings (Shakya and Rankin, 2008). This relates to some of our comments in Chapter 2. Why might some assume that those on the receiving end of 'aid,' in whatever form, are too stupid to recognize the power dynamics and relationships in which they find themselves? And, by that same logic, can we not assume that activists, donors, and students are smart enough to handle the complexities of microfinance, or the complex ways in which to measure and even define success in this industry?[25]

There is, thus, a sort of 'us–them' dynamic as well. Kamau-Rutenberg asserts that 'microfinance makes rich people feel good without understanding how they're implicated in the very system causing poverty elsewhere.'[26] This is provocative and worth thinking about, even for those actively trying to confront and politicize the nuances and complexities of their microfinance work. Western microfinancing initiatives have become, in some ways, the province of newly minted Western-based MBAs who cannot find jobs in a traditional financial sector increasingly in disarray. And, even with the emergence of some studies that challenge the 'success' of microfinance, scholars, policy makers, and activists alike proclaim the triumphs of this tool in helping the destitute (Weber, 2002: 541). What makes the difference between the successes and the failures? Is microfinance generally appealing because we don't want to mess with current financial systems, even when they fall apart before our eyes? Kamau-Rutenberg provides this specific example to challenge the idea of success: think about a $5 cup of Kenyan coffee at Starbucks. Drinking that coffee gives a Kenyan farmer $1 for 100 pounds of product. That same coffee drinker gives a dollar to a microfinance cooperative. But what changed here – for anybody? You could have your own example. Hop onto www.kiva.org, the first, self-described 'person-to-person microlending website,' where you can see pictures of micro-entrepreneurs; you can also see who 'ended with a loss,' or defaulted (about 3,524, compared with 384 fundraising, and 95,844 who have paid back loans). You could easily feel 'connected' (the Kiva website notes that interpersonal connections are facilitated through the Internet) to potentially successful micro-entrepreneurs because of your $50. But for some people, next to a line that says 'defaulted,' you will inevitably read in the person's description, 'X is very hard-working and will be able to pay back the loan.' Thus, while you get to know who has defaulted and what they look like, no one quite knows your consumer, work, and savings habits, so *power relationships still exist*, even with microfinancing initiatives in so-called developed countries. The 90,000+ figure is powerful, but there are other stories to consider.

While solving poverty is not an easy task by any means, it is complicated by premising the solution on the notion that there is always already a singular global space in which to add those 'left out.' This is not helpful because it focuses more on the additive process than on the contradictions and complexities of people's material realities. As we've done in the other chapters, we are trying to hold together the paradoxes and complications of globalization, with the hope of decentering IR.

Chapter Five / Peace and Security

> In times of war, the recognition that teaching neutrality or simply studying systems of domination without taking a stand amounts to complicity is central to serious scholarship and pedagogy. Students need to realize and professors need to teach that spectatorship neither produces a just and peaceful world nor prioritizes dignity over humiliation and humanity over greed. (Abdulhadi, 2005: 157)

> The whole [Iraq] war is like an American movie. You know the end. You know who's the hero. You know the bad guys; they're going to die. But you still watch, because you want to know how it's going to happen and what weapons they're going to use. (Deema Khatib, Al Jazeera producer, quoted in the documentary film *Control Room*, 2004)

Introduction

We both admit it; we have both participated in various movements, ascribed to theories, and chosen to support projects that we thought would help lead to this thing called 'peace and security' for communities around the world and close to home. At the same time, we are a bit uncomfortable with how IR scholarship (and we) can present 'peace and security' as a unitary concern, with surprisingly little attention to the deeper meaning of either. What precisely do universities, think tanks, nongovernmental organizations, activists, and academic journals mean when they focus on ethnic studies and conflict, peace and conflict, peace and justice, peace and security, conflict resolution, security studies, and other variations of the same theme? We think the answers to this question have a lot to do with the kind of world(s) we inhabit.

We claim that 'peace and security' can center IR in three main ways. First, we note IR's tendency to narrate the world teleologically, that is, as purposive and progressing in some sort of linear fashion to an 'end.' As we hope is evident at this point, one of our claims throughout this book is that IR's predominant focus on the North/West and particular political projects is made possible through a particular story arc. As Chapter 2 indicates, the very study of IR starts with the 'birth' of the nation-state, a political organization of the world that all peoples must aim towards but not all are allowed to achieve. Chapter 3 illustrates that the 'origins' of the human rights story enables some in the world to present themselves as more civilized than others. Chapter 4 shows us the evolutionary march of progress for states and peoples as they 'mature' from 'developing' to 'developed;' globalization's insistence on the spatial organization of the world and the disciplining, literally and figuratively, of borders and bodies enables the state to endure as the primary unit of analysis. In this chapter, we show that the 'markers' of progress and historical movement are part of a chronology where only certain events and dates, such as World War Two, the Cold War, and September 11, 2001 matter for both understanding and narrating people's lives and for achieving peace and security. Accordingly, in the second section, we discuss the problems of *temporality*.

The second problem is that IR centers itself precisely by deciding what 'peaceful and secure' looks like. But who gets to be safe, peaceful, and secure? Does 'peace and security' mean that we all get access to affordable health care and housing? Perhaps it means that we have choices about how to live our lives? It could also mean that we do not have to worry about certain forms of violence. For some, peace and security would require rather traumatic upheavals in the usual way of doing things in order to make visible the needs and desires of historically marginalized and oppressed people. For others, those very upheavals or the suggestions of doing something different constitute grave threats to peace and security.

Obviously, we all have a stake in describing what peace and security look like, to us. But we need to say more about the consequences of those world views. Often, there is not much room for contradiction, such as peace achieved through violent means, or a state made insecure by people attempting security for themselves, or different kinds of injustices that arise during 'peacetime.' Whose political sensibilities matter in determining when 'peace and security' have been achieved? The graduate student with field experience in a refugee camp? The refugees in that camp? The PhD in the think tank called upon to consult regarding a conflict-resolution process? The people translating and collecting interviews of displaced peoples? Victims of various kinds of conflicts? Where do we imagine that the analysts live? Where do we imagine that the victims of violence and conflict live? Most importantly, do we ever consider that lurking behind this 'peace and security' discourse are presumptions that we've really got to make sure that certain states or certain people will be safe, even if it means that others will be unsafe? In the third section, we focus our discussion around Cynthia Weber's work, written and film, in order to find out what is 'behind' the category of peace and security as well as to explore what decentering IR might look like.

Finally, through a centered IR, we tend to focus on institutionalized or militarized pathways to peace, and the distinction between 'good' and 'bad' guys. Through IR, we get the idea that peace and security is something that those *over there* do not have, and that, as a result, they could threaten 'our' peace and security *here*. Accordingly, solutions flow in the direction of 'over there,' in the form of a United Nations mission, a Security Council resolution, a set of sanctions, a tribunal (often predicated upon Northern/Western notions of justice), peacekeeping operations (whose troops may come from outside the North/West, but whose material and funding come almost solely from the North/West), multilateral talks, or militarized intervention. 'Peace and security,' in other words, signals the entry of discourses of globalization and development, UN bureaucratic solutions, militarized interventions, and, ultimately, a Northern/Western gaze upon the 'trouble spots' in the world. Certainly, there are examples of how these institutionalized mechanisms work in achieving particular types of goals, such as the disarmament of a particular group, the agreement of leaders to enter a ceasefire, or the beginning of conversations about what constitutes justice. However, in the last section, we examine the consequences of and challenges to 'peace and security' as a category that centers IR through the promotion of international law and institutions, as well as militarized interventions. In each section, we also discuss the strategies and possibilities of decentering IR.

Temporality

We contend that the 'peace and security' field is tied to a kind of temporal reading of pivotal events. As professors, we tend to construct our own syllabi in a temporal format: first, realism and the world wars; second, liberalism and the birth of the United Nations and postwar institutions; third, the end of the Cold War and the ensuing constructivist turn, which examines the 'unleashing' (a revealing construction, since it is non-human animals, at least prior to abuses at Abu Ghraib, that we associate with leashes) of 'cultural,' nationalist, and ethnic issues that accompanied the collapse of the Soviet Union and suddenly threw a wrench into (neo)realist and (neo)liberal assumptions about order and stability. We might assign readings that illustrate how to 'stretch' security from issues regarding the state and interstate politics (disarmament, non-proliferation, arms control, border issues, wars over resources, weapons of mass destruction, emerging powers, rogue states) to intrastate and non-state concerns such as religious and ethnic groups, internal displacement, or conflicts between masses and elites.

The Copenhagen and Welsh schools may enter the conversation, as may the theoretical contributions of 'human security,' constructivism, and feminism.[1] One finds out, at this point, that security can be 'constructed' and learns more about the importance of the relationship between structures and agents in creating political change. A variety of issues may make an appearance on the syllabus to help organize the material and make it more topical: examples include HIV/AIDS and infectious diseases, food, water, sustainable development, climate change, forcible displacement, child soldiers, refugees and internally displaced people, gender violence, and poverty. Some students will learn about the contributions of the more critical strands of IR theory that interrogate discourses of insecurity and representations of danger, ask what those discourses do and accomplish, and reflect upon what it means to even talk about security (Doty, 1996; Doty, 2007; Campbell, 1998b; Wibben, 2009). What we effectively teach our students is that the meaning of 'peace and security' shifts, depending on which school of thought is particularly trendy or legitimized in the major journals or graduate programs.

What also happens in classrooms, programs, and think tanks is that we read people's experiences through the lens of the events that matter the most to the US and those in the North/West. The history of the world is centered, much like most of the world's manufactured maps, on the US and Europe. We tend to see the trench warfare slaughters of World War One or the impressive battlefield and civilian deaths of World War Two, which took so many European lives, as undiluted horrors, made even worse because they happened in the home of civilization, despite the backdrop of colonialism.

The looming threat of the Cold War – which was, of course, often times quite hot outside of the North/West for millions in Southeast Asia and Oceania, in sub-Saharan Africa, and in Latin America and the Caribbean – was the annihilation of civilization (read: the US and Western Europe). When we study the websites of various programs and institutes dedicated to peace and security studies (or variations such as peace and conflict or conflict resolution), we find that the programs' original mandates were to examine US–Soviet relations but eventually extended to 'other' issues to better reflect the changing international environment and to face the challenges of the twenty-first century. We find it odd (and perhaps vaguely pernicious) to see the presentation of issues such as gender, social movements, ethnic conflict, environmental problems, and human development as 'new' and 'recent,' as if the Cold War or the world wars did not impact upon these factors, as if countries and communities directly, indirectly, or marginally involved in these wars did not face challenges other than these particular wars.

These 'ethnic' and other issues are 'newly' discovered but, at the same time, are explained by 'ancient' hate and 'deeply rooted' mistrust (Hansen, 2006). For example, think of the Cold War's heretofore apparently underappreciated role in 'suppressing' primordial, ethnic divisions that were 'always' there (even though they are simultaneously treated as 'post'-Cold War). In this decidedly odd formulation, the US and its European allies (cobbled together in the North Atlantic Treaty Organization) and the Soviet Union and its European allies (united by the Warsaw Pact) somehow forestalled ethnic tensions in Europe (most importantly, of course) as well as around the world; 'order' was in fact the order of the day. The violent collapse of the former Yugoslavia, one of the region's most advanced states and a place where ethnic tensions and rivalries had supposedly been mediated (read: suppressed), is often Exhibit A. Yet even a cursory survey of Africa, both North and sub-Saharan, Southeast Asia, or Oceania suggests that such 'ethnic' challenges hardly dissipated during the Cold War and indeed were often at the center of US–Soviet proxy battles fought out on the bodies and lives of non-Europeans.

The US barely had the time to enjoy its Cold War triumph before the events of September 11, 2001. Jarvis (2008) discusses how political leaders and scholars construct terrorism as a threat to security and peace in a 'timeless' way, so that the fear produced is indefinite. Jarvis focuses particularly on the Bush Administration's deployment of time as a discursive resource for normalizing war. Jarvis mentions specifically *temporal discontinuity, temporal linearity,* and *timelessness. Temporal discontinuity* captures the idea that 9/11 was unprecedented and singularly unique – expected elsewhere but not 'here.' At the same time, however, *temporal linearity* presents 9/11 as part of a larger trajectory of terrorism against the West, one that the West would now win, *of course.* If 9/11 is part of a continuous war against 'the West,' we should all understand that the West *will,* indeed *must,* triumph, just as it did in World War Two and the Cold War. *Timelessness* takes 9/11 as representative of the ongoing battle between good and evil. So, if 9/11 is emblematic of or highlights the war between the civilized and barbaric worlds, then any action, anywhere, can always be justified, because the 'good guys' can be trusted to take out evil, by any means necessary (*ibid.*). It even becomes plausible to claim, in the face of all evidence to the contrary, that the North/West does not torture in its efforts to defeat the 'bad guys,' who, by definition, violate the norms and agreements of warfare.

Critical scholars also invoke a temporality discourse. They might focus on particular events and a *Pax Americana*-style chronology in order to make claims about US imperialism or hegemony. Recently, many have begun to ask whether the second Bush Administration (2001–9) and its responses to 9/11 were a rupture (even some kind of horrible detour) or rather part of a continuous display of how US hegemony has always worked and will continue to work. It is notable that this very question problematically pivots on 9/11 as a central event that we need to 'make sense of' in a different or more diligent way than we would aim for *anything* violent or traumatic that happens to 'other' people elsewhere; this happened to 'us' *here* and hence must be made legible. Consider further our point in Chapter 2 that critiques of post-9/11 US foreign policy are predicated upon the US nation-state 'origin' story: in other words, should it be terribly surprising how the US responded, given its history of using sovereign power? (See James, 1996; Smith, 2008.)

Perhaps 9/11, or at least the responses to it, heralded a 'new' era or way of looking at peace and security. But we claim we should interrogate the temporality of peace and security because, in order to know how power works, we need to understand how it endures, changes, and ultimately often remains the same: same people, same places, same spaces. Jenny Edkins (2003: xv) explores how 'linear, homogeneous time suits a particular form of power – sovereign power.' She examines how sovereign power creates and causes trauma, in the form of wars, genocides, and famines; however, the state hides its involvement through discursively positioning itself as a 'provider not a destroyer of security' and by memorializing those very events (or perhaps ignoring those and focusing on others) within a 'linear narrative of national heroism' (*ibid.*: xv).

As we discussed in Chapters 2 and 3, memory/commemoration and truth-telling are complex processes that can reinscribe structures of power or silence certain stories, thus revealing the difficulties inherent in the categories of indigeneity or human rights. Edkins shows us that remembering or speaking about trauma involves similar difficulties within the category of peace and security. After all, trauma involves a recognition of a betrayal of the promise of security that is supposed to come from one's family, community, or state (*ibid.*: 4). But she reminds us that re-narrating that betrayal, that trauma, can often involve another 'notion of temporality,' where trauma is 'encircled' and politicized by communities rather than subsumed in a linear story (*ibid.*: 15). By 'encircled,' Edkins means surrounding the trauma in a way that is open to 'unanswered and unanswerable questions,' that can mark an event without forcing it to fit in some myth about an army's glory or a state's victory (*ibid.*: 17). Accordingly, some forms of remembering trauma can directly challenge and decenter the very political systems that made possible the violence, insecurity, and war in the first place. As we discussed in Chapter 3, and as Judith Butler notes in *Precarious Life: The Power of Mourning and Violence* (2004), how we choose to grieve and make sense of the loss of life matters profoundly. Why and when do we choose to respond to loss with censorship, surveillance, war, or the attempted annihilation of others?

We accordingly find it important to teach those 'secret histories' behind the neatly presented timeline, to understand the costs and consequences of the 'victories' proclaimed and the 'peace' secured by the US and its allies. These costs matter to professors struggling to teach in the context of wars and national trauma, as some students staunchly support their militaries, while others protest vehemently or are distressed because their family members are deployed or at the receiving end of national security policies (Abdulhadi, 2005; Sharoni, 2008). These costs matter to a significant number of US, Canadian, and European veterans of the Cold War's proxy battles in Korea, Vietnam, and elsewhere, or of the post-9/11 wars in Iraq and Afghanistan, who come home to and continue to suffer from fractured families, homelessness, drug addictions, mental illnesses, or possibly suicide. These costs matter to those detained on and after 9/11, to the surviving victims and families of these various attacks and wars, to Japanese-Americans interned by their own government during World War Two, to those killed and maimed in the attacks on Hiroshima and Nagasaki, to those in Southeast and East Asia who suffered colonialism and militarization at the hands of the very same Allies who defeated fascism in Europe.[2]

These costs matter to Chileans who remember *their* 9/11 in 1973 when a brutal military *coup d'etat* (*golpe d'estado*), supported and fomented by the US, destroyed the democratically elected government. Chileans, along with many others in South America, suffered from the repressive actions of Operation Condor,[3] the world's first international terrorist network, well before Al Qaeda (Burbach, 2003). These costs matter to those affected most by players/events not in the timeline, such as the International Monetary Fund's imposition of a structural adjustment program, a country that diverts funds from emergency relief or infrastructure to amass more weapons, or a coalition of organizations, such as the Save Darfur Coalition discussed in Chapter 3, that focuses more on one conflict zone than another, with deleterious consequences. These multiple stories retell and challenge the triumphant (and myopic) narratives the US and some of its allies (and many in the Global South) put forth about the twentieth and twenty-first centuries.

In effect, we also find it crucial to narrate traumatic events, such as disasters, in ways that don't make it just about the particular event, or only some people's reactions to it. For example, Kanchana Ruwanpura challenges the construction of 'natural' disasters as independent of socio-political, historical, and temporal conditions and factors. In her examination of how Sri Lankan women responded after the 2004 tsunami, Ruwanpura finds that factors such as a then-stalled peace process to bring an end to the civil war as well as socio-economic disparities differently shaped how various coastal communities were able to regain or start anew their livelihoods. She also notes that the disruption and displacement caused by the tsunami may or may not have the same weight as that caused by the war, depending on the kinds of experiences women had during war campaigns (Ruwanpura, 2008: 330–1).

For some, the tsunami may have been a singularly unique event that demanded a reliance on NGOs or the state, whereas for others it called up old coping mechanisms or required a shift in economic work. For some, it inspired 'spaces of optimism,' as some communities recognized that the strategies they had developed throughout the war served them well during the aftermath of the tsunami (*ibid.*: 337). Other countries struggled in different ways because environmental destruction, global warming, and the bulldozing of sand dunes and mangroves to give 'better views' to tourists in hotels destroyed coral reefs that could have minimized, in certain areas, the damage of the tsunami (Keys, Masterman-Smith, and Cottle, 2006: 197). Furthermore, while the suffering of tourists so profoundly raised the stakes for countries providing humanitarian aid, few commentators noticed that countries took advantage of the depoliticization of the tsunami to assert and legitimize militarization, or that trafficking and sexual violence persisted in the immediate aftermath (*ibid.*).

From this and other examples of how communities fare after natural disasters – such as hurricanes, typhoons, or earthquakes – we learn that the devastating event may or may not mark a point in time of 'before' and 'after' for the communities directly impacted. Rather, people's responses reveal more about the type of community-securing strategies and tactics they deploy when facing other types of disruption; countries' responses reveal their own political agendas. While, for some, the 2010 earthquake in Haiti simply highlights how difficult it will be to 'help' people cursed to live in a wretched country of insufferable and endless poverty, hunger, and violence, we think the situation (which is unfolding as this book goes to press) demands a careful analysis of communities' strategies of survival, what happened 'before' the earthquake that rendered Haiti's infrastructure so destructible, and how countries and organizations are appropriating the event to narrate their own versions of Haitian history, the Haitian present, and their vision of their role in Haiti's future, regardless of the various Haitian desires.[4]

When we start disrupting the chronology, we start decentering IR. There are, at any given point, an array of temporalities reflecting different conceptions of time. Our point with this section is to draw attention to the existence of temporal discourses within IR as well as to question how they reproduce Northern/Western conceptions. How do the ways we represent and deploy time deny people's own, often powerful, sense of time, but also put everyone, everywhere, all the time (as it were) on Northern/Western Central Standard Time? Opening ourselves up to other times helps us to decenter IR.

Safe States; Unsafe People

In this section, we essentially ask: who gets to be safe in a 'peaceful and secure' world? In IR, it is states that are to be made safe, with secure borders and a monopoly over the use of force or coercion within those borders, and thus positioned to 'give' security to citizens in exchange for their allegiance. Privileged subjects in the North/West are made to feel safe and comfortable by wars, conflicts, and militarization they do not feel or experience themselves.[5] Who is made unsafe to make another set of people feel safe? What really is security? Who or what is being secured? Whose comfort is guaranteed by a war fueled by a conflict over resources? Does security mean safety? From what? For whom? We question whether IR is prepared to answer – or can even really ask – these kinds of questions. In Chapter 3, we mentioned that IR, particularly in the context of human rights, has a problem talking about dead and dying bodies. Similarly, when we speak about peace and security, we can miss that behind the talk of war, invasion, and ceasefires is killing, murdering, maiming, and lasting trauma.

Several scholars have given us important points of departure for asking the question: *Who gets to be safe?* We point to Cynthia Enloe's scholarship on the militarization of daily life (2000, 2001, 2007), Sjoberg's edited volume on examining security through a gendered lens (2009), as well as Carol Cohn's work on how techno-strategic language within defense communities makes it possible to think of and treat human beings as dispensable (1987). Several journalists have asked what kind of security and protection is possible when the five permanent members of the UN Security Council are some of the largest arms dealers in the world (see Grimmett, 2008). Others have shown that migration is a contested terrain for who protects, who receives protection, and what one has to do – as a refugee, internally displaced person, undocumented migrant, sex worker, child soldier, sex slave, economic migrant, laborer, or any other 'category' – to receive the protection one might get by fitting into said category/label (Malkki, 1995; Hyndman, 2000; Nyers, 2003; Kapur, 2006). In effect, work of this kind shows us the illusory promise of security.

In order to grapple with this 'illusion,' we focus mainly on the exciting, challenging, and difficult decentering work of Cynthia Weber. We are making a political choice here in including Weber's work, particularly as many might ask why we would include the scholarship of someone who focuses on US hegemony and 9/11 in the very chapter in which we critique such a focus. Part of what we're trying to get you (and us) to do here is to 'unlearn' IR theory. If we can unlearn the Western-centric stranglehold on IR, then we can really have hope in decentering IR. We are still a 'we' with passports, residency, jobs, and families in particular locations; by circumstance or chance, we find ourselves assigned to positions as US citizens, and we continue to use the 'we' to navigate our way around the benefits, privileges, and narratives that come with that. We can break the chain of signifiers, but we cannot do so by pretending (or wishing) away US hegemonic existence.

We also need to show how IR theories fail to capture what is happening in the US, much less the world. Are there ways we can imagine 'Third World women' flying to the US to mobilize die-ins and activism around prison rape or domestic violence? Might we have predicted the possibility that about 150 US children 'protected' with citizenship would sue the Obama Administration in 2009 over the deportation of their undocumented parents? There are certain scenarios we cannot 'imagine,' and we believe that Weber joins us in urging students and scholars of IR to ask, Why not? Imagination, curiosity, and experimentation are, as we hope this book demonstrates, key to the practice of decentering.

In effect, Weber's project is to reveal that when the state designs, legitimizes, and packages principles for safe citizenship, it is not to *keep* citizens safe; rather it is to keep the state safe *from* citizens. Weber's work (2008) specifically examines how the state identifies some citizens (and non-citizens) as unsafe and gets 'safe' citizens to secure the state through the principles of 'dying,' 'caring,' and 'immersing.' These design principles are discourses of legitimation, of how people should act towards and within the state of their citizenship. We must be willing to ask whether we want to do what is necessary to be a safe citizen. We must be willing to die or use violence on behalf of the state. We must give consent to societal order by caring for the state and being responsible for ourselves and each other, particularly through civil society. We must immerse ourselves, through Internet technologies, to express our belonging and allegiance. We must continuously prove ourselves to be safe because state security is never 'accomplished,' nor can it be in order for state power to exist (Campbell, 1998b). The state can at any point be 'under attack' from citizens – or outsiders.

Thus, the way states react and 'design' themselves when they feel threatened is important. When we study hegemony, we leave behind Gramsci's original notion[6] and typically look at diplomatic manipulation, economic power (such as controlling the agendas of the international financial institutions), military capability, and similar issues. But IR has yet to study design, marketing, and packaging, which we believe would be a fascinating entry for decentering IR. The social movements literature discusses norm entrepreneurs and how states can be 'shamed' into changing their practices despite their interests. But in order for a state to create a perception of being safe and providing security for the right reasons, it might need more than signing onto international treaties or international legal instruments, or engaging multilaterally.

Accordingly, states seek to 'brand' themselves for a variety of reasons – such as to protect themselves, define themselves, or attract business and tourism. And they are increasingly hiring not political science PhDs but marketing and consulting experts. They are doing so not just to draw in more tourists and investors but rather because of (but at the same time to avoid and deflect) deep ontological crises, fears, and anxieties, not least with regard to their very existence and endurance. States prefer branding because to change policies too much would completely shatter the very way in which states have narrated their origin, history, purpose, and position in the world. It is easier to change the perceptions of the product in a simulation of the real.

Many countries have used branding over the years to sell themselves as places of fashion (France), cars (Germany), watches (Switzerland), or tourism (Jamaica – or Australia, as noted in Chapter 2). It is perhaps more relevant to our discussion here that many countries have long sought to affect how they are perceived abroad: consider the use of the US Information Agency (including Voice of America) or the Soviet Union's reliance on Radio Moscow. More recently, the US, Russia, Turkey, Iran, Honduras, and Israel have used branding experts as well.[7] We have also seen the use of branding by Israel in order to defend its security policy and to appear to be a 'safe' haven for both Jews and non-Jews. Accordingly, Israel created a YouTube channel and the Israeli consulate in New York created a Twitter account to garner support for the 2008–9 invasion of/operation in Gaza, and to combat negative commentaries.

Russia has worked hard to define itself as still including wide swathes of land and millions of non-Russian peoples, and the Turks long sought to present the world with a picture of the Kurds as integral to Turkey's national state and society. In both cases no small part of this has been aimed at their European partners. Iran's creation of Press TV, an English-language international television news channel based in Tehran and broadcast in English 24/7, aims to shape and even control popular perceptions worldwide. In all these and an ever-increasing number of cases, there is a recognition that media in myriad new formats represent a battlefield in which countries must be engaged, particularly if they want to define themselves lest others do so.

Whether social media technology is simply the newest tool for propaganda or fundamentally 'changes the game' remains to be seen. But what we are powerfully reminded of here is that states and citizens, societies and cultures, are commodified, represented, packaged, and designed in particular ways in pursuit of some type of mutual security. There are fissures and cracks in that relationship, and these are gaps that IR theory needs to both explore and better understand. There are so many illusions, manipulations, simulacra; in a sense, the way we decenter is to 'stop believing' in the illusions. How does a state react when it comes to terms with the 'unrealness' of it all and perceives that its image is threatened and that its inability to 'protect' its citizens is blatantly and glaringly obvious? States may launch invasions in search of a 'rally round the flag' approach, such as Argentina's invasion of the Falkland Islands/ Islas Malvinas, or they may seek investment and support from others.

Or, they may go on an offensive with their own citizens. Just ten days after 9/11, the American Ad Council, created in 1941 as essentially the propaganda wing of the US government, launched its 'I am an American' advertising campaign, featuring a series of US citizens from various backgrounds proclaiming 'I am an American.' This advertisement in effect called upon US 'diversity patriots' to participate in and defend the 'illusion' of a tolerant, unified US *nation-state* (see our discussion in Chapter 2) (Weber, 2010: 82). Weber responded with her film *'I Am an American': Video Portraits of Unsafe US Citizens*. The people featured include: Iraq war resister Phil McDowell, who fled to Canada as a political refugee after receiving notice of being stop-lossed; James Yee, former US

Army Muslim chaplin at the Guantanamo Bay detention camp, subjected to but eventually cleared of court-martial charges; undocumented migrant Elvira Arellano, with a US citizen child; Chris Simcox, a founder of Minuteman Civil Defense Corps, a vigilante group preventing migrants from entering US territory; activist Shanti Sellz, a volunteer with No More Deaths, an organization that provides aid to undocumented migrants from Mexico to Arizona; indigenous American Ofelia Rivas, a leader in the Tohono O'odham Nation; Hurricane Katrina evacuees Greg and Glenda Avery; artist Steve Kurtz; retired marine Guadalupe Denogean, who received fast-track citizenship after being injured during the Iraq war; Fernando Suarez del Solar, who refused posthumous US citizenship for his son, Jesus, killed while on duty in Iraq. The videos that comprise the film are available at www.opendemocracy.net. There is no straightforward narrative to be gleaned from the documentary, which makes it all the more difficult to figure out what an 'American' is. Certainly, when one thinks, 'ah, now that's a true American,' the previous examples might not come to mind; and we should ask why not.

Weber's theoretical and film work reveal that the state–citizen relationship is problematically reproduced and undisturbed in discourses about 'safety.' She also explores how people and communities negotiate and engage with unsafe states. Weber notes that US contemporary citizenship is both 'unsettled' and 'unsettling' (2008: 125). In particular, citizens can challenge the state's monopoly over the legitimate use of violence; at the same time, they can be endangered *or* protected by the state (*ibid.*: 126). But the state also needs to be protected from citizens. Citizens enter a social contract, so that they are no longer a potential danger to the state, but this contract protects citizens from each other, not from the sovereign, the state (*ibid.*: 132).

Reading Hobbes through the lens of design, Weber finds Hobbes's answer to the question of what modern liberal citizenship was designed to do: 'Citizenship was designed to provide insecure citizens with protection within a secure state and insecure states with protection from their insecuring citizens' (*ibid.*: 130). We could argue that this is why, some six weeks after 9/11, the usually sluggish US Congress passed the USA PATRIOT[8] Act with virtually no debate, much consensus, and no small amount of self-congratulation. Weber's film, unsafe both for how it could be appropriated but also for how it challenges US hegemony, features interviews not only on 'America' but also on citizenship. She asserts that citizenship is complex and complicated, leading to difficult questions about whether all citizens are equal to each other and how very different types of belonging are supposed to be included under one category of citizenship (*ibid.*: 129). Weber argues that the good citizen gets equated with the good human, but what happens to you, as a human being, if you do not meet the criteria of a good – which by definition includes 'safe' – citizen? Weber notes that 'because the US state [like any state] reserves for itself the power to determine who among its citizens is "safe" or "unsafe" and to reverse this decision at any time, this modern liberal compromise of humanity for citizenship is a compromise too far' (Weber, 2010: 84). Indeed, Peter Nyers (2003) points out that the importance and urgency of Weber's film is that she 'outs' citizenship as a (retractable) condition for being safe, secured, and able to live peacefully in one's community.

In so doing, Weber's film challenges the portrayal by the Ad Council (and thus the US government) of citizens who are without fear *qua* their status as US citizens. The Ad Council failed to include 'the poor, the illegal, the grieving, the dissenting, and the hateful' (Ling, 2010: 100). At the same time, Weber's film powerfully reveals that many of those feeling unsafe, such as Guadalupe Denogean, yearn for an 'America' they believe in, one that lives up to the myth and the legend (Ling, 2010: 100–1).

Indeed, how many of those critical of the Bush Administration bothered to challenge then US presidential candidate Barack Obama's claim that it was necessary to 'return' America to a former glory, that it was possible for the US to be a beacon of light *once again*? As we have argued, temporality is important because during the roughest and most blatant displays of brute force and hegemony, how many citizens, in any state, wistfully recall a 'prior' time that they could 'return' to, that would finally make them feel 'safe' again, if they ever did (and at whose expense)? Accordingly, when we decenter, we need to be cognizant of the attachments to and vehemently defended beliefs in the very concepts and constructs we claim 'center' IR. We should ask, Are we truly willing to 'let go' of certain narratives? How much can we decenter IR when we understand our own lives in terms of our citizenship, our jobs in academia, NGOs, or other organizations that do exactly what we and others critique?

You may quickly become unsafe, because the state is out for itself. And you may never see it coming. Remember how unsafe it is to be a citizen when one's government cannot or will not help after tsunamis (Thailand in 2007), hurricanes (Ike in the Caribbean in 2008), or volcanic activity (Montserrat's Soufrière Hills from 1995 to the present). Consider as well those in the US who had to fend for themselves after Hurricane Katrina (or Rita, or Ike), who find themselves homeless and/ or hungry in one of the world's wealthiest societies, or who currently live without health insurance. It is even more striking, if little remarked upon, when a non-Northern/Western state, such as Cuba, is better able to attend to its citizens' post-hurricane needs than the US, as happened in 2008 with Hurricane Ike.

How are we, as safe and unsafe citizens, intimately bound up with each other? 'Security moms' in the US, with their fears of undocumented migrants, terrorists, and gangs (Faludi, 2008), are safe to shop in a mall – which is what President Bush told Americans to do shortly after the 9/11 attacks – because of another's insecurity as a migrant laborer in the mall's supply chain or as a domestic worker taking care of the shopper's home or children. As Weber's film is available on the Internet (for example, at http//www.youtube.com/user/opendemocracyteam), we could argue that she is 'unsafe' because of how she uses immersion to challenge the state. Indeed, the discourse over her film is not safe, given that one of the subjects of her documentary, Minuteman Simcox, stole a portion of it so that he could promote his political candidacy for state senator in Arizona (Doty, 2010).

For IR, security fundamentally resides with states. Forays into human security, environmental security, and community security cannot be fully understood until citizenship – a real, legal, contract – is understood. IR is centered through peace and security because this concept assumes a particular type of 'security' is forged in the relationship between the state and the citizen. This leaves the international system intact and centered in the North/West. And this is a system that we may critique but might be unwilling to fully challenge, no matter how insecure we are.

Pathways to Peace?

The third way that 'peace and security' centers IR is through a certain positioning of the various players in the world: we rely on international institutions, which pressure, leverage, sanction, shame, and coordinate with states, which are ultimately responsible for creating conditions of peace and security for their citizens. We are not quite sure anyone is clear on what 'peace and security' means for any of the entities involved in this scenario; we just know that the bigger and more far-reaching the global governance framework, the better off people will be, or so we think. As we discussed in Chapter 3, the IR focus on human rights is increasingly about a proliferation of laws, the institutional framework that promulgates and implements those laws, and how to ensure compliance or effect changes in state behavior. It is less and less about radical critique, social movements, and resistance.

We contend that IR's focus on conflict, peace, and security also firmly endorses a similar approach. Accordingly, we call attention to how IR students and scholars may be more likely to look at the International Criminal Court, Security Council resolutions, United Nations agencies, the role of NATO or the Department of Peacekeeping Operations, or the interests of the Permanent 5 and relatively more powerful NGOs, without due attention to local and regional struggles and contestations over and collaborations with this international framework. Our first claim is that IR approaches peace and security by privileging particular 'pathways' to peace within a larger 'governing' framework. The costs are many: reaffirmations of the nation-state; problematic reliance on the very institutions, such as the World Bank, that have severely impeded communities' survival; catapulting situations into an 'international space' for analysis or resolution without attending to possible consequences for the people who are allegedly 'voiceless' and 'powerless'; not enough focus on the political – the radical possibilities of such themes as healing, reconciliation, and sustainability.

Our second claim is that the 'peace and security' category often ushers in the necessity to find the bad guys hurting the good guys. So, the North/West designates and finds war criminals and puts them on trial, or it locates a country or rebel group to disarm and engage in 'peace talks,' or it focuses on a group that must renounce violence. This seems like a simple and straightforward process. And, on the face of it, these actions are advisable and necessary in the context of crises because it is hard to stand up and say, 'Well, wait a minute here, is this the best course?' when everyone else is calling for action. But our point is that we're not always positive that the depictions are accurate or that we have access to full information. Perhaps the designated good guys have marginalized a particular group, or the bad guys are part of a larger system. So, instead we are looking at the kinds of interactions between the institutions set up to address peace and security, the countries that allegedly hold the key to providing peace and security, and the communities contending with instabilities.

We think that IR needs to take more careful account of how communities respond to, ignore, deflect, rely upon, come up against, or otherwise deal with these institutions, instruments, conventions, and commissions. Why do we believe that more laws, more compliance with laws and resolutions, and deeper engagement with large institutions is the way to go? Why do we not question whether even one community might have multiple, contradictory interactions with this larger web of processes, technocrats, and epistemic communities? We are not referring to the simplistic 'international law/institutions' versus 'sovereignty/national security' debate that is often acted out with little regard to the lives lost; we are interrogating how the two key players in IR, institutions and states, came to *be* the key players – and under what circumstances it is desirable to believe that those players can provide 'to' people any semblance of peace and security. We also question which institutions and states have more power than other institutions and states, and why.

Institutional frameworks: international institutions and international law

As discussed in Chapter 2, we can understand international law and institutions in terms of their potential for representing and redressing people's rights, changing countries' repressive behavior, and articulating normative standards. At the same time, legal discourses and the reliance upon international institutional frameworks can have consequences such as depoliticizing or dehistoricizing people's experiences and struggles, or focusing more on some people's grievances than others.[9] When there is war or insecurity in the world, 'centered' IR tends to focus on two themes: (1) creating consensus in international legal remedies, particularly international criminal law, the International Criminal Court (ICC), and *ad hoc* tribunals; (2) making humanitarian interventions more effective. We consider these in turn.

A lot of the international law literature focuses on how to create more 'compliance pull,' or how to frame or institutionalize norms so that more states will sign, ratify, and actually implement the terms of international legal treaties and conventions. The idea is to compel states to legitimize the alleged universality of the practices embodied in these treaties, conventions, and other documents of international law. For example, over five decades after the creation of the United Nations system, activists interested in peace, justice, and rights were elated at the creation of the International Criminal Court (ICC) through the Rome Statute, which entered into force in July 2002. While US politicos grumbled about its unwillingness to sign away its sovereignty and to potentially subject national security policy and US military forces to the political agendas of other countries, advocates of the ICC proclaimed that this was long overdue. Indeed, after the Nuremberg and Tokyo Trials, international criminal law was finally gearing up to go after the perpetrators of the worst atrocities in the world. Certainly, the discourse among international lawyers, practitioners, and NGOs was that the ICC could 'decenter' (or make less important) the US; it was proceeding with or without the blessings of the US. As such, if the international community could build 'consensus' about the importance of upholding principles regarding the most egregious crimes, then, the objections of powerful states notwithstanding, ostensibly peace and security could be better achieved. However, we address three specific problems with building consensus: 1) building the legitimacy of consensus-based institutions at the cost of actually prosecuting crimes; 2) neglecting how international law can be politicized; 3) ignoring the underlying categorizations of international law that cause conflict.

First, the importance of upholding norms can take a backseat to the more 'pressing' goal of legitimizing the institution, such as *ad hoc* tribunals[10] and the International Criminal Court, that is supposed to uphold such norms in the former Yugoslavia, Rwanda, Sierra Leone, East Timor, Iraq, Cambodia, Sudan, the Democratic Republic of the Congo, Central African Republic, Uganda, and others. To be sure, NGOs as well as certain decision makers have been crucial in framing 'rape as a war crime.' They consider, for example, the creation of the International Criminal Court as well as the types of 'gendered crimes' addressed in the International Criminal Tribunal for the former Yugoslavia (ICTY) and the International Criminal Tribunal for Rwanda (ICTR) as remarkable achievements on the part of feminist advocates, the frustrations and setbacks notwithstanding (Halley, Kotiswaran, Shamir, and Thomas, 2006: 342–3). Feminist advocates have showcased the trials of the

Prosecutor v. Dragoljub Kunarac, Radomir Kovac, and Zoran Vukovic in the ICTY and the ICTR case against Jean-Paul Akayesu as emblematic of what women's groups have hoped for: the 'elevation' of rape as an egregious violation of international human rights law.

However, international law and institutions are not *necessarily* and consistently marshaled to address, redress, and deter crimes (war crimes, crimes against humanity, genocide, human rights violations) wherever they may occur. For example, some women's rights advocates and international law practitioners we interviewed pointed to the failure of international courts to bring charges of sexual violence.[11] As one lawyer noted, investigators had 'too much evidence, not enough focus.'[12] In 1995, the ICTR's Office of the Prosecutor decided to create a 'rape database' following the Rwandan genocide in order to get every possible witness to provide testimony; however, because framing rape as a violation of international criminal law was a fairly new phenomenon at that time, some of the important kinds of questions that might link rapes to genocide were not asked.[13]

Furthermore, the very act of asking questions about rape and sexual violence proved to be difficult. As one of our lawyer contacts put it,

> Basically, picture that you're a male investigator. You ask a victim to explain what happened during the genocide, and you get very clear answers, via a translator, of her whole family being killed. You ask her other questions, and find out she was kidnapped and beaten. Looking at the translator, she also says she was 'liberated.' You assume this means they let her go. In fact it means they raped her. She's certainly not going into any more and you're not going to ask.[14]

Our contact further described the realities of the investigation, particularly in terms of the fears investigators felt as they tried to obtain information in unsafe conditions or the assumptions, backgrounds, experiences, and rhetoric they carried about rape. Our contact also mentioned that trying to prove rape in addition to genocide might seem very overwhelming, particularly when 'the sentence for rape could not get any worse than a life sentence for perpetrating genocide. It was also difficult to prove that a superior specifically ordered or knew rape was going on, as it generally did not take place in front of him.'[15] The lack of prosecution, then, does not always mean a lack of concern about rape but has more to do with the exigencies of the case. When investigators for the ICC were collecting evidence in Uganda, for example, a rare opportunity to arrest Thomas Lubanga (former rebel leader in the Democratic Republic of the Congo) arose with enough information to indict him on child soldiers but not on sexual violence.[16] As this was the ICC's inaugural case, it was trying as much as possible not to 'overreach,' particularly as it wanted to prove its legitimacy.[17] The problems (which some may call 'growing pains') notwithstanding, can we create peace in a world *without* this particular pathway, through concerted, collaborative action between the UN, the ICC, and invested NGOs? Advocates answer with a resounding no, and continue to push for including as many victims' cases as possible. As discussed in the film *The Reckoning*, regarding the history and accomplishments of the International Criminal Court, cases are useful for building consensus as well as to demonstrate the commitment of the international community to particular norms and to ending impunity. The film asserts the belief of many lawyers, advocates, and scholars that the ICC, 'done right,' can deter crimes. One powerful scene shows members of the Lord's Resistance Army in Uganda discussing their concerns about pending ICC investigations, illustrating that the very possibility of ICC involvement could deter, shame, or trip up human rights offenders. And, as the film mentions, if the ICC is a court of 'last resort,' it might compel countries to strengthen their judiciary and legal systems to end impunity.

However, because international laws are most often directed towards non-European rather than European perpetrators, thereby incorporating postcolonial and postsocialist societies into a Euro-American order (Philipose, 2009), leaders in these countries, particularly those with ICC investigators in their backyards, can readily politicize international criminal law as an imperial infringement of sovereignty. The charge of intervention cannot be ignored, given the colonial history of international law (see our discussion in Chapter 2). Indeed, a scene in *The Reckoning* shows LRA commanders make overtures towards a 'peace process,' surveying community members ravaged by the civil war about whether they would prefer a peace process or the ICC's 'interference,' with its insistence on holding LRA members accountable. Why would anyone want to stand up and say 'yes, we would prefer you would get arrested' when former killers are watching one's reactions? In such a case, we can't ignore victims of LRA attacks when they think that the threat of ICC action could be negatively leveraged. International criminal law should be politicized as a site for articulating political agendas.

We have a more pressing point here. If the pretext to genocides, rape campaigns, and other sorts of crimes is the strict classification and codification of peoples, then why would that same sort of categorization make sense when prosecuting the crimes that resulted from such constructions? In other words, it is crucial to point out that it was the politicization and marshaling of race, ethnicity, and religion that made violence possible so we don't naturalize those differences through the process of trial. In the context of the fact that international law does in fact legitimize war, using international law to distinguish between 'legal' violence and 'illegal' violence seems rather bizarre, given the presumption *within* international law that war, borders, distinctions among communities are all part and parcel of how we rule ourselves (Philipose, 2009: 198). What is the irony of naming what kind of violence is illegitimate when international law legitimizes many forms of violence, particularly sovereignty, the waging of war, collective military action, the creation of war zones, and sanctions that can and often do result in starving out populations (see Dauphinee, 2008)?

In a more specific example, consider the implications when the ICTY's 'jurisdictional parameters' only examined inter-ethnic conflict: when a Serb raped a Bosnian or Croat, but not the rape of another Serb (Philipose, 2009: 190). Is this not 'committing to a racial taxonomy for the adjudication of sexualized crimes' (*ibid.*: 191)? We may be relieved that international law 'finally' takes sexual crimes seriously, but it does so by (1) differentially racializing the perpetrators and victims; (2) focusing on crimes by citizens rather than foreign peacekeepers or administrators who may have raped during their tenure in the country in question; (3) presuming that any sexual contact between ethnic groups during a conflict must be non-consensual; and (4) assuming that women are necessarily 'innocent' – that is, did not take sides or participate in the conflict (*ibid.*).

Our second point speaks to the use of so-called humanitarian interventions. In particular, we are interested in the institutionalization of 'protection,' at the hands of states, contractors, NATO, and the UN Department of Peacekeeping Operations. For example, peacekeeping missions have evolved from 'just' humanitarian intervention to a 'responsibility to protect, prevent, react, and rebuild' (see the Canadian government-initiated International Commission on Intervention and State Sovereignty Report, the 2004 UN Secretary-General's High-level Plenary Report, the 2005 World Summit Outcome, and interpretations of the United Nations Charter, particularly Articles 24, 25, and 51 and Chapter 7). The new role emerged particularly in response to Somalia, Rwanda, Srebenica, and Kosovo, and in the light of various failures of UN missions, such as the United Nations Organization Mission in the Democratic Republic of the Congo (MONUC) during the Second Congo War. When stories surfaced about UN peacekeepers' crimes – involvement in sexual abuse, trafficking, and prostitution scandals, exchanging food for sex, abandoning the children they fathered, or, more recently, firing upon Haitians waiting for food in post-earthquake relief efforts – various actors, from the UN Secretary-General to NGOs, pushed for reform. The measures suggested include the use of existing international humanitarian and human rights law regarding sexual violence and excessive force, the implementation of UN-mandated codes of conduct, addressing the bureaucratic morass that can make the appropriate action impossible, calling for accountability on the part of troop-contributing countries, 'gender-sensitive' training of troops, and outreach to communities in which troops work (Ndulo, 2009). But the underlying premises of the use of peacekeepers to uphold the stipulations of peace treaties – militarization and the civilian/combatant distinction – were not questioned.

In Chapter 3, we discussed how we might use tragedies to justify militarized intervention (by peacekeepers or other entities). Enloe notes that '[m]ilitarization is a step-by-step process by which a person or thing gradually comes to be controlled by the military or comes to depend for its well-being on militaristic ideas' (Enloe, 2001: 3). Reliance on the institutional framework for protection means that we meet the question 'How can we stop people harming others?' with, on the one hand, getting governments to constrain their powers while, on the other hand, calling for

> increasing intervention by powerful states [which] necessarily rel[y] upon executive governments, militaries and multinational corporations as agents ... While much human rights activism has focused on the exploitative practices of multinational corporations in their operations in the Third World, advocates of humanitarian intervention do not ask whether enabling an increased presence by foreign contractors in the post-conflict period offers the best strategy for ending suffering ... (Orford, 2009: 444–5)

In effect, the problem with the response of militarized, 'humanitarian' intervention is that it privileges top-down decision-making, the investment of resources into war-making and weapons industries, the empowerment of militaries to provide a feeling of safety, and the affirmation that militaries can keep hostile enemies at bay (Ferguson, 2009: 476). We see evidence around the world that these tactics for addressing human rights violations can and often do create more violence. For example, Agathangelou and Ling (2003) and Razack (2004) challenge how and whether UN peacekeepers protect civilians; Agathangelou and Ling examine how peacekeeping maintains a neoliberal regime, while Razack explores the racialization involved in 'saving people from themselves.'

Also, even the undergirding principle of differentiation/discrimination in international humanitarian law is problematic. The just war tradition and the Geneva Protocols of 1977 prohibit military targeting of 'innocent' noncombatants/civilians, who should be 'protected' by peacekeepers and others. Sjoberg's work (2006) reveals that even feminist analysts, when they seek to extend security to those usually not protected, assume that it is indeed possible to protect anyone (see Carpenter's argument (2003) that humanitarian missions rarely protect men, or consider the recent 'women only' food ration cards in Haiti after the January 2010 earthquake). A feminist analysis of the gendered construction of the noncombatant immunity principle reveals that 'innocence' is a category deployed to ensure certain 'masculine' (warriors) and 'feminine' (innocent, supportive of their men) roles in upholding the state's involvement in wars and violence (Sjoberg, 2006). Sjoberg further argues that this distinction pretends that 'innocence' is readily intelligible (are women and children necessarily innocent?) and possible in the context of war (can war be conducted in a 'clean' manner so as to distinguish between combatants and human beings whose lives have been severely disrupted by the very fact of war?).

These are not questions a centered IR asks. This happens, we contend, because of the outrage at what people 'over there' are doing to each other. We point out that the outrage is not consistently experienced and so we might want military intervention in one case but completely ignore another case. Another reason is because of the internalization of the national security imperatives of powerful states that might be called upon to intervene; despite our critiques of state repression, we still have a tendency to believe that precisely because of that power, the state will be able somehow to stop the outrageous event. But we also decenter the assumption that institutions and laws, even when movements and activists have fought for them, will necessarily resolve conflicts. The reason that parallel, complementary, or completely alternative forms of justice, peace, and truth-telling have arisen in the very countries with tribunals and cases at the ICC might have much to do with concerns that international law and domestic law, unintentionally or not, can be more about their own legitimacy and credibility than about the lived experiences of the people affected. Advocates often acknowledge that large institutions and organizations might indeed put as much effort into their own endurance and power as into the declared object of their work, but contend that the potential benefits and resources are hard to live without.

'Alternative' forms of justice and peace-building include the Women's International War Crimes Tribunal assembled in 2000 to address justice for the so-called comfort women, or those subjected to sexual slavery at the hands of the Japanese military before and during World War Two; Courts of Women in various parts of the world that have heard testimony about sexual violence, domestic violence, trafficking, development, nuclear weapons, and other issues; and People's Tribunals, such as the 1966 Russell Tribunal regarding US war crimes in Vietnam (Chinkin, 2006). These forums have no predetermined format or process, point out the failures of state and international legal mechanisms, grapple with difficult issues around 'evidence,' offer ways to incorporate multiple perspectives on war, peace, and justice, and are centered around those directly affected by conflict. They innovatively claim legitimacy by addressing what other formal legal institutions have left out, by using judicial rituals, such as public oaths, with the involvement of reputable lawyers and judges, and through symbolic validation of testimony (*ibid.*). But, despite the room they create for acknowledging and recognizing multiple experiences of oppression, some forms of decidedly non-international justice, such as the Gacaca in Rwanda (Tiemessen, 2004), the Truth and Reconciliation Commission in South Africa (Krog, 1998; Driver, 2005), and memorial projects in Chile (Hite and Collins, 2009), can serve powerful governmental interests, require negotiations with the actors that remain wedded to the *status quo*, and/or draw upon gendered and racialized assumptions that can be divisive.

Essentially, while political actors may rail against 'outside' intervention, they might also restrict and delimit possibilities of reconciliation, healing, and justice in 'post'-conflict/authoritarian societies. But if we are more aware of the consequences of the different types of conflict resolution and peace-building, we are more likely to challenge processes in which we politicize identities in the very ways that led to conflict in the first place. What are the mutual possibilities of healing and trauma in the way we go about securing peace? This is the question we think should be at the forefront of the way we respond to war, conflict, and injustice. In effect, in order to decenter IR, we should explore how multiple actors, including states, institutions, and civil society, create pathways to peace, identify who is privileged as a decision maker, and trace competing understandings of peace, justice, and security.

Good guys and bad guys: dealing with intractable conflict

Mainstream IR, in terms of both scholarship and practice emanating from the North/West, advocates militarization as a way to, ironically enough, guarantee peace and security in areas of the world with deeply entrenched conflicts. We should question two things about this 'pathway' to peace. First, of course, is why it is presumed that deployment of troops or the looming threat of possible military intervention will keep those 'intractable' conflict zones from destabilizing the region or involving nuclear, chemical, or other types of weapons of mass destruction. Second, why are some conflict zones understood to be intractable? What is at stake in naming those regions as always already and forever – backwards and forwards in time – conflictual, without any attentiveness to how various actors may have an interest in continuing the conflict?

The irony is that the conflicts labeled as intractable imply that two sides are equally guilty and equally unwilling to shift, thus resulting in the impasse. However, the discourse underlying the analysis of such conflicts typically singles out one stubborn, incorrigible, ornery player (such as China, Pakistan, Venezuela, Cuba, or Syria). As we sorted through the numerous institutes, think tanks, training programs, and mechanisms directed towards conflict resolution, we were simultaneously intrigued by the efforts of communities to turn upside down the taken-for-granted mainstream discourses about militarization as a means of forcing these particular 'bad' states into 'peaceful' behavior, thus earning the accolade of 'partners in peace.' Not only do we think the good versus bad rhetoric is problematic, as we outlined in Chapter 3, but we are also disturbed by one glaring absence in discussions we hear about ending the wars in Afghanistan and Iraq, ending Israeli occupation, ending Chinese occupation of Tibet, ending the US embargo against Cuba, or discouraging the hawks in US, Israeli, and European policy-making circles from allowing militarized intervention into Iran or Pakistan. To be sure, anti-war, anti-occupation, and peace activists are often engaged in these areas because they contest the demonization of a particular side, but where is the agitation to *end* the intractable conflict that has created a demon like no other?

Ending the Korean War

There are, of course, organizations dedicated to this very cause, but we were curious as to why more broad-based, self-proclaimed peace organizations, particularly in the North/West, have failed so miserably at including the Korean War in the context of their claims about hegemony, the military-industrial complex, and long-lasting oppression and displacement of peoples. If anything, we heard some arguments for the military-based containment of the secretive, isolated state of North Korea, for the 'sake' of the Korean people. Even those who contested the positioning of Iran and Iraq in the 'Axis of Evil' often asked, 'If we are attacking someone, why aren't we attacking North Korea? They *have* weapons of mass destruction, and are proud of it!' At least one answer, oddly enough, seemed to be that North Korea was too dangerous.

When we shift to the issue of the highly militarized Korean peninsula, it seems to us that it is a key conflict for understanding and decentering IR for several reasons.[18] First, the Korean War was the first proxy war in the Cold War, serving as a prototype for conflicts that followed, particularly through the fomenting of a civil war;[19] as such, the resounding claim that the Cold War is over does not seem to be supported by the evidence of a war that is technically still ongoing. The 1953 armistice signed by China, the US, and North Korea was meant to be a temporary document at best, aimed towards a ceasefire until a final peace settlement was achieved. But it never was. Second, about a quarter of the population of South Korea is currently separated from family members in North Korea; the ongoing displacement of about 10 million families is surely as problematic as mass displacements in other parts of the world.

Third, the most compelling aspect of the North Korea–South Korea conflict, and most relevant here, is the rarely questioned premise that this conflict is about North Korea's recalcitrant views and 'bad' behavior, and that, accordingly, militarization is the only way to prevent something catastrophic from happening. North Korea's position as the world's last 'Stalinist' state – heavily militarized, bizarrely hermetic, and simply evil – seems to be given: who argues otherwise? This is not to say that the leadership or policies of North Korea are immune to criticism. However, we argue that rather than seek continued militarization of the Korean peninsula as a pathway to peace, particularly in the context of the nuclear weapons issue, we should consider a more complex, nuanced view of this conflict that decenters the US position and stake in it, and more radically considers the desires within the Korean peninsula for reunification.[20]

How and why do the US and South Korea keep the conflict going? We ask this question to shatter the presumption, accepted by too many, that North Korea is the only antagonist. Even those who would concede that the tensions on the Korean peninsula are due to US and Soviet actions do not go far enough in interrogating the roles of the US and South Korea. For example, is the US more interested in defending South Korea from North Korea or maintaining a military presence in the region, particularly given US perceptions of China's rising profile? Further, as Suh (2007) argues, both the US and South Korea have made long-term investments in their alliance – in equipment, contingency plans, training, and bureaucratic agencies. The two countries are thus so heavily invested in the alliance itself that it would be very disruptive and expensive to alter it, even if they wanted to do so. The intimacy of the relationship deeply influences the negative view both countries have of North Korea. Further, US military policy in the whole region is at stake.

The 1954 US–South Korea mutual defense treaty effectively and indefinitely militarized the conflict, leading to an ongoing presence of 28,000–40,000 US troops, and, consequently, the strategic entrenchment of prostitution to service the US military (Lie, 1995; Moon, 2007). Even a 2003 US–South Korea agreement to move US troops from the demilitarized line gave no timetable or specifics, with redeployment to parts of South Korea a strong possibility. Further, although the US transferred peacetime operational control to the South Korean army in

1994, and aims to transfer wartime operational control in 2012, when the US demanded the expansion of one of its bases in 2004, South Korea actively participated in the displacement of villagers and farmers and the brutal suppression of resistance in Pyongtaek (Vine, 2009: 182).

Also, the Armed Services Committee in the US Congress, which allocates the defense budget and decides where US troops are placed, has continuously ensured the militarization of the border between North Korea and South Korea. This makes sense when many senators on this committee represent states, such as Alaska and Nebraska, with large arms industries.[21] Indeed, South Korea is the fifth largest importer of US weapons and military technology in the world. And while South Korea has been developing an indigenous arms industry, it continues to be a leading recipient of arms from American defense companies located in the Pacific Rim. South Korean politicians have expressed the view that they prefer a stronger US security commitment to South Korea, because US military subsidies allow South Korea to direct its own money to social and economic programs, and because of fears of the economic burden that a potential peace with North Korea might bring. Accordingly, North Korea's militarization and militarized activity can be interpreted in various ways. Some may argue that it is the work of madmen intent on destroying civilization. But most of its military is at the border and in front of the capital city, Pyongyang, which makes strategic sense. North Korea's extensive underground tunnels, as paranoid as they may seem, were a means of escape during US aerial bombing during the early years of the Korea War. And, in comparison, the US has far more nuclear and WMD capacity than much of the world. While we challenge the militarization of conflicts, we suggest that we can view North Korea as being strategic rather than *more* antagonistic than any other player in this conflict.

Furthermore, one could argue that increased tensions in the Korean peninsula could be attributed not only to the aggressive actions of the US but also to the election of conservative, neoliberal President Lee Myung-bak in South Korea in February 2008. Since then, progressive organizations have protested the increasing entrenchment of neoliberal policies, the repression of leftist and union politics, the use of surveillance, and the deployment of riot police.[22] Some have noted that, before his election, people's attitudes towards reunification were substantially different from what they are today: 'Young people were especially talking about reunification as something that is necessary, and there was more openness in South Korean media about portraying North Korean society. There were even lots of different cultural exchanges happening at the time and lots of hope.'[23] Most pressingly, many see the regime as rolling back gains from the June 15 joint declaration between North Korea and South Korea. Indeed, Lee Myung-bak has emphasized and prioritized US–South Korea relations and espouses decidedly anti-North Korea rhetoric.

We should also consider the provocative acts of the US and South Korea, such as the role of CONPLAN 5029, a US–South Korea joint forces command designed to prepare for the collapse of North Korea. CONPLAN 5029 encompassed a commitment to send US troops and equipment in the event of a North Korean invasion as well as a set of military exercises that played out various scenarios assuming North Korean aggression: outflow of weapons of mass destruction, regime change, civil war by coup, the holding of South Korean hostages, mass exodus of North Korean refugees, and natural disasters. In late 2008, this conceptual plan was converted into an operational plan, OPLAN 5029, with the blessing of Lee Myung-bak. These exercises simulate pre-emptive nuclear strike, the deployment of South Korean forces, ground combat, US special operation forces securing North Korean nuclear weapons facilities, and other contingency plans.[24] Furthermore, in 2008, the US brought in nuclear-powered carriers, nuclear submarines, and other nuclear 'hardware,' and staged nuclear war exercises that ostensibly would be directed towards North Korea. The Obama Administration's alleged 'new, respectful stance' in the world notwithstanding, some of the largest military exercises occurred in March 2009 – when US and South Korean troops engaged in Key Resolve/Foal Eagle, simulations of military exercises and tactics that the North Koreans deemed provocative – and at the end of August 2009.

As such, is it the 'bizarre and inexplicable' aggression of Chairman Kim Jong-il, or the military-industrial complex and South Korean–US actions that better explain the *status quo* in the Korean peninsula? In either case, demonization of the players is not useful; rather, we should consider the effects of the purposeful and directed accusations against only one player, North Korea, constructed even in evaluations of possible engagement as *the* 'rogue,' 'adversarial,' or 'target' state (Cha and Kang, 2003; Key-young, 2006; Kim and Kang, 2009). Many authors who promote engagement over coercion or militarization still take it for granted that it is North Korea that the rest of the world must 'engage' (read: if only they would do what 'reasonable' people should – which is, of course, *what we want them to do*). But, in this case it is not just the designated enemy that has engaged in provocative behavior. Harrison (2002) and Hart-Landsberg (1998) acknowledge that North Korean actions are more strategic and 'rational' than its rhetoric may indicate. Journalist Bradley Martin's *Under the Loving Care of the Fatherly Leader: North Korea and the Kim Dynasty* (2006) breaks down the mythologies both within and outside of North Korea. Bruce Cumings, an eminent scholar on Korean politics, points out that North Korea's rhetoric and actions may seem totalitarian or completely antithetical to standards of diplomacy, but it has strategically provoked world players, such as the US, through the use of military weapons in order to gain some leverage towards diplomatic normalization (see Cumings, 2003, 2004).[25] Sigal's *Disarming Strangers* includes a useful appendix, 'North Korea's Tit-for-Tat Negotiating Behavior' (1998: 257–9), which examines how North Korea responds to often erratic policy changes on the part of the US.

In order to grapple with discourses about North Korea, we drew upon the work of the Korea Policy Institute (www.kpolicy.org), an independent research body that insists that US policy be cognizant of Koreans' own reflections upon and desires for sovereignty, reconciliation, and reunification. The Korea Policy Institute also creates key relationships with organizations and groups in both North Korea and South Korea. Indeed, the nexus of academic research, think tanks, and NGOs in 'imagining' and articulating peace, justice, and security is crucial. Hyun Lee, a member of Nodutdol (www.nodutdol.org), a grassroots organization dedicated to peace and reconciliation on the Korean peninsula,[26] emphasizes that the US needs to come to terms with the significance of the North–South declaration in 2000, the first two inter-Korean summits in 2000 and 2007, and the meetings that have now taken place between separated family members. 'The people of North and South Korea will determine their own future. Only they will decide whether they want to demilitarize and reunify.'[27]

Lee claims that a focus on a peace treaty will better lead to disarmament and denuclearization than will increased militarization. With regards to US perceptions, Lee notes that '[a]s long as you're in a state of war, North Korea would never give up nuclear weapons program – why should it?'[28] In addition, when you're in a state of war, how can you influence anyone about your ideas about human rights violations? Accordingly, Lee sees the importance of Nodutdol, particularly through its role in sending Korean Americans to both North and South Korea every other year. The goal is for diasporic Koreans to connect with those working in popular movements, farmers facing the impact of neoliberal policies, environmental activists, women's groups, gay, lesbian, bisexual, and transgendered groups, and young people working towards reunification.

In many ways, as Lee puts it, the people-to-people exchanges help to offer correctives to the distortion of Korean history: 'without that step of this interaction, the solidarity, the mobilization of people in the US and North and South Korea, and understanding the history, reunification becomes meaningless. And healing from the trauma of war requires conversation about reunification.'[29] It is also crucial, in Lee's view, for Korean Americans to help put pressure on the US government to move from focusing on North Korea's withdrawal from the armistice to talks about a peace treaty. Assuredly, this might lead to the framing of those who decenter the US and conservative South Koreans as 'communists' or 'apologists' for North Korea. But we contend that a legitimization of reunification, peace, and reconciliation discourse in IR discussions of North Korea and South Korea would also open the way for a more nuanced reflection upon reunification as a pathway to peace and for defining what peace and security could look like for Koreans in the long term.

It is equally important, then, to be critical of and resist romanticization of reunification so as to examine the hegemonic and marginalized voices even within that movement.[30] This has led Miyoshi Jager, for example, to examine the idealized image of the virtuous Korean woman, set to uphold *chuch'eron* (self-reliance) in the face of adversity and separation from family members. Many reunification dissidents, while representing the division as imposed on the Korean body politic by the West, have either unwittingly or intentionally deployed the Korean woman to stand for the inner core of Korean values, of one Korea, the sanctity of conjugal bliss (read both as marriage in general and the eventual 'marriage' between North Korea and South Korea), and the prosperity of stable households (Miyoshi Jager, 1996).

Kim and Fu (2008) examine how the increasing 'demand' for fair Russian and eastern European women within South Korea's sex industry points to various factors underlying the Korean peninsula conflict.

The internalization of orientalist tropes that prompt Korean women to bleach their skin and promote the fetishization of 'Western' women; the Japanese imperial emasculation of Korean patriarchal authority; the hypersexualization and oppression of Korean women; the creation of prostitution towns to service the US military; increasing neoliberalism with the concomitant increased commodification of women's bodies, and increased 'status' accorded to those who can access and choose 'Western' sex workers – all these factors commingle to explain the incredibly profitable sex industry, and they matter for creating peace.

In effect, nationalisms are constitutive of and reflective of gendered politics. We have tried to suggest here the sorts of questions that emerge for a decentered IR. How do the reunification discourse and the pragmatic politics of reunification deploy and change such gendered narratives and roles? How can reunification and reconciliation rethink and work through these particular gendered traumas and tropes? How would reunification pressure Japan to fully recognize the brutalization of comfort women and the concerns articulated by the Association of Korean Victims of Forcible Drafting and Their Bereaved Families?

We would push IR scholars to be able to discuss such questions as readily as they discuss rogue states and nuclear threats. More to the point, we should identify the states and communities that are 'bad' and rethink whether they are the only provocateurs in a particular conflict. As such, we can decenter IR through a rethinking of so-called intractable conflicts.

Chapter Six / Conclusion

Contentious Cartography: Shifting Sands and the Topography of IR Today

A once rather widely recognized IR theorist on one occasion posed, admittedly in a far different context, the almost always apt and often critical question: 'What is to be done?' (Lenin, 1986). It seems a good place for us to begin here. Lenin may have lifted the question from the title of Nikolai Chernyshevsky's now obscure Russian novel *What Is To Be Done?* (1863/1989). Much like both the characters and readers of a good Russian novel, we find ourselves awash in a dense, complicated story in which there is much suffering, ceaseless struggle, and love lost. There is *a lot* going on, far more than most of us are comfortable thinking about, much less discussing with our relatively limited bases of knowledge. It is complicated and complex, but (as characters and readers) it is worth the struggle. What are we if we do not try? You have to try.

Fernand Braudel, as sophisticated and astute an observer as any and one of the twentieth century's most influential historians and social thinkers, once invoked the nine years (1923–32) he spent living and teaching in Algeria, which during this time (indeed, from 1848 to 1962) was considered, at least politically, an integral part of France. Still, Braudel noted that: 'I believe that this spectacle, the Mediterranean as seen from the opposite side, upside down, had considerable impact on my vision of history' (1972: 450).

By now, no doubt, the phrases 'opposite side' and 'upside down,' jump out at you, framed as they are in opposition to the metropole, the 'mother' (a gendered term of no little moment and rife with implications) colonizing country and its North/West position/ality. This serves, too, as a salutary reminder that even when such a place as Algeria, itself to some

157

degree a Northern/Western construct, is declared 'an integral part' of the state (in the 1848 Constitution of France's Second Republic), and even targeted for 'assimilation' (at the beginning of France's Third Republic in 1870), it remains construed as outside, in opposition, even antagonistic to the powerful and pervasive center. Yet the Northern/Western storyline is that any state can be made part of the center and welcomed into the family of recognized and codified nations and states; or so we tell ourselves, early and often, with force and conviction. But could the place and space that is Algeria ever be *of* the center – the starting point for analysis of global politics? And would it want to be if it could? Or does that simply maintain the problem in some form?

We have come to see many centers or, even better, no centers – but rather people and places and positions. We have been inspired and in a large measure guided by scholars, activists, and 'ordinary' people, many of whom are actually quite extraordinary in the lives they live, outside the center, literally or figuratively. We have met and worked with people in India, Grenada, Mexico, New York, Nicaragua, South Africa, South Texas, and, as a sign of the times, online, and have read scholars all over the world. It is their challenge – challenge*s*, really – to us that we seek to reformulate and (re)present to you here. We ask you what they in essence have asked us: What would it look like to decenter IR? What would it mean to decenter your world?

The field of International Relations was once the province of 'high politics,' both in terms of the issues of concern, such as guns, bombs, borders, and economies, as well as in terms of who the decision makers could and should be. We hope here to join the clarion call for what might be seen as the 'small d' democratization of our discipline (or at least its *perestroika*, both in the more famous Russian sense of restructuring and reform and as applied to the more recent efforts in the field of political science, of which IR is commonly considered a sub-field; see, on the latter, Renwick Monroe, 2005). By this we mean the opening up of IR to the everyday and the ordinary. This is not meant to deny the importance (much less the still impressive if depressive power) of the state, the rise of non-state actors, or the instantiation of both NGOs and multinational corporations as more or less permanent (within the relatively transitory world of international affairs) factors or facets of the contemporary international system. Rather, it is meant to shift where we look, and to whom, and how – dislodging our traditional (a somewhat odd word to use in the context of a field which sees itself as so alive, vibrant, and *au courant*) approaches.

We have endeavored to deploy and employ a number of stories here to try to help you (and us) (re)consider the ways in which IR is centered – indeed, the ways in which we center IR, both consciously and unintentionally. This last is not unimportant, for while we talk about IR being centered, this is not something that just happened, an accident of nature, a by-product of meta-level processes or Braudelian 'structures' of everyday life (1979; see also the notion of environmental differences in Diamond, 1997: 66, or public issues in Mills, 1959: 8), such as hunger, disease, demographic pressures, crop failures, or economic crises. People – we, us – have centered IR, continue to do so (most often unthinkingly and often caught by surprise if or when we are questioned), and predictably have become invested in this very centeredness; its rejection can and does seem strange, a bit distracting, and perhaps vaguely sinister or threatening – who are they to question these fundamental presuppositions which have served us all so well? Indeed, the centering of IR seems 'normal' and 'natural,' a fundamental character/istic – it simply makes sense (and seems comfortably intuitive) that we would write, script, IR from the center. If unusually blunt, Waltz's analysis rings true to us and it thus seems (or is made to seem) 'ridiculous to construct a theory of international politics based on' anywhere but the center, 'written in terms of the great powers of an era' (1979: 72–3). How else would, should, or indeed *could* we proceed? Obviously, we think there may be other ways.

We are not so presumptuous as to believe we alone have somehow escaped the influence, baleful and beneficial, of the usual IR suspects (Morgenthau, Rosenau, Katzenstein, Keohane, Krasner, Waltz, Wendt). These standard(-bearing) authors and others have influenced the entire field and our debt to them at various points is real. While we implicate (and necessarily interrogate) our colleagues' roles in maintaining and expanding domination and control, we are painfully well aware that institutional and structural conditions create and sustain the center through which IR runs. We are also mindful that even the best intentions confront not just the institutions but the socialization we all undergo and the powerful pull of the culture(s) in which we live. We realize IR is populated with (many) fine folks overwhelmingly defined by their good intentions and commitments, neither of which we seek to question here.

While the road to hell may indeed be paved with good intentions, we nonetheless feel most fortunate to work in a discipline where there are so many people we respect and admire, some of them mentors to us (and many others) and many more influential scholars of enormous erudition. Several of these outstanding scholars have proved themselves willing to listen and even consider seriously (we think) some of the ideas that we have proposed here. Indeed, some of these ideas have crept into the IR conversation and have even been treated (by and large) as having a more or less legitimate place at the dinner table, if we may extend Agathangelou and Ling's delightful construction of IR as a house.[1] Nonetheless, it would seem to be the place traditionally reserved for children – seen and not heard unless politely responding to someone's query.

It merits mention and is worth remembering that IR is a 'discipline' and that the attendant implications are not lost on any of us. Thanks, for want of a better word, to Foucault (1977), there is no need to belabor here the ways in which academic disciplines 'discipline' their members, consciously and intentionally or not; Laitin's commentary on King, Keohane, and Verba's *Designing Social Inquiry: Scientific Inference in Qualitative Research* (1994) in the *American Political Science Review* is titled 'Disciplining Political Science' (1995). Still, we should take seriously objections to our project of decentering.

Most responses, however framed, share three common themes. First, there is what we might fruitfully construe as, in homage to another arguably overappreciated IR thinker, the Churchillian response, paraphrasing Churchill's famous quip about democracy being the worst possible form of government except for all the others (1947).[2] The contention here is that, however flawed our current IR theories are, they are much better (or more sophisticated or more nuanced) than anything else we have encountered to date, and with a few adjustments and a tweak here or there we will be fine. We simply need to broaden the tent to bring the dissenters inside, and grow the pie so everyone gets their slice. This would seem to ignore our fundamental concern – leaving intact, as it does, IR's basic premises.

Second is the understandable and familiar if flawed refrain that we, in so many (plaintive) words, have to begin from *somewhere*, so why not here (or, in Waltz's formulation, necessarily from here). Think of it as the 'If not us, who?' response.[3] We certainly recognize that everyone is situated someplace and that we cannot be (nor should anyone pretend to be) everywhere. Still, setting aside the not inconsiderable 'chimera of origins' (Chartier, 1991: 4) this raises, and given that IR does not really have any firm or clear 'beginning,' the question obtains: Why must we begin from the North/West? Even if we agree to disregard the privileging of arboreal models which in no small measure resonate with Northern/ Western conceptualizations of the world, there would seem to be much to recommend an approach to IR which begins elsewhere if, indeed, not elsewhen, rejecting, perhaps, the entire Westphalian frame.

Finally, in homage to yet another IR theorist appreciated more outside of the North/West, is what we might think of as the Zhouian response, in deference to China's Zhou Enlai's famous reply to a question which may or may not have been put to him by one of the twentieth century's most overappreciated IR theorists, then US National Security Advisor Henry Kissinger. Almost certainly an apocryphal anecdote, the most common form of the story has Kissinger in the early 1970s asking Zhou, considered one of the twentieth century's most astute political observers, about the importance of France's 1789 revolution; Zhou's response was that it was too early to tell.[4] The IR version of this is that since we are, in essence, a young discipline and one still working things through and out, just be patient; we will get to you and if we (in the North/West) see some merit, we will invite you to join us.

And now our responses, in brief, to these three beguiling wise men.

(1) Settling with Churchill for what we have *does not give us the best of the worst*. It ignores how much good and interesting work is going on elsewhere which merits our attention and our education. This, by the way, is our responsibility, not theirs. They read us, no? Perhaps we should read them, and wonder how it is that it still remains 'us' and 'them'? It is tempting to blame the author, but perhaps it is the language itself, a human construct, after all, which needs to be interrogated.

(2) Starting from here with Waltz – the 'If not us, who?' option derived from Rabbi Hillel – overlooks a tentative answer: *maybe all of us*. We can (and have begun to) move beyond the *arboreal* model. There is no single, pre-existent pattern which we can explore from 'where we are.' We can (and should) recognize the utility of *rhizomic* models, or other such broader perspectives which seek to put more, not less, into play.

(3) We say to the apocryphal Zhou: *it is not too soon to tell.* We have seen, and tried to review in this book, the damage done. We believe that to continue to operate with an unnecessarily impoverished IR serves no one well. This is why we have endeavored here to offer one way – not *the* way, but *a* way – to 'fix' IR. This, of course, implicates us in the very sort of Northern/Western perspective we have been deriding for the past pages. We think we can duck that charge, but we are not unaware of the baggage we carry.

What we did (or tried to do) here

We began by raising the prospect of 'decentering' IR, moving it away from and beyond a discipline deeply rooted in and inevitably shaped by its North/West position. To this end we rehearsed 'the story of IR,' which is written from and for Northern/Western privilege and power, building around Agathangelou and Ling's (2004) insightful and compelling construction of IR as a house – one that at this point you might perhaps be willing to set on fire, much as firefighters sometimes use 'backburning' to fight larger conflagrations. Second, we called for enriching what we perceive as an impoverished IR that originates – in several senses, none helpful – in the North/West and persists in inserting, referencing, or gesturing towards itself. In this narcissistic project, it is the North/West who are the world's movers and shakers. Thus, it is incumbent upon 'us' to theorize the world and make sense of 'them' or 'those people' 'over there.' Finally, we began to invite our colleagues here and elsewhere, as well as you, into the conversation.

The four chapters that followed represent, we think, not so much the tip of an iceberg as the merest sampling of an ocean in which so much is current – so many ideas, and so many ways of rethinking our world and our community/ies and identity/ies. All of these have profound and serious implications and ramifications for how we can and should do IR. In our sample, it is possible to begin to discern an alternative approach, one that begins not from fiddling around the edges or seeking to soften the blows of the dominators. And if greater complexity only heightens the contradictions we face, that may serve us better than continuing to muddle along in search of 'satisficing' (Herbert Simon's 1947 conflation of sufficient and satisfactory, a delightful portmanteau term with a rather disappointing meaning; see Simon, 1997). As is clear by now, we believe it is time for a serious change, a step-level change, one which fundamentally reassesses IR's basic operating assumptions and decenters the entire enterprise.

Those people over there/back then, they're different: the exoticization and fetishization of 'others'

In the second chapter, on 'indigenous peoples' and our Northern/ Western fascination with and fantasies about them, we sought to do several things. It is imperative that IR scholars recognize that they are tourists (perhaps, at times, even at home, a conundrum beyond the scope of this project but undoubtedly worthy of time and attention), especially when they depart the congenial climes of the North/West for points beyond, interlopers in other people's worlds. To this end, and to set the stage for the project to come, we sought to problematize the concept of indigeneity, perhaps the most powerful centering concept in all of IR. By rejecting the premise that the US and Europe, the North/ West, is the fundamental (arguably, only) reference point and model, we can confront the 'usual' ways IR is done and loosen the powerful grip indigeneity has on the discipline, politics, and people's popular imagination.

Whose 'human' rights: when and where and how?

In the third chapter, on human rights, we tried to open up questions about who defines 'rights' and 'human,' or at least fully human – a not uncontested issue in the sometimes sordid history of IR. In the service of the state, IR scholars such as Henry Kissinger and Samuel Huntington have provided disturbing sustenance to policies and practices that contradict the very claims of 'human rights' central to Northern/Western self-conceptions. More disturbingly for those who see themselves at a remove from such policies and practices in the safe confines of the academy, it is nonetheless the case that both of these issues – who defines human rights and who is indeed human – have been used against billions. None of this is to deny what might be construed as some sort of ethical – not moral, but ethical – imperative to 'do something' when people are being suppressed, oppressed, and repressed. But we do need, desperately, to question such an impetus, which is what we endeavored to do here, and this requires a (deeply) critical stance on human rights.

All around the world

> The need of a constantly expanding market for its products chases the bourgeoisie over the entire surface of the globe. It must nestle everywhere, settle everywhere, establish connexions everywhere. (Marx and Engels, 2002: 223)

There may be no greater double-edged sword – an entirely appropriate image, we fear[5] – in IR than globalization. While people may indeed have a world to win – and, sadly, for billions, remarkably little to lose – and while there is profound and abiding appeal in the universal, the dangers of globalization are manifest and myriad and violent. The reality, a word we are deeply suspicious of and use warily, is that for the immense majority of the world's people – as a powerful US politician with absolutely no pretentions to IR scholarship once suggested – 'all politics is local' (O'Neill, 1993).[6] Indeed, the world we all live in is one of 'small worlds,' the places where we live our lives and make meaning of them. In these worlds and where they connect with the worlds of others, we would contend that the world is not flat (a claim that is hardly novel). Nor is there any inherent, definitional clash of cultures – which, to the extent that any such clashes can be identified, in any case must shift and change over time(s) and place. And, while we have been wary, too, of assuming that people elsewhere are somehow nobler or wiser, it is the case that people all around the world are making their worlds, their lives, meaningful and sustainable in ways that we are only now beginning to appreciate and explore.

International peace and violence: war and more

Have we seen the last of those 'white guys with ties talking about missile size'? There have been salutary shifts in notions of security, often framed now as 'human security,' but the propensity to center the discussion remains deeply embedded in North/West constructs of what security constitutes and who merits such security. There is much about the present debate that is admirable, making a critique even harder. But the problems are persistent and real. The greatest terrorists of the twentieth and twenty-first centuries – and long before – have been and remain states and their minions. It is necessary to ask the 'whose security' questions and also to foreground food and health and housing and education as security, along with readily defensible combat perimeters. And it is well past time for IR to confront its inherent peace deficit: What does peace mean beyond the absence of war, beyond the problems of simple violence? What would a peaceful world look like?

Doing decentered IR

Across all of these topics, we expect to meet with dispute (even denial), disapproval, and dismay. Okay. We certainly share the dismay, primarily about the state of a discipline we love (and, well, hate) and hope we have provided some possible ways to begin to think our way out of the box(es) we are in. While we recognize the academic imperative and know how this project is likely to be met, we hope our colleagues will recognize that arguing over whether we chose the right major areas to focus our attention on, fighting over details, or simply killing the messenger (assuming you think we have a message to deliver) will do little to further necessary discussions about the state of IR. We are well aware, to borrow from Bunce (1985) in a decidedly different context, that the the empire will strike back – and we are hardly even a rebel band, though the imagery may have some merit.

If we are a rebel band of sorts, or seeking to concoct one, we owe a debt of inspiration to one of the most intriguing movements of the late twentieth and early twenty-first century: Mexico's modern day Zapatistas, the EZLN (Zapatista National Liberation Army). Interestingly, these Zapatistas (as opposed to their early twentieth century counterparts) are sometimes appreciated as IR theorists, or at least are read that way by some of their admirers, a role and position they seem to reject. Indeed, even as they embrace their place in global justice movements their very core is the devolution of power back to communities at the local level. The Zapatistas might be honored to be seen as an inspiration, but they want no part of people elsewhere proclaiming themselves Zapatistas, and have urged people to focus on their own struggles and deal with them directly. In both guises they speak to us.

The default position in much of the social sciences, for reasons we are both sympathetic and open to, is to focus on what might be thought of as the 'big, large, huge' (Tilly, 1984); certainly it is possible to discern gargantuan elements in each of the areas we have focused on here. Rather than start from there, however, which is in effect to start from the center, our goal has been to start from nowhere, or perhaps everywhere, and recognize instead the myriad 'small worlds' (Brooks, DeCorse, and Walton, 2008), which are for all intents and purposes *our* worlds, the world of each of us, and hence the world(s) that matters most. Global perspectives and metanarratives rooted in the North/West and prone to replicate a centered perspective demand a one-world approach, albeit a world inevitably of hierarchy, patriarchy, domination, and control. By shifting – or, perhaps more than simply a shift; say, a shove – to the small and local we find ourselves forced to reconceptualize the world, to reconsider our notions, as Braudel did, of what seems to us, at first blush, upside down, inside out, or somehow just wrong, off. The 'large lessons' can and should be 'discovered in small worlds' (Brooks, DeCorse, and Walton, 2008). By moving away from – but note, not outside of, since such language maintains the very sort of dichotomization we seek to remedy – the domination of the center, we believe it is not only possible but absolutely preferable to find/develop/encourage and constitute an IR that is simultaneously everywhere and nowhere, and thus accessible to everyone.[7]

To paraphrase the compelling Zapatista question about democracy, 'Is this the IR you wanted?'[8] If we are to fundamentally reimagine the ontological presuppositions which have guided (and disciplined) IR, what better place to begin than by decentering IR? Such dramatic change does not simply come. It is made by real people living in an all too real world confronted with real and meaningful choices – and it is our obligation to honor and (re)present that; doing any less continues to deny them the very humanity we purport to share with them. As the Zapatistas contend, 'it is not necessary to conquer the world. It is sufficient to make it new. Us. Today.'[9]

Notes

Chapter One / Introduction

1 Agathangelou and Ling (2004) also examine IR in this three-fold manner.

2 Western liberal democracies originated in the eighteenth-century Enlightenment, and owe much to the revolutions in what would become the US and in France. See Selbin (2010) on the 'civilizing and democratizing' story of revolution that emerged from these events. The emerging prototypes helped to articulate political liberalism or constitutional protection of individual rights – particularly from the interference of governments. The concept of 'Western liberal democracy' as a form of government to emulate gained traction during the Cold War because of the contrast between capitalist liberal democracies in the US and Western Europe and communist 'people's republics.'

3 The Global South is a term that generally means formerly colonized and non-aligned (in the context of the Cold War) countries in Central and South America, Africa, South Asia, the Middle East, Oceania, and Southeast Asia, but many scholars include the fifteen so-called post-Soviet countries and territories (the Baltic states, Caucasus, Central Asia, and Eastern Europe), because they bear the brunt of Northern/Western economic policies as well as of Russia's hegemony (see Eichler, 2006). Others might include the countries that emerged with the break-up of the former Yugoslavia, as well as those classified as 'southeastern' Europe. There is, understandably, some confusion about which countries are 'southern' because of various means of categorization. For example, the United Nations uses the terminology 'Global South' to refer to those countries with 'medium' and 'low' human development indices, per the United Nations Development Programme; see, for example: http://tcdc.undp.org/doc/Forging%20a%20Global%20South.pdf. World Bank indicators classify countries in the Global South as less developed countries (LDCs) and heavily indebted poor countries (HIPCs). Another category is newly industrializing countries, such as South Korea, Singapore, Taiwan, and Hong Kong. For our purposes, we generally use Global South to refer to countries and places that are located outside of but have specific hierarchical power relationships with the so-called North/West – see notes 4 and 5. At the same time, we emphasize the need to

understand the different kinds of experiences various people might have – those living, for example, through the Chechen wars with Russia, under the military dictatorship in Myanmar/Burma, or in the Marshall Islands, have different kinds of relationships with the North/West, as well as with powerful actors within their regions.

4   The evocative, problematic, and somewhat controversial phrase 'white settler regime' captures those locales where the Europeans set up shop – that is, invaded and stayed. The most obvious examples would include what became the US but also Canada, Australia, New Zealand, and South Africa (particularly during its domination by Europeans and their descendants).

5   There are, of course, other countries that may read themselves as 'universal' or even as a part of the West. For example, see Arisaka (1997) regarding Japan. Also consider arguments that Israel is the only 'Western-style' liberal democracy in the Middle East.

6   If exactly *how* white were to be debated around the edges, particularly with regard to some of the southern Europeans, maleness would not be; it was a decidedly male enterprise in any number of ways, a dynamic of surprising (and regrettable) persistence.

7   Whether the twentieth century will come to be seen as 'short' (perhaps 1914–89) or 'long' (a case might be made for 1871–2001), most likely it will be framed as one of these: (1) 1898–1989, which would track from the US arrival on the world stage (and entry into neo-colonialism) and the collapse of 'Eastern Europe'; (2) 1905–2003, which might track from Japan's defeat of Russia and the failed revolutions in Russia and Iran to the US invasion of Iraq; (3) 1910–91, which would track from the advent of the Mexican Revolution (followed quickly by the Chinese) to the collapse of the Soviet Union.

8   Many engaged in IR as a form of knowledge, a discipline, and a practical field of politics may contest or disagree with the way Agathangelou and Ling posit the various theories in relationship to each other and the House. We are intrigued by the article's claims and encourage engagement with them. As such, we briefly describe what they mean by each of the terms/relationships and provide some examples of 'canonical' texts aligned with each school of thought. Also, for those readers who are unfamiliar with the questions and schools of thought that typically comprise IR studies, we recommend Weber (2009) and Edkins and Vaughan-Williams (2009). Edkins and Zehfuss (2009) provide a comprehensive overview of major questions and topics in this field.

9   Many of us are certainly aware that publication decisions, tenure, and other aspects of academic life can be affected by the kinds of research questions, epistemologies, and methodologies we use.

10   Ontology is the study of the nature of reality. As such, it deals with the fundamental presumptions about what exists (what is the world made of), how it exists, and, importantly, how to *categorize* existing things. Examples of ontological presumptions include whether one believes that social structures

determine human agency, or vice versa, or that there is a mutual constitutiveness, where structures and agents interact. Epistemology is the study of the nature of knowledge and the validity of knowledge claims. What is the nature of knowledge? How do we know what we know? Positivists, for example, believe that one can study the world based on information gathered 'outside' of oneself through objective assessment and the use of the 'scientific method.' Knowledge is 'out there' and to be acquired. Post-positivist epistemology assumes that what we know is contingent and not 'outside' of ourselves; we do not all 'know' the same reality, and we cannot separate the 'knower' and the 'known.'

11 Realism understands power (measured by capabilities, such as military capacity) as constituted by supposedly objective laws of self-interest. Realism would be the 'father,' as it is considered to be a 'founding' school of the discipline of IR, drawing upon the political theory of Hobbes, Machiavelli, and Thucydides. Realism as a set of theories as well as a form of statecraft recommends actions that signal virility and strength. Strong (and capitalist) states survive and triumph in a world of endless competition over resources through the tool of instrumental rationality. Realists see violence as a norm in international politics. To become familiar with realist IR thinkers, see work by E. H. Carr, Hans Morgenthau, Henry Kissinger, or George F. Kennan.

12 Liberalism and realism are similar because they both emerged out of colonial, capitalist contexts, with the former focusing on the market and the latter on the state. In terms of ontology, they believe in an autonomous individual subject with rational capacity to make choices. Liberalism's focus on preferences, democratic peace, free trade, interdependence, universal rights, and choices may seem diametrically opposed to realism's focus on relative gains, interests, survival, self-help, conflict, and war, but taken together, realism and liberalism both ensure control by certain individual and state actors over the rest of the world. Like the mother and father of a heteronormative household, liberalism and realism work together to govern the world. As such, the majority of the world's decisions are made by strong states engaging in realpolitik and free market liberalism. Liberal thinkers such as Kant and Locke provide inspiration to IR thinkers such as Hedley Bull.

13 Caretaking daughters make sure that everything in the House is in order, doing some of the labor that allows realism and liberalism to rule. They are 'good girls.' (Here it would be useful to see Cindy Weber's superb response (1994) to Robert Keohane's (1989) dismissal of feminism: she claims that he categorizes feminists as 'good girls,' or standpoint feminists, 'little girls,' or empirical feminists, and 'bad girls,' or postmodern feminists. One could also examine Francis Fukuyama's 'Women and the Evolution of World Politics' (1998) – which essentially argues that men are aggressive, women are peaceful, and feminists should really stop trying to change that – and the responses by Ling (2000) and Tickner (1999).) Neoliberalism brings together liberalism's economic cooperation with realism's focus on hegemonic stability, or the usefulness of one powerful country

providing order to the rest of the world. Neoliberalism emphasizes privatization, deregulation, the liberalization of trade, capital controls, and other mechanisms of economic sovereignty, the stripping down of welfare and social support programs, and the disempowerment of workers' rights, and de-emphasizes human rights, labor, environmentalism, etc., through the concerted actions of socio-political forces, including international organizations and institutions, that protect powerful countries' interests and economic practices. According to Agathangelou and Ling (2004: 25), standpoint feminism provides the additive function of (some) women's perspectives while leaving power relations undisturbed, because this strand of feminism equates gender with (mainly white, middle-class, Western) women; liberal feminism advances the myth of universalism (i.e. sisterhood is global, women's rights are human rights, etc.). We think that standpoint feminism and liberal feminism are both quite diverse and have contributed to women's rights movements around the world, but they are also often invested in 'saving' Third World women.

14 Neorealism is a 'bastard heir,' the offspring of a relationship not between realism and liberalism but realism and economics. (Agathangelou and Ling use the word 'bastard' to indicate 'anger due to a sense of robbed patriarchal entitlements . . . convey[ing] a desire on the part of the "illegitimate" son to receive recognition and acceptance from his biological father' (2004: 27, fn. 8).) Realists expect war to happen because of the nature of human beings; neorealists expect war, and conflict and competition for that matter, to happen because there is no world government (Weber, 2001: 16). Neorealists are not concerned with even the pretense of rights but with order. They see the world as an international market and states as firms, competing rationally in a zero-sum world for material resources like money and weapons, thus believing it is possible to strictly separate domestic and international politics. Rational-choice/neorealist theorists use positivist, economistic games such as the prisoner's dilemma to predict and forecast the decisions countries will make, assuming that only 'strong' countries matter in global politics. In the House, neorealism is waiting for realism to keel over and die so that it can take over as the primary school of thought and mode of diplomacy in IR. In other words, neorealism would like IR to focus more on certain economic theories. A key neorealist writer is Kenneth Waltz.

15 The way Agathangelou and Ling explain it, these schools of thought(s) are upstairs because they are sons born of the affair between *liberal (problem-solving) theory*, which is committed to atomistic ontology, positivist epistemology, and a view of world order as a 'given' with problems to be solved, and *critical theory*, which challenges the 'naturalness' of the world order. Marxist IR's focus on dependency theory and world systems theory, Gramscian IR's emphasis on the role of hegemony (i.e. maintaining control not just through political and economic coercion but also ideologically) in international political economy, postmodern IR's focus on the production of knowledge, and pragmatic/

liberal constructivism IR's focus on the construction of state identity and the role of norms, have all offered serious theoretical and empirical challenges to mainstream realist and liberal IR theory. They are certainly 'rebellious': Marxist IR (Immanuel Wallerstein) and Gramscian IR (see Robert Cox) challenge capitalism; postmodern and poststructural thought (James der Derian and Richard Ashley, for example) confront the influence of the Enlightenment, and thus the fiction of the 'free, rational, and private individual' (Agathangelou and Ling 2004: 27); and constructivism (see Alexander Wendt) argues that state interests, described by realists, and preferences, described by liberals, are not given but emerge through interactions and social relationships. Duvall and Varadarajan (2003) are among those who make a distinction between realism, liberalism, and mainstream constructivism, on the one hand, and critical theory, on the other; they eloquently illustrate how the former set of theories have grossly mischaracterized and simplified critical theory and are invested in current, hierarchical relationships of power. Thus, in looking at these theories, while Agathangelou and Ling (2004) would claim that they still rely on Anglocentric thinkers and concepts, Duvall and Varadarajan (2003) make a distinction between the 'modernist' and 'postmodernist' strands within critical theory. For example, they would classify Marxist and Gramscian IR as 'modernist' critical theory because they challenge the given order but also have particular projects of emancipation; postmodern/poststructural theories reject 'foundationalism,' with a focus on unmasking how structures and practices relate and operate (Duvall and Varadarajan, 2003: 83). And there are both liberal and critical strands of constructivism. However, we assert that (1) critical theories, while challenging those in positions of power, can often replicate and draw upon 'centered' ways of doing IR, and (2) critical theories in IR have not gone far enough in taking seriously various feminist and queer theories.

16 These 'fallen daughters' are quite estranged from the House's center, as they show how IR privileges a particular colonial, heteronormative, and patriarchal order (Agathangelou and Ling, 2004: 29–30). Weber's work *Faking It* (1999) is an excellent and compelling example of queering IR.

17 The native informants are non-Western, non-'white' sources of knowledge, 'allowed' into the House as pure, non-threatening outsiders who can 'supplement' mainstream theories. They do the labor of collecting the 'thick descriptions' of the cultures studied in classrooms and think tanks in the West, but they don't challenge Western power.

18 Asian capitalism, the bastard ward, results from combining liberalism and Confucian world order: a combination of capitalist, market development with collective institutions and social hierarchies. Perhaps this school of thought/ perspective could have had a more prominent role in the House, but the so-called East Asian financial collapse confirmed the center's presumptions about corruption in the 'East.' Asian capitalists are a 'ward'– they do not quite matter after their 'failure,' but they are tolerated.

19   The 'bastard twins,' peripheral and transitional economies, result from
      neoliberalism conjoining in odd ways with socialism, particularly in the cases
      of China and Russia, resulting in realist state policies (with aggressive national
      security imperatives) combined with the incorporation of select neoliberal
      economic policies. Peripheral and transitional economies, sometimes called the
      'second world,' continue to be viewed with suspicion, however, by the West due
      to the violence that emerges as a result of the transitions (Agathangelou and
      Ling, 2004: 32).

20   Orientalism is a Western, ideological project that constructs the Self through
      negating the Other. See Said (1979) for an extended discussion. This project
      doesn't propose policies but underwrites the us–them distinctions that we find
      in a multitude of theories.

21   As Agathangelou and Ling (2004) explain, Al Qaeda has learned from neorealism-
      neoliberalism (think of the role of the CIA and narco-trafficking) and is reliant
      on and exists in many ways thanks to Western power (especially through Osama
      bin Laden's businesses) but insists on challenging the North/West center of IR.

22   Postcolonial IR is an extended examination of the intimate relationship between
      Self and Other, focusing on what we can understand about race, class, gender,
      and nation within countries that were formerly colonized, as well as between
      the 'center' and so-called developing world, or Global South. These countries,
      we would add, negotiate their complicated relationships with the West, as well
      as the legacies of colonialism, anti-colonial struggles, and conflict over what it
      would mean to become 'Westernized,' 'modernized,' or 'developed.' Furthermore,
      postcolonial IR encompasses both modernist and postmodernist strands of critical
      thought, by including not only the struggles against domination and colonial
      legacies but also deconstruction of universalism (Duvall and Varadarajan, 2003:
      84). We would also emphasize that feminist postcolonial theory has a specific focus
      on how colonial, anti-colonial, and 'post'-colonial projects essentialize norms of
      gender, sex, and sexuality as they intersect with racialization.

23   Worldism goes even further than postcolonial IR. As Agathangelou and Ling
      propose, worldism presumes that we exist in multiple worlds that live 'through
      us'. It questions IR's 'foundations ["power and interest"], its borders ["in versus
      out"], the presumed identities of its members ["legitimate versus illegitimate"],
      their normative values ["good versus bad"], and asymmetrical positionings ["up
      versus down"]' (2004: 34–5).

24   Many might think of poststructural critical theory with the term 'decentering.'
      Decentering the subject requires a shift from the Enlightenment subject, the
      'unified individual with a center, an inner core that was there at birth and
      developed as the individual grew' to a sociological subject, one that is formed
      in social relation with others and through mediation of multiple cultural
      worlds, to a postmodern subject, with no fixed or essential identity (Edkins,
      1999: 21). To decenter is to critique but also unravel the atomistic, rational
      subject that underlies liberal politics. Accordingly, if subjectivity is never 'pre-

existing,' instead continuously formed and constituted in relation to how we are represented or produced, then what matters are representational practices and the production of knowledge.

25   Regarding the term 'provincializing,' see Chakrabarty's *Provincializing Europe* (2000). He argues that a 'mythical,' imaginary Europe that seems to transcend space and time is often taken as the starting point of modernity. However, there are specific histories behind European experiences with capitalism and the nation-state that cannot be universalized or generalized either for Europe or for other parts of the world. Thus one must be willing to see the limits of 'secular universals.' However, as Muppidi (2010) points out, universalizing narratives that 'center' Europe are persistent and difficult to disrupt, thus compelling him to pose an anti-colonial rather than postcolonial politics and scholarship.

26   Based on Meghana's recollections when attending the panel, 'Global Development Eminent Scholar Panel Honoring Mahmood Mamdani' at the International Studies Association Conference, New York City, New York, 17 February 2009.

27   The India China Knowledge and Capacity Building Institute (affiliated with the New School in New York) and Jacqueline Ala's project to create a curriculum of African international relations at the University of the Witswatersrand in South Africa both challenge 'canonical' IR. They do so by focusing particularly on marginalized issues and populations within those countries. The India China initiative, for example, is an attempt to build a trilateral curriculum between New School, University of Calcutta in India, and Yunnan University in Kunming to rethink Sino-Indian relations through an examination of the populations of northeast India and southwest China. Such an endeavor is not uncomplicated, but the potential payoff is intriguing.

28   We have long known that much that is designated 'fact,' not least societally sanctioned versions of history bolstered by 'official' government (and other) documents, are often little more than thinly veiled fictions in which 'fact' is that which serves the purpose(s) of the author(s) and/or their benefactor(s). There is little about either history or memory or any other 'socially embedded activity' that is 'objective.' Stephen Jay Gould, one of the most influential natural scientists of the late twentieth century, rejected the notion of absolute objectivity: 'Science, since people must do it, is a socially embedded activity. It progresses by hunch, vision, and intuition. Much of its change through time does not record a closer approach to absolute truth, but the alteration of cultural contexts that influence it so strongly. Facts are not pure and unsullied bits of information; culture also influences what we see and how we see it. Theories, moreover, are not inexorable inductions from facts. The most creative theories are often imaginative visions imposed upon facts; the source of imagination is also strongly cultural'. Gould's view should not be misread: 'I do not ally myself with . . . the purely relativistic claim that scientific change only reflects the modification of social contexts, that truth is a meaningless notion outside cultural assumptions, and that science can therefore provide no enduring answers. . . . I share the credo of my colleagues

... that a factual reality exists and that science, though often in an obtuse and erratic manner, can learn about it' (Gould, 1981: 21–2).

29   Email conversation, Simona Sharoni, with Meghana, 20 February 2009.

30   Email conversation, Cynthia Weber, with Meghana, 20 February 2009.

31   Based on Meghana's recollections when attending the panel, 'Diversity and the Teaching of International Relations' at the International Studies Association Conference, New York City, New York, 15 February 2009.

Chapter Two / Indigeneity

1   The interview is quoted in: http://www.utalkmarketing.com/Pages/Article. aspx?ArticleID=12420&Title=Tourism Australia_steers_clear_of_controversy.

2   The story of Northern/Western civilization, very much on the arboreal model, is rooted in the 'familiar' Greco-Roman-(Judeo-)Christian basis of 'Western' culture. 'Western culture, so the story goes (and many of us have a rather disconcerting amount invested in it), is a distinctive and distinguished complement of arts, science(s), political practices, and philosophical and religious principles which set it apart from other civilizations; accurate or not, the story has been pervasive for hundreds of years, carried far and wide by conquest, colonialism, imperialism, neocolonialism, neo-imperialism, and globalization. In this tale, civilization and democracy first emerge among the Greeks, are modified by the Romans, and added to in critical ways by the Hebrew Bible, particularly as it comes to be read by a set of Christians in central Europe' (Selbin, 2010: 96–114).

3   Similar, if less common, invocations of Sun Tzu's sixth century BCE thoughts on military strategy, *The Art of War* (2009), are also meant to steep the field in antiquity.

4   Both of which Tilly (1985) intriguingly contends are a form of 'organized crime.'

5   The Peace of Westphalia treaties, signed on 15 May (Osnabrück) and 24 October (Münster), ended both the Thirty Years War in the Holy Roman Empire and the Eighty Years War between Spain and the Netherlands.

6   To take what might seem an innocuous example, consider the universalization of a convenient and even convivial set of categories which simply sort the world and its ways. So first there are big, broad categories such as African, Asian, or Arab, but smaller ones as well: these people are Rwandan and those Burundi; people living in what the North/West dubbed 'Australia' before the Europeans invaded are called 'Aborigines' and their conquerors (if those who came and took over can be called such) 'Australians'; the people who inhabited what Europeans christened (perhaps more to the point, baptized) 'the Americas' were called 'Indians,' due to a combination of geographic confusion and ethnocentrism – more recently these 'Indians' have been called 'indigenous,' 'first peoples,' 'first nations,' or 'aboriginal.'

7   And hence implicitly contrasted with the 'dead' or 'failed' traditions of the indigenous.

8 Though at least some of those who make such concessions ('mistakes were made') still see a vital and proper role for imperialist and neocolonial policies, particularly to be exercised by the United States. See such notable neoconservative and liberal imperialist scholars as Boot (2002), Johnson (2001), and Ferguson (2003).

9 More recently, Eastern Band Cherokee Hawk Littlejohn asked, 'Who can own the land? The land lives its own life and provides for us all. It cannot be bought or sold or won in war like trade beads or moccasins' (Crowe, 2001).

10 Development, in this sense, is *vis-à-vis* those who have arrived, whose level of development is, arguably, fairly arbitrarily assigned and, of course, based on Northern/Western assumptions about what constitutes 'development.' More on this in Chapter 4.

11 With regard to the undermining, he cites 'the normative scholar Paul Keal (2003).'

12 José Martínez Cobo, Special Rapporteur of the Sub-Commission on Prevention of Discrimination and Protection of Minorities.

13 The Report can be read in full at: http://www.treatycouncil.org/PDFs/CERD_US_Indigenous_Shadow_Report%20amended.pdf.

14 Email interview, Brenda Norrell, with Meghana, 26 August 2009.

15 Like other feminist theories, native/indigenous feminism is not monolithic. See, in particular, the special issue of *Wicazo Sa Review*, Vol. 24, No. 2 (Fall 2009).

16 Interestingly, Xhosa and other Bantu tribes often reference themselves as indigenous or native to Africa, given the long-standing resistance to white Afrikaner revisionist history that proclaimed the settlers to be the true inheritors of South African land. At the same time, however, Khoikhoi and San peoples inhabited the land before some Bantu migrations. Who, in this context, is 'indigenous'?

17 Cokie Roberts, anchor for ABC's *This Week*, 10 August 2008. Others joined in with comments such as 'foreign,' and 'out of touch with Americans.'

18 This point references Walt Whitman's poem, 'I Hear America Singing.'

19 Johnson (2001: 2, fn.): 'There is no graceful ethno-racial nomenclature for describing either south Texas or the border region as a whole . . . I . . . use "Mexican" to refer to Mexican nationals with no deep roots in the United States, "Tejano" or "Texas-Mexican" to refer to Texas residents of Mexican descent and "ethnic Mexicans" to subsume both groups. The label "Mexican American" is reserved for those of Mexican descent who considered themselves to be US citizens. . . . "Anglo," following the common practice in Texas, refers to Euro-Americans not of Mexican descent. It is a more useful term than "white" because many Tejanos were in fact very light in complexion and in some circumstances considered themselves "white." Racial and ethnic categories present themselves as natural and commonsensical . . . [but] they are the products of history rather than the inherent or immutable properties of groups of people – how else could it be that a "white" woman can give birth to a "black" child, but the reverse

is impossible under American racial terminology? I . . . use the term "racial" to describe conflicts between Anglos and ethnic Mexicans not to impute a biological basis to early twentieth-century social distinctions, but . . . to capture the deep social gulf that . . . separate(d) the two groups.'

20   The concept of 'tribe' in the Israeli-Palestinian conflict is particularly interesting because Semitic tribes encompassed both Arabs and Jews. We foreground the concept of *tribal* loyalties because many of the discourses around the presumable convictions of an Israeli or a Jew or a Palestinian center around something ancient, indigenous, long-standing, connected to land, a bounded nation of peoples.

21   Butler (2004: 113–14) comments: 'There are sources of American Jewish identification, for instance . . . in civil rights and social justice struggles that may exist in relative independence from the question of the status of Israel. What do we make of Jews, including myself, who are emotionally invested in the state of Israel, critical of its current form, and call for a radical restructuring of its economic and juridical basis precisely because they are so invested? Is it always possible to say that such Jews do not know their own best interests, that such Jews turn against other Jews, that such Jews turn against their own Jewishness?'

22   Shulman speaks about a 'Jewish past with its dead voices whispering in my memory. "Bind the wounds. Heal the sick. Don't forget you were slaves. To save one person is to save a world. Don't be afraid. All that lives is holy. Forgive. Wake up. Shake off the dust and stand up. Feed the hungry. Bring the poor into your home. Cover the naked. Break their chains." Did I invent these voices? They seem to speak from a buried, dreamlike domain, as distant and insistent as childhood. It is nothing to be right, and a true disaster to be righteous, but it is everything to do what you can' (2007: 212).

23   Email interview, Emelia Markovich, with Meghana, 17 October 2009.

24   Email interview, Or Ben David, with Meghana, 9 October 2009.

25   Email interview, Efi Brenner, with Meghana, 8 October 2009.

26   Hussein Ibish offers an interesting analysis of various Palestinian positions on the two-state solution in his *What's Wrong with the One-State Agenda?* (2009). In particular, he challenges the strategic usefulness of the politics of 'demography,' and outlines why it's in the best interest of both Palestinians and Israelis, of various political positions, to promote the two-state solution.

27   Interview, Ora Wise, with Meghana, 17 September 2009, Brooklyn, New York. Ora suggested that readers visit http://youthsolidarity.net and http://indigenous delegation.wordpress.com for a better sense of the kinds of creative projects in which the delegates engaged.

28   Email interview, Nathalie Handal, with Meghana, 3 December 2009.

Chapter Three / Human Rights

1 Email interview, Nathalie Handal, with Meghana, 3 December 2009.

2 This propensity blithely ignores that, as Selbin (2010: 98–9) argues, 'the Greeks' were diverse and ensconced in hundreds of city-states around the region, and much that we associate with them is derived from what we know of Athens. The modern conceit in the North/West is that our notions of democracy derive from Athens. Yet it merits mention that democracy was suspect at best and associated with threats of mob rule. Indeed, Aristotle saw it 'as a perverted form of government . . . likely inevitable and . . . better than an oligarchy or tyranny, [but] . . . in practice it would be a disaster, the rule of the needy who have neither the time nor inclination.' Athens's democracy was exclusive (male citizens only), direct, and, some distinctive features (such as ostracism) aside, readily recognizable in its form and format, and a plausible base from which Northern/Western liberal bourgeois democracy may be dated.

3 On these 'civilizing and democratizing' revolutions, see Selbin (2010: 96–114), who also suggests the French case is more commonly read as the first great social revolution (*ibid.*: 118–25).

4 But see Ishay (2007) for examples of non-Western human rights texts and documents.

5 For an explicit challenge to the Northern/Western stranglehold on human rights, with the aim of integrating North–South dialogue, see the work of North–South XXI, at: http://sites.google.com/site/nordsudxxi/.

6 It would be many years before often grudging recognition was accorded the Nazi's unrelenting attacks on homosexuals, Romanies, the mentally ill, the disabled, and others.

7 To this end, Kathryn Sikkink offers a unique and compelling analysis of why countries incorporate human rights in foreign policy, showing that states are performing sovereignty when they do so, thus getting us past the stale 'sovereignty versus human rights' debate (2004: 6).

8 The existence of the International Tribunal of the Far East is all the more interesting because of the focus by those who had fought the Japanese on war crimes but silence on many other issues, such as the Allies' crimes, comfort women, sexual violence, the number of Chinese killed, and other issues that fail to get much attention when discussing atrocities during World War Two.

9 We recommend Campbell (1998a) to help understand the break-up of the former Yugoslavia. Ramet's book (2005) is useful for its long list of references. Rather than present a narrative about the players and who did what, we prefer to encourage readers to use the questions we pose as a point of entry into the vast complexities of these wars and this particular region.

10 Relevant for this discussion is an analysis of Hegel's master–slave dialectic and whether he was referencing Haiti in any of his work, in Fischer (2004: 26–33).

11 Such fear is evident in the words of Simón Bolívar, South America's famed nineteenth century 'Liberator' who led the independence struggles against Spain

but also wrote that 'a slave insurrection was "a thousand times worse than a Spanish invasion"'(McAuley, 1997: 174).

12   Accordingly, we have been following the various debates about whether the US is participating in an aid mission or a militarized intervention/occupation.

13   In a story well known both in the English-speaking Caribbean and among Britain's 'martial' peoples (Gurkhas, Kenyans, and southern African troops who have done much fighting and dying for them), on 17 December 1918 fifty-plus West Indian sergeants fighting as part of British forces in Europe organized the 'Caribbean League.' With members from British Guiana in the south and west to the Bahamas in the north and east, and most places in between, the League demanded self-determination for the Caribbean and pledged to organize a general strike or more when they got home. In 1919, several did, most notably in Trinidad and Belize. See, among others, James (1999: 63–4).

14   Dr King's speeches, including this one, are available widely in multiple texts and online.

15   It is crucial to note how various thinkers are 'written out,' not only of human rights analysis, but also of various disciplines or, more broadly, academia. Consider, for example, how the University of Michigan denied tenure to Andrea Smith, author of numerous books and articles about the intersection of indigeneity, feminism, and violence and co-founder of INCITE! Women of Color Against Violence and the Chicago chapter of Women of All Red Nations.

16   These remarks are widely available online and elsewhere. See http://www.nytimes.com/2007/10/06/us/nationalspecial3/06interrogate.html?_r=2&scp=1&sq=%E2%80%9CThis%20government%20does%20not%20torture%20people,%E2%80%9D&st=cse or http://www.cnn.com/2007/POLITICS/10/05/bush.torture/index.html.

17   Sikkink (2004), while committed to a different kind of political project about human rights, points out that we cannot easily dismiss human rights as necessarily disciplinary or imperial. She notes that the 'key protagonists' of the global human rights movement were located outside of the US, particularly in Latin American countries, and developed 'principled' ideas in reaction to colonialism or US-sponsored state repression.

18   This does not mean that Citgo has not come under fire in the US, nor does it mean that we should not think critically about the relationship between the US and Venezuela. As a result of anger by citizen groups and some politicians, Citgo launched a 'social responsibility' campaign, and Joseph Kennedy, chairman of Citizens Energy, aired ads in the US with Americans thanking Venezuela and Citgo. See also: http://www.citgo.com/WebOther/CommunityInvolvement/HeatingHomesWarmingHearts.pdf for an example of how Citgo describes its work.

19   Email interview, Omer Shah, with Meghana, 20 June 2009.

20   Email interview, Omer Shah, with Meghana, 20 June 2009.

21   The Portuguese first called the city Bombaim, which the British later Anglicized

to Bombay. In 1995, the name was changed to the Marathi pronunciation of 'Mumbai' because of the insistence by right-wing Hindu nationalists, namely the Shiv Sena political party, on the need to reclaim India as a *Hindu* country/ nation and to promote the Marathi language in Bombay and the state of Maharashtra. Because of the violent, chauvinistic, and exclusionary politics of Shiv Sena in renaming Mumbai and attempted desecularizing of the city, many continue to call the city Bombay.

22 See the discussion in the April 2008 issue of the *International Judicial Monitor*, at http://www.judicialmonitor.org/archive_0408/asilsidebar.html.

23 The full report is available here: http://www.un.org/News/dh/sudan/com_inq_darfur.pdf.

24 See the 2001 letter 'Report of the Panel of Experts on the Illegal Exploitation of Natural Resources and Other Forms of Wealth of the Democratic Republic of the Congo,' from the Secretary-General to the President of the Security Council at http://www.un.org/News/dh/latest/drcongo.htm.

25 Another seemingly *non sequitur* charge from Kristof is that he saw 'missionaries and diamond-buyers, warlords and US peacekeepers, but never a US colonist of any kind' (2009). This is a bizarre claim, considering the complexities of colonialism, much less the ability to identify a 'colonist.'

26 There is a vast variety of feminist theories. There are standpoint, postcolonial, poststructural, queer, liberal, and radical feminisms, for a start. Some feminists see queer theory as separate, while others see that queer and feminist concerns necessarily go 'together' because of the mutual concern with sex, gender, and sexuality. We try to be precise about how the theorists/activists identify themselves. Even the term 'queer' is controversial, depending on whether one may identify as gay or queer, because of debates over what queer theory and activism should or should not entail, or because some gay activism has not adequately addressed transphobia, for example. We acknowledge that the terms themselves are inadequate, imprecise, and flawed.

27 In the case of India, for example, many feminists were surprised when right-wing Hindu nationalist political parties started to mobilize scores of women in the 1990s. How is it, they asked, that larger numbers of women would take to the streets to fight for nationalism rather than to protest patriarchy (Nayak, 2003)? However, Indian women's networks and Hindu nationalists both used gender violence to mobilize women to fight patriarchy, in the first instance, and to support Hindu political parties, in the second instance. The latter were successful in blaming and deflecting the existence of gender violence onto threats, such as Muslims writ large, to India (Nayak, 2003).

28 Feminists and queer activists may also lend themselves purposely to cooptation, because they seek to use a feminist lens to 'expose' something about which they claim to have an 'insider' view. Take, for example, Irshad Manji, gay, feminist, Canadian author of *The Trouble with Islam* (2003). While many have embraced her for telling ugly 'truths' about her religion and others have viewed her as

a traitor, still others are troubled by the implications of her interpretations, particularly given her reception by the Northern/Western press. The *New York Times* described her as 'Osama bin Laden's worst nightmare,' perhaps because she claims she is trying to reconcile her faith in Allah with her love of freedom – implying that the two need to be reconciled, in a way that Jesus or Yahweh or Buddha and freedom might not. Azar Nafisi, an American woman of Iranian origin, documents her experiences teaching middle-class, urban Iranian women about Western literature in *Reading Lolita in Tehran* (2004), a book heralded by US neoconservatives Fouad Ajami and Bernard Lewis as allowing readers to 'understand' the situation of Iranian women (Bahramitash, 2008: 105). The way these 'native informants' have been eagerly consumed warns us that we should be careful about how we frame, consciously or not, our social justice and human rights talk.

29 Hamid Dabashi, author of *Iran: A People Interrupted*, notes that the overwhelming majority were not well-off but rather unemployed youths 'who cannot even afford to rent an apartment, let alone marry and raise a family and join the middle class in a principally oil-based economy that is not labor-intensive to begin with.' Other supporters included war veterans with no respect for incumbent Ahmadinejad's policies but 'unsurpassed admiration' for Hussein Mousavi's role as prime minister during the 1980s war with Iraq. See Dabashi's commentary at: http://www.cnn.com/2009/WORLD/meast/06/22/dabashi.iran.myths/index.html.

30 We attribute this observation to Rabab Adulhadi, based on her comments at a panel entitled 'Feminist Research, Pedagogy and Activism after 9/11,' International Studies Association Conference, New York, 15 February 2009.

31 While Partition officially occurred in 1947, the 'two-nation' ideas emerged and found traction over a period of time during British colonialism. Partition continues to be invoked by citizens, particularly those separated from their family members, and by India and Pakistan, during the wars between the two countries, communal riots, the Kashmir situation, and peace efforts.

32 Email interview, Tehila Wise, with Meghana, 2 September 2009.

33 Email interview, Tehila Wise, with Meghana, 2 September 2009.

34 We reproduce the entire poem here:

When my ink spills its lyrical libations
So I guess my lines are wine that you're tasting
One drop for that name you forgot but through your veins their blood is racing
One drop for the names you're not taught cuz the past they're steadily erasing
My verse is a whole glass I crush and put the days in
Then spread
Not just for those that are dead
For those imprisoned
For souls not yet envisioned

For the minds that aren't fed
Cuz I see it as a duty
To let any voice that's been stripped mute speak through me
So when I wake and fill my lungs it's whose tongue will I be today that's the question
Pressing against your consciousness – that's the teeth
The sound released
I move as a message
So when I spit at open mic my words come with a whole guest list
Not cocky or restless when I say these gems are precious
Cuz they were handed to me
Entrusted, gold-crusted with my contribution
The minerals that made them are the millions
The tech needed to wreck them would cost billions
Each time I wrote I soaked up the stories, the horrors and glories
The silence screaming from my history books
Though they were full of anecdotes
Each time I wrote I soaked up the time we all lost believing our sins put Jesus on the cross
And why to me that even mattered
While every year one in four women get raped and even more get battered
When they preach they don't teach how AIDS got unleashed
Priest or rabbi
It's a lie if they tell you Darfur is genocide and sit silently watching Iraqis die
While the funding gets bigger to back triggers that turn people into numbers and figures
Blinded
But then I'm narrow-minded
When I expose that, though it's been a while, for a black man on trial today the gavel can be the same as a rope
Each time I wrote I soaked up the hope
The vision, the precision of quiet riots to get someone to listen
Of movement
After being kept from walking so long realizing you have legs is an improvement
So many voices I gotta spit fast to avoid getting choked
Each time I wrote I soaked up
And now I spill
Over their borders, onto my pages
Fuck them defining time I spill into ancient ages
Give the Nile's current a push, visit Kush, get feedback from real sages
This shit is contagious
Call it what it is

Cuz if you ain't healthy then you're ill
If you're not moving you're standing still
I spill something real that you can feel
Cuz for so long we've been isolated
Thought it was each other that we hated
The fight faded into the shadow of a thrill
Now captivated cuz I spill
Pen-points dripping hemlock
I even drop my points like stock in the lingo of Dow Jones
These poems are 747 Boeings
Ignorance's frame just got melted by my mental plane
To this day I spill for every person told to pray
Instead of make solutions with their own ten fingers
Steered not towards scholars but towards singers
The thought still lingers
That some decades ago my flow would be useless, my use nothing more than a cook
the first time I was told it's not intelligence it's looks
And I love my faith but I turned to books
To fill in the spaces not covered by the Bible
Soaked each word spoke
Then I unlocked
Some shocks are small waves but this one was tidal
Yet still wanna fit me in a title
Claimed it was suicidal
When I stripped gender from my bones, gay and straight from my heart, fat and thin from my skin
But more importantly I stripped them from within
For once felt alive
I had defied their lie
Put no adjective before my pride
I had cried too much cuz the point I had missed
They don't run this
And like Columbus
They did not discover me
Their lines on maps and railroad tracks will never cover me
I won't be left standing with some beads in my palm and my land is gone
Cuz they won't steal my name, reduce me to a Disney movie or song
But
I wasn't born strong
I was made
Path paved by others who have walked this way
I am a tribute, a monument, an anthem

To a person, thought, idea
Never awarded a street, college, or grant from
Those who wished we would disappear
if they prove our mortality through assault on our flesh
Our words they never heard spoken
Because we were moving
When I spill I'm proving scientific theory
Hear me
The water in me has always been there
Even if at one point its form was air
That I did not breathe
Because when a soul leaves it offers a space to be filled
Takeover looms – the masses enter the room
When I spill
(Tehila Wise, 'Spill')

Chapter Four / Globalization

1   See explanation in Chapter 1, fn. 2.
2   Industrialized society is essentially predicated upon mass production and, concomitantly, mass consumption. Post-industrialized states are those in which the service sector of the economy is dominant, and information processing and technology crucial – Japan, Germany, the US, and the Scandinavian countries are oft-cited examples. The concept derives from Bell (1973); see also Ritzer (2007).
3   Selbin has argued elsewhere that '(1) the (putative) "Washington Consensus" . . . had little to do with Washington and far more to do with global capital markets, and the "consensus" was largely among elites in Latin America and the Caribbean and North America; (2) The "Washington Consensus" trope, in any case, quickly turned from more narrow (wide repercussions aside) neoliberal economic "reforms" championed by those in the United States to political "reforms" based on the United States' model of Western liberal democracy and social "reforms" and expectations rooted in the United States' socio-political and cultural milieu; (3) Despite the relative lack of attention by politicians, the popular press, and many academics, even at the height of the "Washington Consensus" millions of people in Latin America and the Caribbean dissented, engaging in acts of everyday resistance and even rebellion, though these were commonly read by those in the North and their regional allies/minions as either nearly inexplicable actions of scared and confused people or "last gasps" of recalcitrant "cold warriors" foolishly resisting the inevitable (and obviously salutary) neoliberal tide which would lift all boats' (2007: 33).
4   Our two concerns here are similar, in certain ways, to those of the Transnationalism Project at the Center for International Studies, University of Chicago. Towards the end of developing new theoretical frameworks for examining globalization

and transnational movements, they look at (1) 'global governance,' specifically the 'multiplication of cross-border governance mechanisms,' or how various global regimes, national laws, international laws, and informal and private systems intersect, and the various 'democracy deficits' that arise: see http://transnationalism.uchicago.edu/gov.html; (2) migration patterns linked to economic conditions, economic 'bridges' between rich and poor countries, increased immigration to supplement depleted workforces in Western Europe and Japan, and restrictions on immigration: see http://transnationalism.uchicago.edu/migration.html.

5   The ILO creates and ratifies international law regarding labor rights and standards. Core labor standards include conventions 29, 87, 98, 100, 105, 111, and 138. The US has ratified 105, regarding forced labor. However, 105 references Convention 29 (which the US has not signed), which details that prison labor for private purposes is against international law. Kang (2009) explains that because of the 105 reference to 29, the US is legally bound to these standards.

6   In 2002, as Hindu nationalist volunteers (those challenging the secularism of India and the supposed 'takeover' by Muslims by proclaiming that Indians must articulate an allegiance to the Hindu nation in order to authentically be a part of the country) were traveling by train in Gujarat, a state in India, a carriage caught on fire. The next day, upon allegations that a 'Muslim mob' had started the fire, Hindu nationalists slaughtered and raped Muslims. But this was no spontaneous 'outburst'; Hindu nationalists were well armed and had names and addresses of Muslims, compiled well before the attacks, indicating months of careful planning and thought. Government leaders, particularly Chief Minister Narendra Modi, were both complicit and grossly negligent in addressing the violence. See also the film *Final Solution*, directed by Rakesh Sharma, for a narration of these events.

7   For more on the role of diasporas in peace processes, see http://www.diaspora-centre.org/DOCS/PILPG_Engaging_Dia.pdf.

8   Email interview, Roohi Choudhry, with Meghana, 2 June 2009.

9   Email interview, Roohi Choudhry, with Meghana, 2 June 2009.

10 Imagine what the world would look like if, rather than *tracing*, which is what modern borders (and maps) do, there was a genuine effort to *map*. For Deleuze and Guattari (1987: 12) this would mean trying to 'contact with the real' rather than reproducing the un/conscious real of the North/West. Perhaps it would involve trying to forget maps even exist. The Situationists' theory of the *dérive* may point to another way to decenter (see Debord, 2006). The *dérive* is a sort of passive, drifting movement through society and culture. Yet, at its base, the concept reflects the intention consciously to regard your environment without preconceptions, prepared to see what you have not seen previously and imagine and accept the (im)possible.

11 Gayatri Spivak's seminal piece, 'Can the Subaltern Speak' (1988), helped to

define the Subaltern Studies collective, which sought to intervene in South Asian historiography that neglects and erases 'history from below,' from the standpoint of the subaltern. For Gramsci, the subaltern is any person/group in the 'less powerful' position in hierarchical power relationships. Subaltern Studies examine the subaltern, say, the 'masses,' as agents of change and resistance.

12   Grovogui (2001) argues that the 1991 collapse of the Soviet Union, with the resulting 'end' of the Cold War and alleged inevitability of neoliberal globalization and US hegemony (remember: 'there is no alternative'), has affected IR theory so profoundly that 'comparative analysts have rid themselves of the theories of imperialism, dependency, uneven development, and others that once sought to explain the political and institutional context of late-modern inequities between states, nations, classes, and genders' (*ibid.*: 425). Instead, they rely upon the inevitability of 'civilizational attainments, cultural dispositions, and work ethics' rather than an analysis of 'social relations, power, and the nature of material transactions among entities' to understand justice. Grovogui's thesis sets the stage for showing how, through what might be deemed 'globalization talk,' IR theory 'compares' levels of development as if it is some sort of objective enterprise with impartial measures – and usually without any sort of rigorous and systematic investigation. In some cases, this brings back unfortunate memories of the unpleasant years (1950s and 1960s) when comparative politics all too often resorted to sordid and unhelpful 'cultural explanations.'

13   It is interesting in this regard to note the fascination in the US in the late twentieth and early twenty-first century with how the Irish (Ignatiev, 1995) and Jews (Brodkin, 1998) 'became white,' whether Italians are white (Guglielmo and Salerno, 2003), and how immigrants to the US work to become white (Roediger, 2006). This is also a salutary reminder that in the US being 'American' remains in no small part defined by one's literal and figurative 'whiteness.'

14   Based on our conversations with people who work on projects affiliated with the World Bank, there are also a variety of tensions and conflicts within the World Bank over policies and approaches to issues of poverty, food, and water. As such, it, like any other institution, is not a monolithic, singular entity.

15   Wanjiru Kamau-Rutenberg notes that the West spent the 1980s, 1990s, and the early part of the 2000s telling African farmers to position themselves in the global market. But now, because of global warming, are Western consumers going to stop buying green beans, for example, from Kenya? Where will that leave Kenyan farmers, she asks. Phone interview, Wanjiru Kamau-Rutenberg, with Meghana, 21 January 2010.

16   Phone interview, Wanjiru Kamau-Rutenberg, with Meghana, 21 January 2010.

17   Phone interview, Wanjiru Kamau-Rutenberg, with Meghana, 21 January 2010.

18   Our interviews and conversations with those working in the microfinance industry concur that while their anecdotal evidence indicates qualitative differences in the lives of their clients, there are multiple successes and failures, ranging from opportunities for women trying to get out of sex work to

recognition that people living in abject poverty are decidedly left out of the pool of 'potential,' trainable entrepreneurs who could benefit from microfinance.

19 Phone interview, Wanjiru Kamau-Rutenberg, with Meghana, 21 January 2010.

20 Phone interview, Wanjiru Kamau-Rutenberg, with Meghana, 21 January 2010.

21 Phone interview, Wanjiru Kamau-Rutenberg, with Meghana, 21 January 2010.

22 Phone interview, Wanjiru Kamau-Rutenberg, with Meghana, 21 January 2010.

23 Phone, email, and in-person informal conversations with people working in microfinance.

24 Phone interview, Wanjiru Kamau-Rutenberg, with Meghana, 21 January 2010.

25 Phone interview, Wanjiru Kamau-Rutenberg, with Meghana, 21 January 2010.

26 Phone interview, Wanjiru Kamau-Rutenberg, with Meghana, 21 January 2010.

Chapter Five / Peace and Security

1 The 'Copenhagen School' (Barry Buzan and Ole Waever) focuses on social aspects of security, regional security communities (or security interdependence within geographical regions), and securitization, or the intersubjective process of how people respond to perceptions of and speech acts about security threats. The 'Welsh School' (Ken Booth, Richard Wyn Jones, and Andrew Linklater), offers critical approaches to security, focusing on the key issue of emancipation and examining how key structural issues, such as ongoing war, oppression, and poverty, 'constrain' people; there is, instead, hope for common humanity. The concept of 'human security' emerged to address the violence and quality of life issues individuals and populations face. Constructivists explore the role of norms and identity in shaping both what constitutes a threat as well as the possibilities of political change and cooperation. Feminist theories have a vast variety of approaches to security, ranging from examining the gendered effects of war to the relationship between masculinity and war-making, to the role of women and men in creating the conditions of peace.

2 Here is a salutary reminder of the History we tell as opposed to the history millions know. After Japan's unconditional surrender in 1945, the Viet Minh, Vietnamese nationalists, moved to take power and declared the country's independence from its former French colonial taskmasters. Unwilling to accept this, the victorious Allies, led by the UK, the USA, and the Soviet Union, struck a deal (one of many strokes of *real politik* at this time; see Neale, 2003: 25–6 for details) that sent Nationalist Chinese (anti-communist) troops in to occupy the north and British troops to occupy the south. The arriving British not only rearmed the interned French forces, but released and armed defeated Japanese forces to help defeat the Viet Minh and 'restore order.' It was thus considered (vastly) preferable to have defeated Japanese troops in control rather than the independence-minded Vietnamese, who had been foolish enough to believe that they had been fighting the Japanese alongside the Allies in part for the right of self-determination.

3 Operation Condor consisted of the orchestrated, systematic attempts by the

authoritarian regimes in Argentina, Bolivia, Brazil, Chile, Ecuador, Uruguay, Paraguay, and Peru to eradicate and control suspected 'socialist' and 'communist' players. The US provided both approval and supervisory support.

4 The struggle, for example, between the US and Brazil for direction of the rescue – some might say occupation – efforts, is a particularly noteworthy and intriguing example.

5 We think here of Baudrillard's *The Gulf War Did Not Take Place* (1995).

6 Antonio Gramsci's concept of cultural hegemony is meant to explain not only the domination of one class over the others in a society, but how that domination is manufactured, embraced, and even self-imposed by those who are dominated.

7 See Interbrand's 2003 report on 'Branding a Country,' at http://www.brand channel.com/images/papers/Country_Branding.pdf. Interbrand is a brand consulting firm that works with over twenty countries.

8 The deliciously contrived acronym for Uniting and Strengthening America by Providing Appropriate Tools Required to Intercept and Obstruct Terrorism Act of 2001.

9 While we could certainly debate these issues here, we believe that the very way the resolutions and rulings are framed is problematic; this is why we do not consider seemingly 'progressive' resolutions as any more innocent. For example, let's look at Security Council Resolution 1325 on 'Women, Peace and Security' and the consequent efforts of UNIFEM's program to implement 1325's plans. The Security Council unanimously adopted 1325 in 2000. UNIFEM then created a toolbox to explore the role of women and the effects on women and children (sometimes only girls are mentioned) of preventing conflict, the negotiation of peace agreements, the planning of refugee camps and peacekeeping operations, and the reconstruction of war-torn communities. In her analysis of the politics of 1325, Shepherd reveals how United Nations terminology and organizational dynamics center Northern/Western perspectives and the quasi-mythical nation-state (Shepherd, 2006).

Ostensibly a document that recognizes the gendered impact of conflict as well as women's contributions to creating peace, 1325 and its development reaffirms Westphalian sovereignty. It also sets aside 'women and girls' as a category; indeed, the Resolution describes and pivots on gender roles that are understood in rather uni-dimensional and unproblematized ways (Hudson, 2009). Why examine gender as some type of tangible resource in peace-building efforts rather than (or in addition to) using a critical gender analysis to rethink policies around peace-making (creating an end to the fighting), peacekeeping (ensuring and implementing the provisions of peace treaties), and peace-building (rebuilding society's infrastructure and rethinking divides among formerly warring factions)? Resolution 1325 also problematically invokes 'global governance' and 'global civil society,' follows conventional assumptions about 'where' development and conflict occur, reaffirms international law as a

188 / DECENTERING INTERNATIONAL RELATIONS

source of authority, and promotes 'gender mainstreaming' (Shepherd, 2008a; 2008b). We think part of what global governance does is to make it seem that we really need to focus on the 'bad' or 'weak' states and empower key actors, such as NGOs, to deal with the unpleasant by-products (harm of 'women and children') of larger security concerns (war and conflict). In the light of this, it would be interesting to add to the conversation the recently released *Gender and International Security: Feminist Perspectives* (Sjoberg, 2009), along with the working papers of UN consultants; see, for example: http://www.un.org/womenwatch/osagi/cdrom/documents/Background_Paper Africa.pdf.

10 See the Human Rights Watch compendium on the International Criminal Tribunal for Rwanda at: http://www.hrw.org/sites/default/files/reports/ictr0110webwcover.pdf. See also the websites of the various courts and tribunals at: www.icty.org, www.ictr.org, www.sc-sl.org, www.global policy.org, www.yale.edu/cfp, www.iraq-iht.org/en/orgenal.html, and www.ICC.org.

11 These people preferred to remain anonymous.

12 The lawyer who spoke with Meghana preferred to remain anonymous. We chose to not provide any identifying information about the date of interview, the lawyer's previous or current positions, or the location and background. We will refer to this person as 'ICTR lawyer,' because of this person's experiences working with the ICTR.

13 Email interview, ICTR lawyer, with Meghana, n.d.

14 Email interview, ICTR lawyer, with Meghana, n.d.

15 Email interview, ICTR lawyer, with Meghana, n.d.

16 Email interview, ICTR lawyer, with Meghana, n.d.

17 Email interview, ICTR lawyer, with Meghana, n.d.

18 We developed major points in this section in consultation and conversation with Dr Thomas Kim, Associate Professor of Politics and International Relations at Scripps College and Executive Director of the Korean Policy Institute. We bear ultimate responsibility for the content.

19 While one might fruitfully debate various post-World War Two interventions and intercessions, such as the Allied involvement in Greece and Italy in forestalling their erstwhile local allies who had been communists in favor of those who were not, or who in some cases had even fought against the Allied forces, Korea seems the first clear-cut case of a proxy war, if complicated by China's involvement and the US utilization of the United Nations as a fig leaf.

20 Three major turning points stand out. First, we can trace much of the disagreement to US President Clinton's Geneva Agreed Framework in 1994, which aimed to diffuse the first North Korea nuclear crisis. The two countries agreed to the non-binding agreement in the wake of North Korea's notification that it was withdrawing from the Non-proliferation Treaty and of US plans to bomb the Yongbyon nuclear reactor. North Korea agreed to freeze the nuclear facilities in exchange for two light water reactors. Those light water reactors were never delivered because of US Congressional opposition, and the agreement

very quickly fell apart. Thereafter, North Korea cooperated when Washington did and retaliated when the US reneged on promises, such as lifting sanctions. Second is North Korean Chairman Kim Jong-il and South Korean President Kim Dae-jung's agreement in the June 15, 2000 North–South Joint Declaration to solve independently the questions of reunification, to settle humanitarian issues such as visits between separated families, to promote cooperation in a number of areas, and to implement authority-to-authority negotiations to expedite and facilitate the agreed-upon points. Third is US President Bush's decision to break with Kim Dae-jung's policy of reconciliation and adopt a more hawkish stance towards North Korea. After he designated North Korea part of the 'Axis of Evil' in a January 29, 2002 speech, tensions between North Korea, South Korea, and the US increased dramatically. But it is worth noting that South Korea and North Korea continued negotiating, as North Korea even entertained some talk of normalizing relations with Japan. However, in the context of an increasingly militarized US, reflected in its rhetoric regarding the Korean peninsula, North Korea eventually tested an intercontinental ballistic missile and a nuclear device in 2006. North Korea purposely did so on US Independence Day. So, while the UN responded with Security Resolutions 1695 (2006), the Bush Administration 'got the message,' and quickly shifted from a promotion of regime collapse to engagement with North Korea. Consequently, the Six-Party Talks soon reached an agreement in February 2007 aiming towards denuclearizing North Korea.

21 Phone interview, Hyun Lee, member of Nodutdol (see below), with Meghana, 19 August 2009.

22 Phone interview, Hyun Lee, with Meghana, 19 August 2009.

23 Phone interview, Hyun Lee, with Meghana, 19 August 2009.

24 Phone interview, Hyun Lee, with Meghana, 19 August 2009.

25 See a 29 May 2009 interview with Bruce Cumings regarding this issue on *Democracy Now;* the program and the transcript are available at http://www.democracynow.org/2009/5/29/north_korea.

26 Nodutdol aims to bring justice to those Koreans traumatized by the division and to connect the protests against war and militarism in both US and Korean societies. It has also been active in the Peace Treaty Campaign, invigorated by the Korean Policy Institute's Reunification Conference in Fall 2008.

27 Phone interview, Hyun Lee, with Meghana, 19 August 2009.

28 Phone interview, Hyun Lee, with Meghana, 19 August 2009.

29 Phone interview, Hyun Lee, with Meghana, 19 August 2009.

30 Or to consider, as Dr Kim points out, that the push for unification is also coming from corporations, like Samsung, hoping to exploit cheap labor from North Korea.

Chapter Six / Conclusion

1 The notion of the table also resonates with Laitin (1995: 454), whose work we will invoke shortly, and who in a different context similarly notes that 'we need

not, as Almond (1990) has suggested, eat at "separate tables" any longer; it is now possible productively to consume across cuisines.'

2 'Many forms of government have been tried and will be tried in this world of sin and woe. No one pretends that democracy is perfect or all-wise. Indeed, it has been said that democracy is the worst form of government except all those other forms that have been tried from time to time.' Churchill (1947; 1974: 566); Shapiro (2006: 154); Jay (1996: 93).

3 Attributed originally to Hillel the Elder ('If I am not for myself, who will be for me? And when I am for myself, what am "I"? And if not now, when?' – Rabbi Hillel, from the Pirkay Avot, a book of the Mishnah, the first part of the Talmud). In the US this has come to be associated with a certain 'American exceptionalism' rooted in Tocqueville's somewhat overwrought, epic rendition of the US. Robert Kennedy reportedly liked to quote the saying, and it is particularly popularly associated in the US with President Ronald Reagan, who invoked it in his second inaugural address.

4 Tracking down any sort of authoritative source for this is elusive, perhaps because it never happened; see Gittings (2007: 61). Most versions attribute the remark to Zhou, some to Mao Zedong; most versions include US Secretary of State Henry Kissinger, though some name French Ambassador André Malraux. Unsourced accounts are rife, including those given by respected scholars; see, for example, Sick (1995: 145); Prins (1998: 793); Rosenberg (1999: 91); Vatikiotis (2005/6: 27); Fischer (2006: 340); or Aron (2006: 443).

5 See Hoffman and Weiss (2006).

6 This political axiom has, in the US, long been associated with the former Speaker of the US House of Representatives, though he liked to credit his father. It is clearly a maxim of some antiquity.

7 A phrase and a sense borrowed from Burckhardt's description of an old story as 'one of those which are true and not true, everywhere and nowhere' (1860/1958: 40). This authoritative, dense, problematic work was published in 1860 as *Die Cultur der Renaissance in Italien: ein Versuch*.

8 The famous question posed by the Clandestine Revolutionary Indigenous Committee General Command (CCRI-CG) of the EZLN is in a communiqué sent out January 31, 1994 (30 days after their uprising began), in which they asked, 'Why is everyone so quiet? Is this the democracy you wanted?' Often dated February 4, 1994 in the US.

9 Clandestine Indigenous Revolutionary Committee General Command of the Zapatista Army of National Liberation, 'First Declaration of La Realidad for Humanity and against Neoliberalism,' Mexico, January 1996.

References

Abdulhadi, R. (1998) 'The Palestinian Women's Autonomous Movement: Emergence, Dynamics, and Challenges,' *Gender and Society*, Vol. 12, No. 6, pp. 649–73.
—— (2005) 'Tread Lightly: Teaching Gender and Sexuality in Time of War,' *Journal of Women's History*, Vol. 17, No. 4, pp. 154–8.
Abu-Lughod, L. (2001) 'Orientalism and Middle East Feminist Studies,' *Feminist Studies*, Vol. 27, No. 1, pp. 101–13.
—— (2002) 'Do Muslim Women Really Need Saving? Anthropological Reflections on Cultural Relativism and Its Others,' *American Anthropologist*, Vol. 104, No. 3, pp. 783–90.
Acharya, A. and B. Buzan (2009) *Non-Western International Relations Theory.* New York NY: Routledge.
Adeleye-Fayemi, B. (2005) 'Creating a New World with New Visions: African Feminism and Trends in the Global Women's Movement,' in J. Kerr, E. Sprenger, and A. Symington (eds), *The Future of Women's Rights: Global Visions and Strategies.* New York NY: Zed Books, pp. 38–55.
Adler, E. (1997) 'Imagined (Security) Communities: Cognitive Regions in International Relations,' *Millennium*, Vol. 26, No. 2, pp. 249–77.
Agathangelou, A. (2006) 'Colonizing Desires: Bodies for Sale, Exploitation and (In)security in Desire Industries,' *Cyprus Review*, Vol. 18, No. 2, pp. 37–73.
Agathangelou, A. and L. Ling (2003) 'Desire Industries: Sex Trafficking, UN Peacekeeping, and the Neo-Liberal World Order,' *Brown Journal of World Affairs*, Vol. 10, No. 1, pp. 133–48.
—— (2004) 'The House of IR: from Family Power Politics to the Poisies of Worldism,' *International Studies Review*, Vol. 6, No. 4, pp. 21–49.
Aguilar, D. and A. Lacsamana (eds) (2004) *Women and Globalization.* Amherst MA: Humanity Books.
Ahmed, L. (1992) *Women and Gender in Islam: Historical Roots of a Modern Debate.* New Haven CT: Yale University Press.
Aidi, H. D. (2005) 'Slavery, Genocide and the Politics of Outrage: Understanding the New Racial Olympics,' *Middle East Report*, 234. Available at: http://www.merip.org/mer/mer234/aidi.html.
Anderson, K. (2002) 'Microcredit: Fulfilling or Belying the Universalist Morality of Globalizing Markets?' *Yale Human Rights and Development Law Journal*, Vol. 5, pp. 85–122.
Ang, I. (2003) 'I'm a Feminist but . . . "Other" Women and Postnational Feminism,' in Reina Lewis and Sara Mills (eds), *Feminist Postcolonial Theory: A Reader.* New York NY: Routledge, pp. 190–206.
Anghie, A. (2005) *Imperialism, Sovereignty and the Making of International Law.* Cambridge: Cambridge University Press.

Anzaldúa, G. (1999) *Borderlands/La Frontera, the New Mestiza*. San Francisco CA: Aunt Lute Books.

Arendt, H. (1963) *Eichmann in Jerusalem: A Report on the Banality of Evil*. New York NY: Penguin Books.

Arias, A. (ed.) (2001) *The Rigoberta Menchú Controversy*. Minneapolis MN: University of Minnesota Press.

Arisaka, Y. (1997) 'Beyond "East and West": Nishida's Universalism and Postcolonial Critique,' *The Review of Politics*, Vol. 59, No. 3, pp. 541–60.

Aron, L. (2006) 'Ideas of Revolutions and Revolutionary Ideas,' *Demokratizatsiya*, Vol. 14, No. 3, pp. 435–59.

Aronowitz, S. (2001) *The Knowledge Factory: Dismantling the Corporate University and Creating True Higher Learning*. Boston MA: Beacon Press.

Bacchetta, P. (2000) 'Reinterrogating Partition Violence: Voices of Women/Children/Dalits in India's Partition,' *Feminist Studies*, Vol. 26, No. 3, pp. 567–85.

Bahramitash, R. (2008) 'Saving Iranian Women: Orientalist Feminism and the Axis of Evil,' in B. Sutton, S. Morgen, and J. Novkov (eds), *Security Disarmed: Critical Perspectives on Gender, Race, and Militarization*. Piscataway NJ: Rutgers University Press, pp. 100–10.

Banerjee, A., E. Duflo, R. Glennerster, and C. Kinnan (2009) 'The Miracle of Microfinance? Evidence from a Randomised Evaluation.' Available at: www.povertyactionlab.com/projects/project.php?pid=44.

Barber, B. (1992) 'Jihad vs. McWorld,' *The Atlantic Monthly*, Vol. 269, No. 3, pp. 53–65.

Barnett, M. (1999) 'Peacekeeping, Indifference, and Genocide in Rwanda,' in J. Weldes, *et al.* (eds), *Cultures of Insecurity: States, Communities, and the Production of Danger*. Minneapolis MN: University of Minnesota, pp. 173–202.

Baudrillard, J. (1995) *The Gulf War Did Not Take Place*. Bloomington IN: Indiana University Press.

Becker, E. (2003) 'US Corn Subsidies Said to Damage Mexico,' *The New York Times*, 27 August, p. C4.

Bedford, K. (2009) *Developing Partnerships: Gender, Sexuality, and the Reformed World Bank*. Minneapolis MN: University of Minnesota Press.

Beier, J. (2005) *International Relations in Uncommon Places: Indigeneity, Cosmology, and the Limits of International Theory*. New York NY: Palgrave Macmillan.

Bell, D. (1973) *The Coming of Post-Industrial Society*, New York NY: Harper Colophon Books.

Béteille. A. (1998) 'The Idea of Indigenous People,' *Current Anthropology*, Vol. 39, No. 2, pp. 187–91.

Bhasin, K. and R. Menon (1998) *Borders and Boundaries: Women in India's Partition*. New Delhi: Kali for Women.

Biswas, S. and S. Nair (2009) *International Relations and States of Exception: Margins, Peripheries, and Excluded Bodies*. New York NY: Routledge.

Boot, M. (2002) *The Savage Wars of Peace: Small Wars and the Rise of American Power*. New York NY: Basic Books.

Bowden, B. (2005) 'The Colonial Origins of International Law, European Expansion and the Classical Standard of Civilization,' *Journal of the History of International Law*, Vol. 7, No. 1, pp. 1–23.

Boyce Davies, C. (2007) *Left of Karl Marx: the Political Life of Black Communist Claudia Jones*. Durham NC: Duke University Press.

Braudel, F. (1972) 'Personal Testimony,' *The Journal of Modern History*, Vol. 44, No. 4, pp. 448–67.

—— (1979) *Civilization and Capitalism, 15th–18th Century, Vol. I: The Structure of Everyday Life*, trans. by S. Reynolds. New York NY: Harper and Row.

Brodkin, K. (1998) *How Jews Became White Folks: and What That Says about Race in*

America. New Brunswick NJ: Rutgers University Press.

Brooks, J., C. DeCorse, and J. Walton (2008) *Small Worlds: Method, Meaning, and Narrative in Microhistory.* Santa Fe NM: School for Advanced Research Press.

Brown, Wendy (1995) *States of Injury: Power and Freedom in Late Modernity.* Princeton NJ: Princeton University Press.

Brown, William (2006) 'Africa and International Relations: a Comment on IR Theory, Anarchy and Statehood,' *Review of International Studies,* Vol. 32, No. 1, pp. 119– 43.

Bruyneel, K. (2007) *The Third Space of Sovereignty: the Postcolonial Politics of US– Indigenous Relations.* Minneapolis MN: University of Minnesota Press.

Brysk, A. (2000) *From Tribal Village to Global Village: Indian Rights and International Relations in Latin America.* Stanford CA: Stanford University Press.

Buck-Morss, S. (2003) *Thinking Past Terror: Islamism and Critical Theory on the Left.* London: Verso.

Bunce, V. (1985) 'The Empire Strikes Back: the Evolution of the Eastern Bloc from a Soviet Asset to a Soviet Liability,' *International Organization,* Vol. 39, No. 1, pp. 1–46.

Burbach, R. (2003) 'Two 9/11s, One Story,' *The Guardian,* 11 September.

Burckhardt, J. (1860/1958) *The Civilization of the Renaissance in Italy,* Vol. I, trans. S. Middlemore. New York NY: Harper and Brothers Publishers.

Burke, A. (2008) 'Postmodernism' in C. Reus-Smit and D. Snidal (eds), *The Oxford Handbook of International Relations.* New York NY: Oxford University Press, pp. 359–77.

Butalia, U. (1998) *The Other Side of Silence: Voices from the Partition of India.* New Delhi: Penguin India.

Butler, J. (1993) *Bodies That Matter: On the Discursive Limits of 'Sex.'* New York NY: Routledge.

—— (2004) *Precarious Life: the Power of Mourning and Violence.* London: Verso Books.

Campbell, D. (1998a) *National Deconstruction: Violence, Identity, and Justice in Bosnia.* Minneapolis MN: University of Minnesota Press.

—— (1998b) *Writing Security: United States Foreign Policy and the Politics of Identity.* Minneapolis MN: University of Minnesota Press.

—— (2007) 'Geopolitics and Visuality: Sighting the Darfur Conflict,' *Political Geography,* Vol. 26, No. 4, pp. 357–82.

Carpenter, R. C. (2003) '"Women and Children First": Gender, Norms and Humanitarian Evacuation in the Balkans, 1991–1995,' *International Organization,* Vol. 57, No. 4, pp. 661–94.

—— (2007) 'Setting the Advocacy Agenda: Theorizing Issue Emergence and Non-emergence in Transnational Advocacy Networks,' *International Studies Quarterly,* Vol. 51, pp. 99–120.

Cha, V. and D. Kang (2003) *Nuclear North Korea: a Debate on Engagement Strategies.* New York NY: Columbia University Press.

Chakrabarty, D. (2000) *Provincializing Europe: Postcolonial Thought and Historical Difference.* Princeton NJ: Princeton University Press.

Chartier, R. (1991) *The Cultural Origins of the French Revolution,* trans. Lydia Cochrane. Durham NC: Duke University Press.

Chatterton, P. (2006) '"Give up Activism" and Change the World in Unknown Ways: or, Learning to Walk with Others on Uncommon Ground,' *Antipode,* Vol. 38, No. 2, pp. 259–81.

Chen, B., C.-C. Hwang and L. H. M. Ling (2009) 'Lust/Caution in IR: Democratising World Politics with Culture as Method,' *Millennium,* Vol. 37, No. 3, pp. 743–66.

Chernyshevsky, N. (1863/1989) *What Is to Be Done?* trans. M. Katz. Ithaca NY: Cornell University Press.

Chinkin, C. (2006) 'People's Tribunals: Legitimate or Rough Justice,' *Windsor Yearbook of*

Access to Justice, Vol. 24, pp. 202–20.

Chong, A. and N. Hamilton-Hart (2009) 'Teaching International Relations in Southeast Asia: Historical Memory, Academic Context, and Politics – an Introduction,' *International Relations of the Asia Pacific,* Vol. 9, No. 1, pp. 1–18.

Chowdhry, G. and S. Nair (eds) (2002) *Power, Postcolonialism and International Relations: Reading Race, Gender and Class.* London: Routledge.

Churchill, W. (1947) Speech in the House of Commons (1947-11-11), cited in *The Official Report, House of Commons* (5th Series), 11 November 1947, vol. 444, cc. 206–07.

—— (1974) *W. S. Churchill: His Complete Speeches, 1897–1963,* Vol. 7, R. James (ed.). New York NY: Chelsea House Publishers.

Clairmont, B. (2008) 'Sexual Assault Response Teams: Resource Guide for the Development of a Sexual Assault Response Team (SART) in Tribal Communities' (occasional publication of the Tribal Law and Policy Institute), pp. 1–118. Available at: http://www.tribal-institute.org/download/SART_Manual_09_08.pdf.

Clavin, M. (2008) 'A Second Haitian Revolution: John Brown, Touissant Louverture, and the Making of the American Civil War,' *Civil War History,* Vol. 52, No. 2, pp. 117–45.

Cohn, C. (1987) 'Sex and Death in the Rational World of Defense Intellectuals,' *Signs,* Vol. 12, No. 4, pp. 687–718.

Collier, P. (2007) *The Bottom Billion: Why the Poorest Countries are Failing and What Can Be Done about It.* New York NY: Oxford University Press.

'Concept of Indigenous Peoples' (2004) Workshop on Data Collection and Disaggregation for Indigenous Peoples, Secretariat of the Permanent Forum on Indigenous Issues, Department of Economic and Social Affairs. New York, NY. Available at: http://www.un.org/esa/socdev/unpfii/documents/workshop_data_ background.doc.

Connolly, W. E. (1996) 'Tocqueville, Territory and Violence' in M. J. Shapiro and H. Alker (eds), *Challenging Boundaries: Global Flows, Territorial Identities.* Minneapolis MN: University of Minnesota Press, pp. 141–64.

Consultative Group to Assist the Poor (2006) 'Financial Inclusion 2015: Four Scenarios for the Future of Microfinance,' *Focus Notes,* No. 39. Washington, DC: CGAP.

Convention Concerning Indigenous and Tribal Peoples in Independent Countries (1989) International Labour Organisation. Available at: http://www.ilo.org/ilolex/cgi- lex/convde.pl?C169.

Crawford, N. (1994) 'A Security Regime among Democracies: Cooperation among Iroquois Nations,' *International Organization,* Vol. 48, No. 3, pp. 345–85.

Crowe, T. (2001) 'Hawk Littlejohn Embraced the Old Ways in the Modern World,' *The Smoky Mountain News,* 17 January.

Cruz, C. Z. (2005) 'Four Questions on Critical Race Praxis: Lessons from Two Young Lives in Indian Country,' *Fordham Law Review,* Vol. 73, No. 5, pp. 2133–60.

—— (2007) 'Law of the Land: Recognition, Resurgence, and Place of Indigenous Legal Tradition in Indigenous Law and Justice Systems.' Lecture at Hamline University. Podcast available at: http://law.hamline.edu/conversations-law-hamline-audio/international-indigenous-forum-featuring-professor-christine-zuni-cr.

—— (2008) 'Shadow War Scholarship, Indigenous Legal Tradition, and Modern Law in Indian County,' *Washburn Law Journal,* Vol. 47, No. 3, pp. 631–52.

Cumings, B. (2003) 'Wrong Again,' *London Review of Books,* Vol. 25, No. 3, pp. 9–12.

—— (2004) *North Korea: Another Country.* New York NY: The New Press.

Currie, J. and J. Newson (eds) (1998) *Universities and Globalization: Critical Perspectives.* Thousand Oaks CA: Sage.

Daes, E. (1997) 'Protection of the Heritage of Indigenous People,' Human Rights Studies Series, No. 10. New York NY: United Nations.

Darby, P. (ed.) (2000) *At the Edge of International Relations: Postcolonialism, Gender and Dependency.* New York NY: Wellington House.

—— (2006) 'Introduction,' in P. Darby (ed.), *Postcolonizing the International: Working to Change the Way We Are*. Honolulu HI: University of Hawai'i Press, pp 1–10.

Das, V. (1997) 'Language and Body: Transactions in the Construction of Pain,' in A. Kleinman, V. Das, and M. Lock (eds), *Social Suffering*. Berkeley CA: University of California Press, pp. 67–92.

Dauphinee, E. (2007) *The Ethics of Researching War: Looking for Bosnia*. Manchester: Manchester University Press.

—— (2008) 'War Crimes and the Ruin of Law,' *Millennium*, Vol. 37, No. 1, pp. 49–67.

de Soto, H. (2000) *The Mystery of Capital: Why Capitalism Triumphs in the West and Fails Everywhere Else*. New York NY: Basic Books.

de Waal, A. (2004a) 'Counter-Insurgency on the Cheap,' *London Review of Books*, Vol. 26, No. 15, pp. 25–7.

—— (2004b) 'Tragedy in Darfur: on Understanding and Ending the Horror,' *Boston Review*, October/November.

—— (2006) '"I Will Not Sign,"' *London Review of Books*, Vol. 28, No. 23, pp. 17–20.

Debord, G. (2006), 'Theory of the Dérive,' in K. Knabb (ed. and trans.), *Situationist International Anthology*, revised edition. Berkeley CA: Bureau of Public Secrets, pp. 50–4.

Deer, S. (2009) 'Decolonizing Rape Law: a Native Feminist Synthesis of Safety and Sovereignty,' *Wicazo Sa Review*, Vol. 24, No. 2, pp. 149–67.

Deleuze, G. and F. Guattari (1987) *A Thousand Plateaus: Capitalism and Schizophrenia*, trans. B. Massumi. Minneapolis MN: University of Minnesota Press.

Denzin, N., Y. Lincoln, and L. Tuhiwai Smith (eds) (2008) *Handbook of Critical and Indigenous Methodologies*. Beverley Hills CA: Sage Publications.

Diamond, J. (1997) *Guns, Germs, and Steel: The Fates of Human Societies*. New York NY: W. W. Norton.

Didur, J. (2000) 'At a Loss for Words: Reading the Silence in South Asian Women's Partition Narratives,' *Topia*, No. 4, pp. 53–71.

Diez, T. and K. Hayward (2008) 'Reconfiguring Spaces of Conflict: Northern Ireland and the Impact of European Integration,' *Space and Polity*, Vol. 12, No. 1, pp. 47–62.

Diez, T., S. Stetter, and M. Albert (2006) 'The European Union and Border Conflicts: the Transformative Power of Integration,' *International Organization*, Vol. 60, No. 3, pp. 563–93.

Doty, R. (1996) *Imperial Encounters: the Politics of Representation in North/South Relations*. Minneapolis MN: University of Minnesota Press.

—— (2004) 'Maladies of Our Souls: Identity and Voice in the Writing of Academic International Relations,' *Cambridge Review of International Affairs*, Vol. 17, No. 2, pp. 377–92.

—— (2007) 'States of Exception on the Mexico–US Border: Security, Decisions, and Civilian Border Patrols,' *International Political Sociology*, Vol. 1, No. 2, pp. 113–37.

—— (2010) '"Do You Know If Your Borders Are Secure?"' *International Political Sociology*, Vol. 4, No. 1, pp. 92–5.

Driver, D. (2005) 'Truth, Reconciliation, Gender: the South African Truth and Reconciliation Commission and Black Women's Intellectual History,' *Australian Feminist Studies*, Vol. 20, No. 47, pp. 219–29.

Dunn, K. (2008) 'Never Mind the Bollocks: the Punk Rock Politics of Global Communication,' in C. Constantinou, O. Richmond, and A. Watson (eds), *Cultures and Politics of Global Communication*. Cambridge: Cambridge University Press, pp. 193–210.

Dunn, K. and T. Shaw (eds) (2001) *Africa's Challenge to International Relations Theory*, New York NY: Palgrave Macmillan.

Duvall, R. and L. Varadarajan (2003) 'On the Practical Significance of Critical International Relations Theory,' *Asian Journal of Political Science*, Vol. 11. No. 2, pp. 75–88.

Edkins, J. (1999) *Poststructuralism and International Relations: Bringing the Political Back In.* Boulder CO: Lynne Rienner Publishers.
—— (2003) *Trauma and the Memory of Politics.* Cambridge: Cambridge University Press.
Edkins, J. and N. Vaughan-Williams (eds) (2009) *Critical Theorists and International Relations.* New York NY: Routledge.
Edkins, J. and M. Zehfuss (2009) *Global Politics.* New York NY: Routledge.
Edney, M. (1997) *Mapping an Empire: the Geographical Construction of British India, 1765–1843.* Chicago IL: University of Chicago Press.
Ehrenreich, B. (2004) 'To Defeat Terrorists, Try Listening to Feminists,' *Common Dreams online,* available at http://www.commondreams.org/views04/0803-02.htm.
Eichler, M. (2006) 'Russia's Post-Communist Transformation: a Gendered Analysis of the Chechen Wars,' *International Feminist Journal of Politics,* Vol. 8, No. 4, pp. 486–511.
Eichler-Levine, J. and R. R. Hicks (2007) '"As Americans against Genocide": the Crisis in Darfur and Interreligious Political Activism,' *American Quarterly,* Vol. 59, No. 3, pp. 711–35.
Enloe, C. (2000) *Maneuvers: the International Politics of Militarizing Women's Lives.* Berkeley CA: University of California Press.
—— (2001) *Bananas, Beaches, and Bases: Making Feminist Sense of International Politics,* updated edition. Berkeley CA: University of California Press.
—— (2007) *Globalization and Militarism: Feminists Make the Link.* Lanham MD: Rowman and Littlefield Publishers, Inc.
Entzinger, H., M. Martiniello, and C. Wihtol de Wenden (eds) (2004) *Migration Between States and Markets.* Burlington VT: Ashgate.
Escobar, A. (1988) 'Power and Visibility: Development and the Invention and Management of the Third World,' *Cultural Anthropology,* Vol. 3, No. 4, pp. 428–33.
—— (1995) *Encountering Development: the Making and Unmaking of the Third World.* Princeton NJ: Princeton University Press.
—— (2008) *Territories of Difference: Place, Movements, Life, Redes.* Durham NC: Duke University Press.
Faludi, S. (2008) *The Terror Dream: Myth and Misogyny in an Insecure America.* New York NY: Picador.
Fauriol, G. (1996) 'Haiti: the Failures of Governance' in H. Wiarda and H. Kline (eds), *Latin American Politics and Development,* fourth edition. Boulder CO: Westview Press, pp. 517–30.
Feiner, S. and D. Barker (2007) 'Microcredit and Women's Poverty,' *The Dominion,* No. 42, 17 January.
Fenelon, J. and T. Hall (2008) 'Revitalization and Indigenous Resistance to Globalization and Neoliberalism,' *American Behavioral Scientist,* Vol. 51, No. 12, pp. 1867–1901.
Fenelon, J. and S. Murguía (2008) 'Indigenous Peoples: Globalization, Resistance, and Revitalization,' *American Behavioral Scientist,* Vol. 51, No. 12, pp. 1656–71.
Ferguson, J. (2006) *Global Shadows: Africa in the Neoliberal World Order.* Durham NC: Duke University Press.
Ferguson, K. E. (2009) 'The Sublime Object of Militarism,' *New Political Science,* Vol. 31, No. 4, pp. 475–86.
Ferguson, N. (2003) *Empire: the Rise and Demise of the British World Order and the Lessons for Global Power.* New York NY: Basic Books.
Fischer, J. (2006) 'The Free Will Revolution (Continued),' *Journal of Ethics,* Vol. 10, No. 3, pp. 315–45.
Fischer, S. (2004) *Modernity Disavowed: Haiti and the Cultures of Slavery in the Age of Revolution.* Durham NC: Duke University Press.
Foran, J. (2005) *Taking Power: on the Origins of Third World Revolutions.* Cambridge: Cambridge University Press.
Foucault, M. (1977) *Discipline and Punish: the Birth of the Prison,* trans. A. Sheridan. New York NY: Pantheon Books.

Franklin, M. (ed.) (2005) *Resounding International Relations: on Music, Culture and Politics.* New York NY: Palgrave Macmillan.

Friedman, T. (2000) *The Lexus and the Olive Tree: Understanding Globalization,* revised and updated edition. New York NY: Farrar, Straus, and Giroux.

—— (2005) *The World is Flat: a Brief History of the Twenty-First Century.* New York NY: Farrar, Straus, and Giroux.

—— (2008) 'Calling All Pakistanis,' *The New York Times,* 3 November.

Fukuyama, F. (1998) 'Women and the Evolution of World Politics,' *Foreign Affairs,* Vol. 77, No. 5, pp. 24–40.

Ganguly-Scrase, R., G. Vogl, and R. Julian (2005) 'Neoliberal Globalisation and Women's Experiences of Forced Migrations in Asia,' paper presented at conference on 'Social Change in the 21st Century,' Queensland University of Technology, Brisbane, 28 October. Available at: http://eprints.qut.edu.au/3461/1/3461.pdf.

Gibson-Graham, J. K. (2002) 'Beyond Global vs. Local: Economic Politics outside of the Binary Frame' in A. Herod and M. Wright (eds), *Geographies of Power: Placing Scale.* Oxford: Blackwell Publishers, pp. 25–60.

Gilly. A. (2005) 'Bolivia: a Twenty-first-century Revolution,' *Socialism and Democracy,* Vol.19, No. 3, pp. 41–54.

Gittings, J. (2007) 'A Historical View of Western Reporting on China,' *China Media Research,* Vol. 3, No. 1, pp. 61–4.

Global Trade Watch (2001) 'Down on the Farm: NAFTA's Seven Years War on Farmers and Ranchers in the US, Canada, and Mexico,' Public Citizens Global Trade Watch.

Gokhale, K. (2009) 'Group Borrowing Leads to Pressure,' *Wall Street Journal,* 13 August.

Gonzalez, C. G. (2003) 'Seasons of Resistance: Sustainable Agriculture and Food Security in Cuba,' *Tulane Environmental Law Journal,* Vol. 16, pp. 685–732.

Gott, R. (2007) 'Latin America as a White Settler Society: the 2006 SLAS Lecture,' *Bulletin of Latin American Research,* Vol. 26, No. 2, pp. 269–89.

Gould, S. (1981) *The Mismeasure of Man.* New York NY: W. W. Norton.

Gourevitch, P. (1998) *We Wish to Inform You That Tomorrow We Will Be Killed with Our Families: Stories from Rwanda.* London: Picador.

Grimmett, R. F. (2008) 'Conventional Arms Transfers to Developing Nations, 2000–2007,' Congressional Research Service Report for Congress, 23 October. Available at: http://www.fas.org/programs/ssp/asmp/factsandfigures/government_data/2008/RL34723.pdf.

Grovogui, S. (2001) 'Come to Africa: a Hermeneutics of Race in International Theory,' *Alternatives,* Vol. 26, No. 4, pp. 425–48.

Guglielmo, J. and S. Salerno (eds) (2003) *Are Italians White? How Race is Made in America.* New York NY: Routledge.

Hall, L. K. (2008) 'Strategies of Erasure: US Colonialism and Native Hawaiian Feminism,' *American Quarterly,* Vol. 60, No. 2, pp. 273–80.

Halley, J., P. Kotiswaran, H. Shamir, and C. Thomas (2006) 'From the International to the Local in Feminist Legal Responses to Rape, Prostitution/Sex Work, and Sex Trafficking: Four Studies in Contemporary Governance Feminism,' *Harvard Journal of Law and Gender,* Vol. 29, pp. 335–423.

Handal, N. (2005) *The Lives of Rains.* New York NY: Interlink.

Hansen, L. (2006) *Security as Practice: Discourse Analysis and the Bosnian War.* New York NY: Routledge.

Harvey, D. (2005) *A Brief History of Neoliberalism.* Oxford: Oxford University Press.

Harrison, S. (2002) *Korean Endgame: a Strategy for Reunification and US Disengagement.* Princeton NJ: Princeton University Press.

Hart-Landsberg, M. (1998) *Korea: Division, Reunification, and US Foreign Policy.* New York NY: Monthly Review Press.

Hite, K. and C. Collins (2009) 'Memorial Fragments, Monumental Silences and Reawakenings in 21st-Century Chile,' *Millennium,* Vol. 38, No. 2, pp. 379–400.

Hodge, M. and C. Searle (eds) (1981) *'Is Freedom We Making': the New Democracy in Grenada.* St Georges: Government Information Service.

Hoffman, P. and T. Weiss (2006) *Sword and Salve: Confronting New Wars and Humanitarian Crises.* Boulder CO: Rowman and Littlefield.

Holmgren, D. (2002) *Permaculture: Principles and Pathways beyond Sustainability.* Cambridge MA: Holmgren Design Press.

Honig, B. (2001) *Democracy and the Foreigner.* Princeton NJ: Princeton University Press.

Hudson, D. (2008) 'Developing Geographies of Financialisation: Banking the Poor and Remittance Securitisation,' *Contemporary Politics,* Vol. 14, No. 3, pp. 315–33.

Hudson, N. F. (2009) 'Securitizing Women's Rights and Gender Equality,' *Journal of Human Rights,* Vol. 8, No. 1, pp. 53–70.

Huntington, S. (1993) 'The Clash of Civilizations,' *Foreign Affairs,* Vol. 72, No. 3, pp. 22–49.

—— (1996) *The Clash of Civilizations and the Remaking of World Order.* New York NY: Simon and Schuster.

Hyndman, J. (2000) *Managing Displacement: Refugees and the Politics of Humanitarianism.* Minneapolis MN: University of Minnesota Press.

Ibish, H. (2009) *What's Wrong with the One-State Agenda? Why Ending the Occupation and Peace with Israel Is Still the Palestinian National Goal.* Washington DC: American Task Force on Palestine. Available at: http://www.americantaskforce.org/.

Ignatiev, N. (1995) *How the Irish Became White.* New York NY: Routledge.

Inayatullah, N. and D. Blaney (2004) *International Relations and the Problem of Difference.* New York NY: Routledge.

—— (2007) 'Doing International Relations from Below' in C. Reus-Smit and D. Snidal (eds), *The Oxford Handbook of International Relations.* New York NY: Oxford University Press, pp. 663–74.

Ishay, M. (2007) *The Human Rights Reader: Major Political Essays, Speeches, and Documents from Ancient Times to the Present,* second edition. New York NY: Routledge.

—— (2008) *The History of Human Rights: from Ancient Times to the Globalization Era.* Berkeley CA: University of California Press.

James, C. L. R. (1989) *The Black Jacobins: Toussaint L'Ouverture and the San Domingo Revolution,* second edition. New York NY: Vintage.

James, J. (1996) *Resisting State Violence.* Minneapolis MN: University of Minnesota Press.

James, W. (1999) *Holding Aloft the Banner of Ethiopia: Caribbean Radicalism in Early Twentieth Century America.* London: Verso.

Jarvis, L. (2008) 'Times of Terror: Writing Temporality into the War on Terror,' *Critical Studies on Terrorism,* Vol. 1, No. 2, pp. 245–62.

Jay, A. (1996) *The Oxford Dictionary of Political Quotations.* Oxford: Oxford University Press.

Jessepe, L. (2009) 'University of Kansas Tribal Law Conference,' *Indian Country Today,* 5 March.

Johnson, P. (2001) *Modern Times: the World from the Twenties to the Nineties,* revised edition. New York NY: Harper Perennial Modern Classics.

Kalhan, A. (2009) 'Constitution and "Extraconstitution": Colonial Emergency Regimes in Postcolonial Pakistan and India' in V. Ramraj and A. Thiruvengadam (eds), *Emergency Powers in Asia.* Cambridge: Cambridge University Press, pp. 89–120.

Kamat, S. and B. Mathew (2003) 'Mapping Political Violence in a Globalized World: the Case of Hindu Nationalism,' *Social Justice,* Vol. 30, No. 3, pp. 4–16.

Kamola, I. (2007) 'The Global Coffee Economy and the Production of Genocide in Rwanda,' *Third World Quarterly,* Vol. 28, No. 3, pp. 571–92.

—— (2009) 'Producing the Global Imaginary: Academic Knowledge, Globalization and the Making of the World.' Unpublished dissertation, University of Minnesota.

Kang, S. (2009) 'Forced Prison Labor: International Labor Standards, Human Rights and the Privatization of Prison Labor in the Contemporary United States,' *New Political Science*, Vol. 31, No. 2, pp. 137–61.

Kapur, R. (2002) 'The Tragedy of Victimization Rhetoric: Resurrecting the "Native" Subject in International/Postcolonial Feminist Legal Politics,' *Harvard Human Rights Journal*, No. 15.

—— (2006) 'Human Rights in the Twenty-first Century: Take a Walk on the Dark Side,' *Sydney Law Review*, Vol. 28, No. 4, pp. 665–87.

Karlan, D. and J. Zinman (2009) 'Expanding Microenterprise Credit Access: Using Randomized Supply Decisions to Estimate the Impacts in Manila.' Available at: http://www.dartmouth.edu/~jzinman/Papers/expandingaccess_manila_jul09.pdf.

Keal, P. (2003) *European Conquest and the Rights of Indigenous Peoples: the Moral Backwardness of International Society*. Cambridge: Cambridge University Press.

Keck, M. and K. Sikkink (1998) *Activists Beyond Borders: Advocacy Networks in International Politics*. Ithaca NY: Cornell University Press.

Keohane, R. (1989) 'International Relations Theory: Contributions of a Feminist Standpoint,' *Millennium*, Vol. 18, No. 2, pp. 245–53.

Keys, A., H. Masterman-Smith, and D. Cottle (2006) 'The Political Economy of a Natural Disaster: the Boxing Day Tsunami, 2004,' *Antipode*, Vol. 38, No. 2, pp. 195–204.

Key-young, S. (2006) *South Korean Engagement Policies and North Korea: Identities, Norms, and the Sunshine Policy*. London: Routledge.

Khasnabish, A. (2007) 'Insurgent Imaginations,' *Ephemera*, Vol. 7, No. 4, pp. 505–25.

Kim, J. and M. Fu (2008) 'International Women in South Korea's Sex Industry: a New Commodity Frontier,' *Asian Survey*, Vol. 48, No. 3, pp. 492–513.

Kim, S. and D. Kang (eds) (2009) *Engagement with North Korea: a Viable Alternative*. Albany NY: State University of New York Press.

King, G., R. Keohane, and S. Verba (1994) *Designing Social Inquiry: Scientific Inference in Qualitative Research*. Princeton NJ: Princeton University Press.

Kinsella, H. (2006) 'Gendering Grotius: Sex and Sex Difference in the Laws of War,' *Political Theory*, Vol. 34, No. 2, pp. 161–91.

Knight, F. (2000) 'The Haitian Revolution,' *The American Historical Review*, Vol. 105, No. 1, pp. 103–15.

Koskenniemi. M. (2002) '"The Lady Doth Protest Too Much": Kosovo and the Turn to Ethics in International Law,' *Modern Law Review*, Vol. 65, No. 2, pp. 159–75.

Kozol, W. (2004) 'Domesticating NATO's war in Kosovo/a: (In)visible Bodies and the Dilemma of Photojournalism,' *Meridians*, Vol. 4, No. 2, pp. 1–38.

Krishna, S. (1993) 'The Importance of Being Ironic: a Postcolonial View on Critical International Relations Theory,' *Alternatives*, Vol. 18, No. 3, pp. 385–417.

—— (1999) *Postcolonial Insecurities: India, Sri Lanka, and the Question of Nationhood*. Minneapolis MN: University of Minnesota Press.

—— (2001) 'Race, Amnesia, and the Education of International Relations,' *Alternatives*, Vol. 26, No. 4, pp. 401–24.

—— (2002) 'An Inarticulate Imperialism: Dubya, Afghanistan and the American Century,' *Alternatives: Turkish Journal of International Relations*, Vol. 1, No. 2.

Kristof, N. (2007) 'Darfur and Congo,' *The New York Times*, 20 June.

—— (2009) 'What to Do about Darfur,' *The New York Review of Books*, Vol. 56, No. 11.

Krog, A. (1998) *Country of My Skull: Guilt, Sorrow, and the Limits of Forgiveness in the New South Africa*. Johannesburg: Random House.

Kumar, P. (1999) 'Testimonies of Loss and Memory: Partition and the Haunting of a Nation,' *Interventions*, Vol. 1, No. 2, pp. 201–16.

Kushner, T. and A. Solomon (eds) (2003) *Wrestling with Zion: Progressive Jewish-American Responses to the Israeli-Palestinian Conflict*. New York NY: Grove Press.

Kuokkanen, R. (2008) 'Globalization as Racialized, Sexualized Violence,' *International Feminist Journal of Politics*, Vol. 10, No. 2, pp. 216–33.

Laitin, D. (1995) 'Disciplining Political Science. (The Qualitative–Quantitative

Disputation: Gary King, Robert O. Keohane, and Sidney Verba's Designing Social Inquiry: Scientific Inference in Qualitative Research),' *American Political Science Review*, Vol. 89, No. 2, pp. 454–7.

Lalu, P. (2009) *The Deaths of Hintsa: Postapartheid South Africa and the Shape of Recurring Pasts*. Cape Town: HSRC Press.

Lebow, R. (1994) 'The Long Peace, the End of the Cold War, and the Failure of Realism,' *International Organization*, Vol. 48, No. 2, pp. 249–77.

Lenin, V. (1986) *What Is to Be Done?* New York NY: International Publishers.

Lie, J. (1995) 'The Transformation of Sexual Work in 20th Century Korea,' *Gender and Society*, Vol. 9, No. 3, pp. 310–27.

Ling, L. H. M. (2000) 'Hypermasculinity on the Rise, Again: a Response to Fukuyama on Women and World Politics,' *International Feminist Journal of Politics*, Vol. 2, No. 2, pp. 277–86.

—— (2010) 'Who is an American?' *International Political Sociology*, Vol. 4, No. 1, pp. 100–4.

Lorde. A. (2007) 'The Master's Tools Will Never Dismantle the Master's House,' *Sister Outsider*. Berkeley CA: Crossing Press, pp. 110–13.

—— (2009) 'Poetry Makes Something Happen' in R. Byrd, J. Cole, and B. Guy-Sheftall (eds), *I Am Your Sister: Collected and Unpublished Writings of Audre Lorde*. New York NY: Oxford University Press. pp. 184–7.

Lowenthal, I. (1976) 'Haiti: Behind Mountains, More Mountains,' *Reviews in Anthropology*, Vol. 3, No. 6, pp. 656–69.

Malik, M. (2007) 'Not Motivated by Politics,' *Dawn*, 11 May.

Malkki, L. (1995) *Purity and Exile: Violence, Memory, and National Cosmology among Hutu Refugees in Tanzania*. Chicago IL: University of Chicago Press.

Mamdani, M. (2002) *When Victims Become Killers: Colonialism, Nativism, and the Genocide in Rwanda*. Princeton NJ: Princeton University Press.

—— (2007) 'The Politics of Naming: Genocide, Civil War, Insurgency,' *London Review of Books*, Vol. 29, No. 5, pp. 5–8.

—— (2009a) 'Dissent On Darfur,' *The New York Review of Books*, Vol. 56, No. 13.

—— (2009b) *Saviors and Survivors: Darfur, Politics, and the War on Terror*. New York NY: Pantheon Books.

Mani, L. (1998) *Contentious Traditions: the Debate on Sati in Colonial India*. Berkeley, CA: University of California Press.

Mani, B. and L. Varadarajan (2005) '"The Largest Gathering of the Global Indian Family": Neoliberalism, Nationalism, and Diaspora at Pravasi Bharatiya Divas,' *Diaspora*, Vol. 14, No. 1, pp. 45–73.

Manji, I. (2003) *The Trouble with Islam*. New York NY: St Martin's Press.

Marcos, Subcomandante and Ejército Zapatista de Liberación Nacional (1998) *Zapatista Encuentro: Documents from the 1996 Encounter for Humanity and Against Neoliberalism, La Realidad, Mexico*. New York NY: Seven Stories Press.

Martin, B. (2006) *Under the Loving Care of the Fatherly Leader: North Korea and the Kim Dynasty*. New York NY: St Martin's Press.

Marx, K. and F. Engels (2002) *The Communist Manifesto*. New York NY: Penguin Classics.

Mbembe, A. (2001) *On the Postcolony*. Berkeley CA: University of California Press.

McAuley, C. (1997) 'Race and the Process of the American Revolution' in J. Foran (ed.), *Theorizing Revolutions*. New York NY: Routledge, pp. 168–202.

McKie, R. (2008) 'How the Myth of Food Miles Hurts the Planet,' *The Observer*, 23 March.

McKinley, M. (2004) 'The Co-option of the University and the Privileging of Annihilation,' *International Relations*, Vol. 18, No. 2, pp. 151–72.

Menchú, Rigoberta (trans. Ann Wright) (1984) *I, Rigoberta Menchú: an Indian Woman in Guatemala*. London, Verso.

Menon, R. and K. Bhasin (1996) 'Abducted Women, the State and Questions of Honour,' in K. Jayawardena and M. Alwis (eds), *Embodied Violence: Communalizing Women's Sexuality in South Asia*. London: Zed Books.

Mills, C. Wright (1959) *The Sociological Imagination*, London: Oxford University Press.

Mills, Charles W. (1997) *The Racial Contract*. Ithaca NY: Cornell University Press.

Minow, M. (1998) *Between Vengeance and Forgiveness: Facing History after Genocide and Mass Violence*. Boston MA: Beacon Press.

Misra, J., J. Woodring, and S. N. Merz (2006) 'The Globalization of Care Work: Neoliberal Economic Restructuring and Migration Policy,' *Globalizations*, Vol. 3, No. 3, pp. 317–22.

Miyoshi Jager, S. (1996) 'Women, Resistance and the Divided Nation: the Romantic Rhetoric of Korean Reunification,' *The Journal of Asian Studies*, Vol. 55, No. 1, pp. 3–21.

Mojab, S. and R. Gorman (2007) 'Dispersed Nationalism: War, Diaspora and Kurdish Women's Organizing,' *Journal of Middle East Women's Studies*, Vol. 3, No. 1, pp. 58–85.

Moon, K. (2007) *Sex among Allies: Military Prostitution in US–Korea Relations*. New York NY: Columbia University Press.

Morduch, J. (1998) "Does Microfinance Really Help the Poor: New Evidence from Flagship Programs in Bangladesh.' Available at: http://www.nyu.edu/projects/morduch/ documents/microfinance/Does_Microfinance_Really_Help.pdf.

Morgenthau, H. (1948) *Politics among Nations*. New York NY: Alfred Knopf.

Munir, D. (2009) 'Struggling for the Rule of Law: the Pakistani Lawyers' Movement,' *Middle East Report Online*, No. 251. Available at: http://www.merip.org/mer/mer251/mer251.html.

Muppidi, H. (2010) *The Colonial Signs of International Relations*. New York NY: Columbia University Press. Forthcoming manuscript, pp. 1–195.

Mutume, G. (2007) '"Indigenous" People Fight for Inclusion: Press for an End to Discrimination and Marginalization,' *Africa Renewal* (United Nations Department of Public Information), Vol. 21, No. 1, pp. 6–8. Available at: http://www.un.org/ecosocdev/geninfo/afrec/vol21no1/ar-21no1.pdf.

Nafisi, A. (2004) *Reading Lolita in Tehran: a Memoir in Books*. New York NY: Random House.

Nair, M. (2006) 'Defining Indigeneity: Situating Transnational Knowledge,' World Society Focus Paper Series, World Society Foundation, Zurich, Switzerland, pp. 1–20. Available at: http://www.uzh.ch/wsf/WSFocus_Nair.pdf.

Narayan, U. (1997) *Dislocating Cultures: Identities, Traditions, and Third World Feminism*. New York NY: Routledge.

—— (2000) 'Essence of Culture and a Sense of History: a Feminist Critique of Cultural Essentialism' in Uma Naryan and Sandra Harding (eds), *Decentering the Center: Philosophy for a Muticultural, Postcolonial, and Feminist World*. Bloomington IN: Indiana University Press, pp. 80–100.

Nayak, M. (2003) 'The Struggle over Gendered Meanings in India: How Indian Women's Networks, the Hindu Nationalist Hegemonic Project, and Transnational Feminists Address Gender Violence,' *Women and Politics*, Vol. 25, No. 3, pp. 71–96.

Nayak, M. and C. Malone (2009) 'American Orientalism and American Exceptionalism: a Critical Rethinking of US Hegemony,' *International Studies Review*, Vol. 11, No. 2, pp. 253–76.

Nayak, M. and J. Suchland (2006) 'Gender Violence and Hegemonic Projects: Introduction,' *International Feminist Journal of Politics*, Vol. 8, No. 4, pp. 467–85.

Ndulo, M. (2009) 'The United Nations Responses to the Sexual Abuse and Exploitation of Women and Girls by Peacekeepers during Peacekeeping Missions,' *Berkeley Journal of International Law*, Vol. 27, No. 1, pp. 127–61.

Neale, J. (2003) *A People's History of the Vietnam War*. New York NY: The New Press.

Nesbitt, N. (2008) 'Turning the Tide: the Problem of Popular Insurgency in Haitian Revolutionary Historiography,' *Small Axe*, No. 27, pp.14–31.

Neuman, S. (ed.) (1998) *International Relations Theory and the Third World*, New York NY: Palgrave Macmillan.

Newson, J. A. (2004) 'Disrupting the "Student as Consumer" Model: the New Emancipatory Project,' *International Relations*, Vol. 18, No. 2, pp. 227–39.

Nnaemeka, Obioma (2005) 'African Women, Colonial Discourses, and Imperialistic Interventions' in Obioma Nnaemeka (ed.), *Female Circumcision and the Politics of Knowledge: African Women in Imperialist Discourses*. Westport CT: Praeger Publishers, pp. 27–46.

Norchi, C. (2000) 'Indigenous Knowledge as Intellectual Property,' *Policy Sciences*, Vol. 33, Nos. 3–4, pp. 387–98.

Nyers, P. (2003) 'Abject Cosmopolitanism: the Politics of Protection in the Antideportation Movement,' *Third World Quarterly*, Vol. 24, No. 6, pp. 1069–93.

Obiora, L. A. (1997) 'The Little Foxes That Spoil the Vine: Revisiting the Feminist Critique of Female Circumcision' in O. Oyewumi (ed.), *African Women and Feminism: Reflecting on the Politics of Sisterhood*. Trenton NJ: Africa World Press, pp. 197–229.

'Off the Grid in Cuba: Renewable Energy on a Budget' (2008) World Security Institute US–Cuba Cooperative Security Project. Available at: http://www.wsicubaproject.org/RenewableEnergyBudget08.cfm.

O'Neill, T. (1993) *All Politics Is Local: and Other Rules of the Game*. Avon NY: Adams Media Corporation.

Orford, A. (2002) 'Feminism, Imperialism and the Mission of International Law,' *Nordic Journal of International Law*, Vol. 71, pp. 275–96.

—— (ed.) (2006) *International Law and Its Others*. Cambridge: Cambridge University Press.

—— (2009) 'What Can We Do to Stop People Harming Others?' in J. Edkins and M. Zehfuss (eds), *Global Politics: a New Introduction*. New York NY: Routledge, pp. 427–53.

Parpart, J. and M. Zalewski (eds) (2008) *Rethinking the Man Question: Sex, Gender and Violence in International Relations*. London: Zed Books.

Patel, R. (2008) *Stuffed and Starved: the Hidden Battle for the World Food System*. Brooklyn NY: Melville House.

Peet, R. (2003) *Unholy Trinity: the IMF, World Bank and WTO*. London: Zed Books.

Philipose, E. (2009) 'Feminism, International Law, and the Spectacular Violence of the "Other": Decolonizing the Laws of War' in R. Heberle and V. Grace (eds), *Theorizing Sexual Violence*. New York NY: Routledge, pp. 176–204.

Plummer, B. (1982) 'The Afro-American Response to the Occupation of Haiti, 1915–1934,' *Phylon*, Vol. 43, No. 2, pp. 125–43.

Pogrebinschi, T. (2007) 'Ordinary Democracy: Marx and Dewey on the Political Subject,' paper presented at the Annual Meeting of American Political Science Association.

Pollan, M. (2008) 'Farmer in Chief,' *The New York Times*, 9 October.

Prasad, V. (2007) *The Darker Nations: a Biography of the Short-lived World*. New Delhi: Left Word Books.

Pratt, M. (1986) 'Fieldwork in Common Places' in J. Clifford and G. E. Marcus (eds), *Writing Culture – the Poetics of Ethnography*. Berkeley CA: University of California Press, pp. 27–50.

—— (2001) '*I, Rigoberta Menchú* and the "Culture Wars"' in A. Arias (ed.), *The Rigoberta Menchu Controversy*. Minneapolis MN: University of Minnesota Press, pp. 29–51.

Pringle, P. (2005) *Food, Inc.: Mendel to Monsanto – the Promises and Perils of the Biotech Harvest*. New York NY: Simon and Schuster.

Prins, G. (1998) 'The Four-stroke Cycle in Security Studies,' *International Affairs*, Vol. 74, No. 4, pp. 781–808.

Puar, J. (2007) *Terrorist Assemblages: Homonationalism in Queer Times.* Durham NC: Duke University Press.

Quinn, M. (2006) 'The Power of Community: How Cuba Survived Peak Oil,' *Energy Bulletin.* Available at: http://www.energybulletin.net/node/13171.

Rai, S. (2008) *Gender Politics of Development: Essays in Hope and Despair.* London: Zed Books.

Raj, K. (2006) 'Paradoxes on the Borders of Europe,' *International Feminist Journal of Politics,* Vol. 8, No. 4, pp. 512–34.

Ramet, S. (2005) *Thinking about Yugoslavia: Scholarly Debates about the Yugoslav Breakup and the Wars in Bosnia and Kosovo.* Cambridge: Cambridge University Press.

Rankin, K. N. (2001) 'Governing Development: Neoliberalism, Microcredit, and Rational Economic Woman,' *Economy and Society,* Vol. 30, No. 1, pp. 18–37. Available at: http://unpan1.un.org/intradoc/groups/public/documents/apcity/unpan011685. pdf.

Razack, S. (2004) *Dark Threats and White Knights: the Somalia Affair, Peacekeeping, and the New Imperialism.* Toronto: University of Toronto Press.

Renwick Monroe, K. (2005) *Perestroika! The Raucous Rebellion in Political Science.* New Haven CT: Yale University Press.

Richter-Montpetit, M. (2007) 'Empire, Desire and Violence: a Queer Transnational Feminist Reading of the Prisoner "Abuse" in Abu Ghraib and the Question of "Gender Equality,"' *International Feminist Journal of Politics,* Vol. 9, No. 1, pp. 38–59.

Risse, T., S. Ropp, and K. Sikkink (eds) (1999) *The Power of Human Rights: International Norms and Domestic Change.* Cambridge: Cambridge University Press.

Ritzer, G. (2007) *The Coming of Post-Industrial Society,* second edition. New York NY: McGraw-Hill.

Rodney, W. (1981) *How Europe Underdeveloped Africa.* Washington DC: Howard University Press.

Roediger, D. (2006) *Working Toward Whiteness: How America's Immigrants Became White – the Strange Journey from Ellis Island to the Suburbs.* New York NY: Basic Books.

Roodman, D. and J. Morduch (2009) 'The Impact of Microcredit on the Poor in Bangladesh: Revisiting the Evidence,' Working Paper 174, Centre for Global Development. Available at: http://ideas.repec.org/p/cgd/wpaper/174.html.

Rosenberg, T. (1999) 'The Unfinished Revolution of 1989,' *Foreign Policy,* No. 115, pp. 91–106.

Rosow, S. J. (2003) 'Toward an Anti-Disciplinary Global Studies,' *International Studies Perspectives,* Vol. 4, No. 1, pp. 1–14.

Rosset, P. and M. Benjamin (1994) *The Greening of the Revolution: Cuba's Experiment with Organic Agriculture.* San Francisco CA: Global Exchange.

Roy, A. (2008) '9 is not 11,' 12 December. Available at: http://www.huffingtonpost.com/arundhati-roy/9-is-not-11_b_150637.html.

Rupert, M. (2000) *Ideologies of Globalization: Contending Visions of a New World Order.* New York NY: Routledge.

Russo, A. (2006) 'The Feminist Majority Foundation's Campaign to Stop Gender Apartheid: the Intersections of Feminism and Imperialism in the United States,' *International Feminist Journal of Politics,* Vol. 8, No. 4, pp. 557–80.

Ruwanpura, K. N. (2008) 'Temporality of Disasters: the Politics of Women's Livelihoods "after" the 2004 Tsunami in Sri Lanka,' *Singapore Journal of Tropical Geography,* Vol. 29, No. 3, pp. 325–40.

Said, E. (1979) *Orientalism.* New York NY: Vintage Books.

Sajed. A. (2008) 'Securitized Migrants and Postcolonial (In)difference,' paper presented at Canadian Political Science Association Conference, Vancouver, Canada, 4–6 June.

Sassen, S. (2006), *Territory, Authority, Rights: from Medieval to Global Assemblages.* Princeton NJ: Princeton University Press.

'Saving Amina Lawal: Human Rights Symbolism and the Dangers of Colonialism' (2004) *Harvard Law Review,* Vol. 117, No. 7, pp. 2365–86.

Scarry, E. (1985) *The Body in Pain: the Making and Unmaking of the World.* New York NY: Oxford University Press.

Searle, C. (1984) *Words Unchained: Language and Revolution in Grenada.* London: Zed Books.

Selbin, E. (2007) 'Making the World New: Latin American Studies after the Washington Consensus,' *LASA Forum,* Vol. 38, No. 4, pp. 33–5.

—— (2010) *Revolution, Rebellion, Resistance: the Power of Story.* London: Zed Books.

Shah, O. (2008) 'Dear Thomas Friedman, You're Wrong (Again),' *SAMAR,* 15 December.

Shakya, Y. B. and K. Rankin (2008) 'The Politics of Subversion in Development Practice: an Exploration of Microfinance in Nepal and Vietnam,' *Journal of Development Studies,* Vol. 44, No. 8, pp. 1214–35.

Shani, G. (2008) 'Toward a Post-Western IR: the Umma, Khalsa Panth, and Critical IR Theory,' *International Studies Review,* Vol. 10, No. 4, pp. 722–34.

Shapiro, F. (2006) *Yale Book of Quotations.* New Haven CT: Yale University Press.

Sharoni, S. (2006) 'Compassionate Resistance: a Personal/Political Journey to Israel/Palestine,' *International Feminist Journal of Politics,* Vol. 8, No. 2, pp. 288–99.

—— (2008) 'Teaching about Gender, Race and Militarization after 9/11: a Pedagogy of Dissent, Compassion, and Hope' in B. Sutton, S. Morgen, and J. Novkov (eds), *Security Disarmed: Critical Perspectives on Gender, Race, and Militarization.* Piscataway NJ: Rutgers University Press, pp. 259–79.

Shaw, K. (2002) 'Indigeneity and the International,' *Millennium,* Vol. 31, No. 1, pp. 55–81.

—— (2003) 'Whose Knowledge for What Politics?' *Review of International Studies,* Vol. 29, pp. 199–221.

—— (2008) *Indigeneity and Political Theory: Sovereignty and the Limits of the Political.* New York NY: Routledge.

Shepherd, L. (2006) 'Veiled References: Construction of Gender in the Bush Administration Discourse on the Attacks on Afghanistan Post-9/11,' *International Feminist Journal of Politics,* Vol. 8, No. 1, pp. 19–41.

—— (2008a) *Gender, Violence and Security: Discourse as Practice.* London: Zed Books.

—— (2008b) 'Power and Authority in the Production of United Nations Security Council Resolution 1325,' *International Studies Quarterly,* Vol. 52, No. 2, pp. 383–404.

Shilliam, R. (2008) 'The Enigmatic Figure of the Non-Western Thinker in International Relations,' *Antepodium: Online Journal of World Affairs.* Available at http://www.victoria.ac.nz/atp/articles/ArticlesWord/Shilliam-2008.doc.

Shiva, V. (2000) *Stolen Harvest: the Hijacking of the Global Food Supply.* Cambridge MA: South End Press.

Shor, I. (1992) *Empowering Education: Critical Teaching for Social Change.* Portsmouth MA: Heinemann.

Shulman, D. (2007) *Dark Hope: Working for Peace in Israel and Palestine.* Chicago IL: University of Chicago Press.

—— (2009) 'Israel without Illusions: What Goldstone Got Right,' *The New York Review of Books Blog,* 17 November. Available at: http://blogs.nybooks.com/post/247398486/israel-without-illusions-what-goldstone-got-right.

Sick, G. (1995) 'Iran: the Adolescent Revolution,' *Journal of International Affairs,* Vol. 49, No. 1, pp. 145–66.

Sidhu, R. K. (2006) *Universities and Globalization: to Market, to Market.* Mahwah NJ: Lawrence Erlbaum Associates, Inc.

Sigal, L. (1998) *Disarming Strangers: Nuclear Diplomacy with North Korea.* Princeton NJ: Princeton University Press.

Sikkink, K. (2004) *Mixed Signals: US Human Rights Policy and Latin America.* Ithaca NY: Cornell University Press.

Simon, H. (1997) *Administrative Behavior,* fourth edition. New York NY: Free Press.

Sjoberg, L. (2006) 'The Gendered Realities of the Immunity Principle: Why Gender Analysis Needs Feminism,' *International Studies Quarterly,* Vol. 50, No. 4, 889–910.

—— (ed.) (2009) *Gender and International Security: Feminist Perspectives.* New York NY: Routledge.

Smith, A. (2008) 'American Studies without America: Native Feminisms and the Nation-State,' *American Quarterly,* Vol. 60, No. 2, pp. 309–15.

Smith, A. and J. K. Kauanui (2008) 'Native Feminisms Engage American Studies,' *American Quarterly,* Vol. 60, No. 2, pp. 241–9.

Smith, H. and P. Stares (2007) *Diasporas in Conflict: Peace-makers or Peace-wreckers.* New York NY: United Nations University Press.

Smith, S. (2002) 'The United States and the Discipline of International Relations: "Hegemonic Country, Hegemonic Discipline,"' *International Studies Review,* Vol. 4, No. 2, pp. 67–85.

Spivak, G. (1988) 'Can the Subaltern Speak?' in C. Nelson and L. Grossberg (eds), *Marxism and the Interpretation of Culture.* Urbana IL: University of Illinois Press, pp. 271–313.

Stoll, D. (1999) *Rigoberta Menchú and the Story of All Poor Guatemalans.* Boulder CO: Westview Press.

Suggs, H. (2002) 'The Response of the African American Press to the United States Occupation of Haiti, 1915–1934,' *Journal of African-American Studies,* Vol. 87, No. 1, pp. 70–82.

Suh, J. (2007) *Power, Interest and Identity in Military Alliances.* New York NY: Palgrave Macmillan.

Sun Tzu (2009) *The Art of War,* ed. and trans. J. Minford. New York NY: Penguin.

Sunder, M. (2003) 'Piercing the Veil,' *Yale Law Journal,* Vol. 112, pp. 1399–1472.

Tétreault, M. and R. Lipschutz (2005) *Global Politics as if People Mattered.* Boulder CO: Rowman and Littlefield Publishers.

Thucydides (2009) *The Peloponnesian War,* trans. M. Hammond. New York NY: Oxford University Press.

Tickner, J. (1999) 'Why Women Can't Run the World: International Politics According to Francis Fukuyama,' *International Studies Review,* Vol. 1, No. 3, pp. 3–11.

Tiemessen, A. (2004) 'After Arusha: Gacaca Justice in Post-Genocide Rwanda,' *African Studies Quarterly,* Vol. 8, No. 1. Available at: http://www.africa.ufl.edu/asq/v8/v8i1a4.htm.

Tilly, C. (1984) *Big Structures, Large Processes, Huge Comparisons.* New York NY: Russell Sage Foundation.

—— (1985) 'War Making and State Making as Organized Crime' in P. B. Evans, D. Ruschemeyer, and T. Skoepol (eds), *Bringing the State Back In.* Cambridge: Cambridge University Press, pp. 169–87.

Tsygankov, A. P. and P. A. Tsygankov (2007) 'A Sociology of Dependence in International Relations Theory: a Case of Russian Liberal IR,' *International Political Sociology,* Vol. 1, No. 4, pp. 307–24.

Turner, V. (1967) 'Betwixt and Between: the Liminal Period in Rites de Passage' in *The Forest of Symbols: Aspects of Ndembu Ritual.* Ithaca NY: Cornell University Press, pp. 93–111.

United Nations (2008) 'United Nations Peacekeeping Operations: Principles and Guidelines.' Available at: http://peacekeepingresourcehub.unlb.org/Pbps/Library/Capstone_Doctrine_ENG.pdf, pp. 1–100.

Vatikiotis, M. (2005/6) 'The Architecture of China's Diplomatic Edge,' *Brown Journal of World Affairs,* Vol. 12, No. 2, pp. 25–37.

Vine, D. (2009) *Island of Shame: the Secret History of the US Military Base on Diego Garcia.* Princeton NJ: Princeton University Press.

206 / DECENTERING INTERNATIONAL RELATIONS

ghEschen, P. (1997) *Race against Empire: Black Americans and Abolitionism, 1937–1957.* Ithaca NY: Cornell University Press.
Waever, O. (1998) 'The Sociology of a Not So International Discipline: American and European Developments in International Relations,' *International Organization,* Vol. 52, No. 4, pp. 687–727.
Waever, O. and A. Tickner (2009) *International Relations Scholarship around the World.* New York NY: Routledge.
Walker, A. and P. Parmar (1993) *Warrior Marks: Female Genital Mutilation and the Sexual Blinding of Women.* New York NY: Harcourt Brace.
Waltz, K. (1979) *Theory of International Politics.* New York NY: McGraw-Hill.
Wanyeki, L. M. (2007) 'Microcredit Makes Women Poor,' *The East African,* July. Available at: http://www.mailarchive.com/ugandanet@kym.net/msg24516.html.
Watson, A. (2007) 'Children Born of Wartime Rape: Rights and Representation,' *International Feminist Journal of Politics,* Vol. 9, No. 1, pp. 20–34.
Wayland, S. (2004) 'Ethnonationalist Networks and Transnational Opportunities: the Sri Lankan Tamil Diaspora,' *Review of International Studies,* Vol. 30, No. 3, pp. 405–26.
Weber, C. (1994) 'Good Girls, Little Girls, and Bad Girls: Male Paranoia in Robert Keohane's Critique of Feminist International Relations,' *Journal of International Studies,* Vol. 23, No. 2, pp. 337–49.
—— (1999) *Faking It: US Hegemony in a 'Post-Phallic' Era.* Minneapolis MN: University of Minnesota Press.
—— (2001) *International Relations Theory: a Critical Introduction,* New York NY: Routledge.
—— (2008) 'Designing Safe Citizens,' *Citizenship Studies,* Vol. 12, No. 2, pp. 125–42.
—— (2009) *International Relations Theory: a Critical Introduction,* third edition. New York NY: Routledge.
—— (2010) 'Citizenship, Security, Humanity,' *International Political Sociology,* Vol. 4, No. 1, pp. 81–6.
Weber, H. (2002) 'The Imposition of a Global Development Architecture: the Example of Microcredit,' *Review of International Studies,* Vol. 28, No. 3, pp. 537–55.
Weldes, J. (ed.) (2003) *To Seek Out New Worlds: Exploring Links between Science Fiction and World Politics.* New York NY: Palgrave Macmillan.
Wibben, A. (2009) 'Who Do We Think We Are?' in J. Edkins and M. Zehfuss (eds), *Global Politics: a New Introduction.* New York NY: Routledge, pp. 70–96.
Yegenoglu, M. (1998) *Colonial Fantasies: Towards a Feminist Reading of Orientalism.* Cambridge: Cambridge University Press.
Yiftachel, O. (2006) *Ethnocracy: Land and Identity Politics in Israel/Palestine.* Philadelphia PA: University of Pennsylvania Press.
Zizek, S. (2000) *The Fragile Absolute, or, Why Is the Christian Legacy Worth Fighting for?* London: Verso.

Index

bad guys discourse, 126; intellectual origins, 24; narratives decentering, 4; phraseology of, 65; postcolonial theory, 30; postmodern thought, 29; scholars' tourist recognition, 163; stories of, 85; teleological narratives, 124; temporal discourse, 132; textbooks, 23, 67; theorists, 127, 165; theory myopias, 16; theory self-representation, 17; USA knowledge 'export', 14; Western-centric stranglehold, 134
International Studies Association, composition of, 13
International Studies Quarterly, 65
Internet, 105
Iran, 112, 150; branding experts use, 135; military intervention opposed, 150; pariah discourse, 80; post-election uprisings, 80
Iraq, 142, 150; human rights underplayed, 73; war, 124, 131
Ireland, 5; partition legacy, 96
Iroquois League, cooperative security, 30
Ishay, M., 61
Islam, 66-7; critical Islamic discourses, 17
Isleata Pueblo people, 37
Israel, 150; branding experts use, 135; anti-Semitism accusations, 46; Palestinian citizens, 50; -Palestinian peace work, 47; -Palestinian Ta'ayush, 48; state of, 49; US Aid and commitment, 45

Jager, Miyoshi, 155
Jamaica,, American country, 45
James, C.L.R., 59
Janjaweed, 71
Japan, 24, 151; comfort women brutalized, 155-6; military abuses, 148
Japanese Americans, interned, 131
Jarvis, Lee, 128-9
Jewish Holocaust, 53-4
Jharkhand region, India, 26
jihadists, Arab, 70
job losses, outsourced, 108
Jones, Claudia, 62
Jones, Tim, 21
journalism, 104; Northern/Western, 106
justice, 126
Justice and Equality Movement, Darfur-based, 71

Kamat, S., 99

Kamau-Rutenberg, Wanjiru, 117-18, 119-3
Kamola, Isaac, 106-7, 115
Kang, S., 98
Kennedy, Anthony, 38
Keohane, R., 160
Kerry, John, 81
Khalsa Panth, critical Sikh discourses, 17
Khatib, Deema, 124
Kim Jong-il, 153
Kim, J., 155
King, G., 160
King Jr, Martin Luther, 'Birth of a Nation' speech, 62
Kissinger, Henry, 161, 163
Knight, E., 59
knowledge production, 41, 44, 91, 101, 115; contestation need, 106; development discourse, 102; journalism, 104; Northern/Western locus, 6; of 'others' creation, 4
Korea: people-to-people exchanges, 155; Policy Institute, 154; War, 131, 150
Kosovo, 146; Liberation Army, 56; war, 54-5
Kovac, Radomir, 143
Krishna, Sankaran, 5, 18-19, 77
Kristof, Nicholas, 70-1, 73-5
Kunarac, Dragoljub, 143
Kurdistan, 101; Kurds, 136
Kushner, Tony, 47

Laitin, D., 160
Lakota Sioux, money-for-land rejection, 27
Lalu, Premesh, 42, 44
land: and culture thefts, 19; indigenous legal notions, 38; Northern/Western ownership obsession, 23, 32; relating to, 28
language, techno-strategic, 133
Latin America, 'pink tide', 112
Law Association for Asia and the Pacific, 69
law: indigenous traditions, 39; nation-state, 40; strategic use of, 34, 37
Lawal, Amina, 79
Laws of Manu, Hindu, 52
Lee Myung-bak, 152-3
Lee, Hyun, 154-5
legitimation, discourses of, 134
Lenin, V.I., 157
liberal democracy, 2
liberalization, trade and finance, 94

Obama, Barack, 87, 112, 138;
    Administration, 134, 153
Obiora, L. Amede, 118
'objectivity', critical analysis of 41-2
Ogoni people Nigeria, international links
    use, 35; oil company resistance, 79
Oliphant v. Suquamish Indian Tribe, 39
Operation Condor, 131
Orientalism, 7, 29, 66
'Others': domination construction, 25;
    'Othering', 82; 'Otherness', 27
'ownership', 121

pain, 85
Pakistan, 68, 100; girls' education, 81;
    military intervention opposed, 150;
    postcolonial, 77; 'terrorist' label, 69
Pakistani Lawyers' Movement, 68
Palestine: dehumanized people, 46; Israeli
    conflict, 45; right of return, 49
Palestine Education Project, Brooklyn-
    based, 49
Pan-African Congress, Manchester 1945
    meeting, 62
Parmar, Pratibha, 117-18
participatory research, pitfalls of, 42
peace: and security discourse, 4, 9, 11,
    22, 126; militarized, 149; privileged
    'pathways', 140
Peace of Westphalia, 23
pedagogy, critical, 14-15
People's Tribunals, 148
permaculture, 113-15
'perpetuity', Jewish sense of, 47
Persian Empire, human rights
    formulations, 52
Peru, 45
Pilots Group, Israel, 47
Pogrebinschi, T., 14
Pollan, Michael, 112
Portugal, 4
post-Cold War, new 'other, 66
postcolonialism: International Relations, 7;
    studies, 16
poverty, 104, 121-3; 'banking' on the
    poor, 120; local complexities, 118; root
    causes, 120
power, 'centres' of, 3; problematized
    relationships, 102; sovereign, 130;
    working of, 11
Prasad, Vijay, 102
Pratt, Mary Louise, 44, 88
Press TV, Iran, 136
prison labor, 98

prisoners of war, Bosnian Muslim, 55
private property, 27; as 'human right', 61;
    capitalist rights, 34; concepts of, 39;
'problem', definition power, 7
Puar, J., 80-1, 83
Puerto Rico, 45
punk politics, 16

queer theorists, 16
Quran, 52

race: dehistoricized, 61; International
    Relations racialization role, 18; racism,
    116
radio propaganda, Rwanda genocide, 56
Rai, S., 103
rape, 143-5; USA law, 39
Razack, S., 147
redemption, US nationalist narratives, 74
refugees, 98
refuseniks, Israel, 47
regional stereotyping, global, 106
remittances, 118
resistance, academic claims to, 12-13
Review of International Studies, 65
revolution, 'traditional' conceptions of, 13
Revolutionary Association of Women in
    Afghanistan, 79
rhizomic models, 161
Rice, Condoleeza, 87
Robespierre, Maximilian, 60
romanticization: ahistorical, 28; 'of
    disposable people', 22; paternalistic, 27
Roy, Arundhati, 68-9
Rushdie, Salman, 69
Russell Tribunal, 148
Russia, 5-6, 26, 135, 136
Ruwanpura, Kanchana, 131
Rwanda, 142, 146; Gacaca, 148; genocide,
    56; 'rape database', 143; Rwandan
    Patriotic Front, 57; Tutsi government,
    73

Sachs, Jeffrey, 93
Said, Edward, 66; *Orientalism*, 13
Sajed, Alina, 84
Salim, Salim Ahmed, 73
San people, Southern Africa, 28
Sangatte, refugee centre, 98
Save Darfur Coalition, 74, 131;
    composition of, 74; US-based, 70
saving, multiple forms of, 119
Sayeret Matkal dissidents, 47
Scarry, Elaine, 85

www.ingramcontent.com/pod-product-compliance
Lightning Source LLC
Chambersburg PA
CBHW031130270326
41929CB00011B/1570